Explorations in Communication and History

When and how do communication and history impact each other? How do disciplinary perspectives affect what we know?

Explorations in Communication and History addresses the link between what we know and how we know it by tracking the intersection of communication and history. Asking how each discipline has enhanced and hindered our understanding of the other, the book considers what happens to what we know when disciplines engage.

Through a critical collection of essays written by top scholars, the book addresses the engagement of communication and history as it applies to the study of technology, audiences and journalism. Driven by fundamental questions about disciplinary knowledge and boundary-marking, such as how communication and history change what the other notices about the world, how particular platforms encourage scholars to look beyond their disciplinary boundaries, and which cues encourage them to reject old paradigms and embrace new ones, the book both navigates the terrain connecting communication and history and raises meta-questions about its shaping. In so doing, it elaborates our understanding of what communication and history have to give each other, how they build off of each other's strengths and often subvert each other's weaknesses, and what we can expect from the future of disciplinary engagement.

Contributors: S. Elizabeth Bird, Richard Butsch, James Curran, Susan J. Douglas, Anna McCarthy, Robert McChesney, John Nerone, David Paul Nord, John Durham Peters, Michael Schudson, Peter Stallybrass, Paul Starr.

A comprehensive introduction by Barbie Zelizer contextualizes these debates and makes a case for the importance of disciplinary engagement for teaching as well as research in media and cultural studies. Each section also provides a brief introduction to contextualize the essays and highlight the issues they raise, making this an invaluable collection for students and scholars alike.

Barbie Zelizer is the Raymond Williams Professor of Communication and Director of the Scholars Program in Culture and Communication at the University of Pennsylvania's Annenberg School for Communication. A former journalist, Zelizer is known for her work in the area of journalism, culture, memory and images, particularly in times of crisis. Previous publications include *Reporting War: Journalism in Wartime* (2004) and *Journalism After September 11* (2002) (both co-edited with Stuart Allan).

Shaping Inquiry in Culture, Communication and Media Studies

Series Editor: Barbie Zelizer (University of Pennsylvania)

Dedicated to bringing to the foreground the central impulses by which we engage in inquiry, the Shaping Inquiry in Culture, Communication and Media Studies series attempts to make explicit the ways in which we craft our intellectual grasp of the world.

Explorations in Communication and History
Edited by Barbie Zelizer

Explorations in Communication and History

Edited by Barbie Zelizer

Routledge
Taylor & Francis Group

LONDON AND NEW YORK

First published 2008
by Routledge
2 Park Square, Milton Park, Abingdon, Oxon OX14 4RN

Simultaneously published in the USA and Canada
by Routledge
270 Madison Ave, New York, NY 10016

Routledge is an imprint of the Taylor & Francis Group, an informa business

Editorial selection and material © 2008 Barbie Zelizer
Individual chapters © 2008 the contributors

Typeset in Sabon by
Taylor & Francis Books
Printed and bound in Great Britain by
CPI Antony Rowe, Chippenham, Wiltshire

British Library Cataloguing in Publication Data
A catalogue record for this book is available from the British Library

Library of Congress Cataloging in Publication Data
Explorations in communication and history / edited by Barbie Zelizer.
    p. cm. – (Shaping inquiry in culture, communication and media studies)
Includes bibliographical references.
1. Communication–History. 2. Mass media–History. I. Zelizer, Barbie.
    P90.E89 2009
    302.2–dc22
                        2008019117

ISBN10: 0-415-77733-X (hbk)
ISBN10: 0-415-77734-8 (pbk)
ISBN10: 0-203-88860-X (ebk)

ISBN13: 978-0-415-77733-9 (hbk)
ISBN13: 978-0-415-77734-6 (pbk)
ISBN13: 978-0-203-88860-5 (ebk)

Contents

When disciplines engage

Barbie Zelizer

The optimum shape of disciplines in engendering certain ways of thinking about the world has haunted us ever since specialized knowledge first emerged as a contender for general intellectualism. Debates over the value of disciplines – their placement, their role, their power – oscillate between a broad-based celebration of the capacity to think in rigorous, trained ways and a condemnation of the power of disciplines to enforce and police knowledge acquisition. One given of disciplinary knowledge is its naturalization, the way in which disciplinary modes of thinking become unquestioned aspects of the default setting for academic inquiry. At times, the naturalization of disciplinary perspective becomes so entrenched that we can forget how much of what we know in the academy is driven without a clear correspondence to how we came to the knowledge we possess.

This book is an attempt to force our attention to the linkage between what we know and how we know it, and it makes that attempt on the back of the intersection, strong in some quarters and uneven in others, between communication and history. Posited in this book as two approaches to knowledge that have formed at different times on the backs of different conceptual prisms, epistemologies and methodological tools, the book traces what happens to what we know when the two disciplines engage. The possibilities associated with their engagement – indifference, negotiation, contestation, adaptation, even collision – introduce a rearrangement of the longstanding relationship between content and form, bringing issues of form – *how* we think – to the forefront of our attention and making the questions at the heart of this project clear-cut and necessary: When and how do communication and history impact each other? When and how does each change what the other notices about the world? More specifically, when and how do particular kinds of platforms encourage historians and communication scholars to look beyond their disciplinary boundaries? Which kinds of cues encourage them to reject old paradigms and embrace new ones?

One might ask why paying heed to disciplinary boundaries ultimately matters. In that all of us experience knowledge in far more integrated ways than our disciplinary boundaries suggest, we need to do better at offering an understanding of knowledge acquisition that in part parallels what happens to knowledge in the world at large. If how we think inhabits a critical space in relationship to what we think we know, we need to account for it in the models that we present to the public, to our students and ultimately to ourselves. If we do not, the notion of the ivory tower, anathema for many contemporary academics, will persist as the outstanding prism through which to consider scholarly work.

On disciplines as interpretive communities

For those who have long trafficked in the dissemination of knowledge, it comes as no surprise that knowledge is shared in patterned ways. The idea of disciplinary knowledge is pervasive, an organizing tool that has been recognized and revered across large sectors of the academy since the earliest days of the university. When C.P. Snow wrote of what he called two cultures nearly half a century ago, he offered a persuasive argument for the inherent distinctions between different modes of knowledge, and the logic he applied to distinguishing between the natural sciences and the humanities has over the years been extended to the social sciences and the various particular disciplines and academic fields that stretch across the curriculum.[1]

And yet the picture of disciplinary knowledge and the consequent recognition of disciplinary borders today are far more complicated than they were in C.P. Snow's time. Developments associated with globalization, with an increased managerialism in universities, with the intrusion of market considerations into the curriculum and with a trend toward centralized university relations all render an insistence on disciplines existing in pristine isolation from each other as much a tendency of the past as the academy's formerly prevalent repair to notions of the ivory tower. Inquiry today takes shape in circumstances that are by and large porous, permeable, engaged, internally contradictory, unstable and dynamic, and there is a need to address these attributes in our scholarly discussions of it.

Thus, considerations of disciplinary borders must by necessity give equal due to disciplinary crossings. How disciplines matter, which disciplines matter more and which matter less, which disciplines yield to their neighbors and on which grounds, whether disciplines need refurbishing in today's state of knowledge acquisition are all questions that have begun to undermine the more traditional disciplinary project of days of yore.

Perhaps for these reasons, contemporary scholars now regularly admit that disciplinary knowledge is negotiated for reasons having as much to do with serendipity, circumstance and people as with expertise. Characterized by both their content and their methodology, disciplines are "as much about what they study as they are about how they study".[2] Though the dissemination of knowledge follows routes which play to the known, familiar and, over time, broadly predictable, how we share what we know and our adaptation to the novel and unknown are assumed to take place incrementally, alongside attentiveness to the environment and what it facilitates and impedes. This is how Thomas Kuhn saw the growth of science, when he argued that individuals and then collectives develop shared paradigms gradually by appealing repeatedly to those involved in their development. Problems and procedures are named and labeled in ways that can generate consensus, while battles ensue over competing insights that might alter existing classifications. Such battles linger in reduced form long after the new paradigms seem set in place.[3]

All of these notions have less to do with knowledge itself and more to do with those who shape it, a point addressed by other scholars too – Peter Berger and Thomas Luckmann, Emile Durkheim, Michel Foucault, Nelson Goodman, G. Nigel Gilbert and Michael Mulkay, and Mary Douglas.[4] Coming from different vantage points, each independently argued that knowledge's development has as much to do with social forces – like integration, power, solidarity, notions of suitability – as with cognitive ones.

Such a backdrop helps explain many of the tensions surrounding disciplinary knowledge. Scholars exist within the boundaries – and confines – of separate interpretive communities,[5] where tacit knowledge and shared ways of knowing rule in certain aspects of a phenomenon and rule out others for members of the group. Invoking the interpretive strategies of like-minded individuals, each group determines what counts as evidence and in which ways, making judgment calls about the focal points worth thinking about and the kinds of research that count.

It is no surprise, then, that disciplinary knowledge produces its own set of strengths and weaknesses. Though scholars residing in disciplines may have well-traveled paths for speaking with each other, through the academic conventions of cross-citation, conferencing and other practices,[6] they tend to make little headway in sharing that knowledge beyond the boundaries of their own disciplinary frames or of those belonging to neighboring disciplines that are regularly frequented. The result is discrete bodies of knowledge, whose supporters largely preach to the converted but do not do enough to create a shared frame of reference about the focal point at hand.

And yet, the contemporary dissemination of knowledge takes shape in increasingly patterned ways. Three premises guide its sharing:

- no single identified group, field or individual knows all that there is to know;
- the adoption of new conceptual frameworks is dynamic and continually requires refinement and adaptation;
- the forces behind the concepts we develop – whether they are individuals, organizations, professional lobbies, or informal groups – are critical to the knowledge that ensues. In most cases, such forces tend to be hierarchical, politicized, and reflect an enactment of cultural power, hindering and

fermenting the development and dissemination of knowledge in certain ways and not others.

All of this raises critical questions about the relevance of inquiry to the world at large, where phenomena take shape not according to disciplinary perspectives but in spite of them. In a world which necessarily blends demarcations across personal history, training and bias, the academy needs to do a better job of linking its views on the world with the world itself.

History and communication

As two discrete bodies of disciplinary inquiry, history and communication make different kinds of claims about the world. Each does so in ways integral to internally constituted ways of thinking: One is as old as the academy; the other is a relatively recent inhabitant of the disciplinary horizon. One is heralded as one of the bona fide premier disciplines of the humanities; the other makes its mark as a new kind of hybrid discipline that borrows equally from the humanities and social sciences. One has endured ongoing chatter about its crustiness; the other suffers from claims that it panders too easily to the trendy and contemporary. One resides in the hallowed and distanced settings of archives, museums and private collections of documents; the other navigates the connections – and disconnects – between scholarly grey matter and its application in real settings. In each case, scholars use internally recognized intellectual prisms, epistemological rationales and methodological tools to engage with the world around them, so as to better elucidate its trappings.

How do history and communication maintain their singularity? Positioning the past as constitutive, history leads the parade of disciplines in situating its foci of engagement in earlier times. Presuming that those times have much to say about the world that extends beyond history's borders, history and its purveyors insist on a one-on-one link between acts of analysis and the temporal periods that preceded them. Recognizing the capacity of the past to tell us about the world, historians lend the past both implicit and explicit forms, using it to shape inquiry by grounding fundamental assumptions over time through recognizable, patterned and often durable cues. Central in establishing the longevity of values, beliefs, practices and ethics, historians have tended to use the past – its lessons, triumphs, and tragedies – as a way to understand contemporary conditions, suggesting that what has drawn academic attention has tended to be that which has persisted. Largely dependent on documents rather than people, historical inquiry has ranged from history writ small, as in memoirs or biographies, through histories that are organized around temporal periods, themes and events, and across history writ large, where the concern primarily surrounds the linkage between large-scale institutions. Not surprisingly, much of this scholarship has had to wrestle with the question of who can lay claim to the past, paving the way for social and cultural histories that offer a bottoms-up view of the past and allow for greater consideration of contingency.

Enter communication. One of the more recent residents of the disciplinary environment, communication situates itself against the world in myriad ways. Touted as the study of the communicative actions, values, beliefs and practices by which people engage with others, communication concerns itself with the relay of messages across time and space and the ways in which that relay creates community, produces effect, and lends meaning to the world at large. Borrowing from both the humanities and social sciences, communication – and its ancillary assists of media studies, journalism studies, and speech communication, among others – positions rhetoric alongside positivism, the study of organizational strategy alongside the examination of marginalization in popular culture. Bridging across the communicative exchanges between people, across groups, within organizations and formal settings, through institutions and structures, media and numerous symbolic modes of exchange, communication underlies nearly every aspect of human activity. In much the same way that the past is constitutive for historians, human exchange of some type is constitutive for communication scholars. And yet both – the past and communicative exchange – go far beyond the specific disciplinary boundaries that house them. Larger than the disciplines that claim their ownership, these originary concepts leak outward and in so doing herald the blending of the disciplines that follow in their stead.

At the same time, both disciplines offer handshakes to the other that call to mind a distant, disliked relative. For both communication and history, the other constitutes no better than a choice among alternatives, across topic, focus, method and theory. Communication historians mirror historians of communication, in that history's orientation toward communication and communication's orientation toward history display a similar marginalization of the other. Neither of the fields moves strongly beyond its own disciplinary nearsightedness to engage with the other head-on, and neither offers a clear response to the role, impact or relevance of the other. The mainstream of historical inquiry uses communication – and its related focal points of the media, journalism and popular culture – with some degree of skepticism, and often only when other venues do not readily present themselves for analysis. The mainstream of communication research relates hesitantly to history, which challenges both its primary orientation to the present and its lack of recognition that an interest in contemporary times draws boundaries around a point in the present in parallel fashion to historians' drawing of boundaries around a point in the past. For each, the other is part of the landscape of inquiry, but unevenly so.

And yet, inquiry has begun to travel with increasing ease across disciplinary boundaries, with some of the most relevant interdisciplinary endeavors such as "the history of the book" or "the history of technology" prompting us to ask whether we have thought enough about what happens when different disciplines meld together into new modes of knowledge acquisition. The questions implied here are manifold. How are historical topics addressed within communication, and what does it mean when we say our research "has a historical component"? In which ways can different historical perspectives be useful in shaping that address? What is historical communication research and what could it be if we were to invest some effort at clarifying its parameters?

This book attempts to force a connection between communication and history so as to provoke discussion of what happens when they do engage. In addressing the intersection between communication and history, it asks the fundamental question of what happens to our understanding of both disciplines when they are brought together in inquiry. *Explorations in Communication and History* attempts to discern the shape of that intersection. The questions it tackles are multiple and diverse. What do we understand differently about history by virtue of its connection with communication? What impact does history have on communication? How does each deepen, enhance and complicate our understanding of the other? What about history and communication independently shapes academic exploration? How do historians and communication theorists occupy and maintain ground in thinking through the issues, problems and events of the world around them? Equally important, how do communication and history come together in many of the projects that we find them intertwined?

The idea for this volume evolved in part from a measure of frustration with existing disciplinary boundaries. Both communication and history have seemed to be the ever growing focus of inquiry across the academic curriculum but not always in ways that call attention to the disciplines from which they originally evolved. As other modes of scholarly attention successfully incorporate historical inquiry into their projects or delve into the areas integral to communication without calling them as such, communication and history seem to have been pushed to the backdrop of academic inquiry, where their basic impulses and premises are subtly invoked but largely unarticulated.

Explorations in Communication and History constitutes an attempt to draw communication and history back to the foreground of academic thought. In asking why care about the intersection of communication and history, the book aims to invigorate thinking about disciplinary boundaries and what happens when we cross them, mix them up and challenge them.

Structure of the book

Explorations in Communication and History originated as a conference, held at the University of Pennsylvania's Annenberg School for Communication. Sparked by a concern articulated by then-graduate student Josh Lauer, who worried over the lack of sufficient address to the intersection between communication and history, the school's Scholars Program in Culture and Communication joined forces with the Graduate Working Group in

Communication and History to mount a one-day symposium devoted to the topic.[7]

Four frequently traveled roads have engaged communication theorists and historians in conceptual ways – the general link between the two disciplines, audiences, technology and journalism. Inherent in each have been questions about method: what were the relevant issues of access, sampling and data retrieval? Who left the better paper trail, and what was one to do about the trail if it did not yield the fullest understanding of the problem at hand? Questions have been also raised about existential certainty, as in the fundamental question of how can we know that what we know is worth knowing? How are we to craft an analytical setting that pushes us beyond the obvious – connecting odd bedfellows of discipline, methodology, time period, geographic diversity or parallel problem?

Four panels were set up to reflect these engagements. Speakers were purposefully juxtaposed in ways that forced them to engage across their disciplinary differences – communication scholars who worked in a historical paradigm, historians who focused on topics germane to communication, scholars from other disciplines whose interests drew from both communication and history.

Explorations in Communication and History reflects that structure, and four sections mirror the panels originally charged with addressing the engagement of communication and history.

Overview: communication and history

Three papers open the conversation on the engagement between communication and history, asking about the ways in which the general link between them has impacted upon the structure of knowledge. Querying how each discipline shapes its targets of inquiry and what happens to inquiry when it draws from both disciplines, this section offers the opportunity to consider history and communication across their broadest cues of engagement.

It is fitting that noted communication theorist John Durham Peters begins the conversation. In "History as a communication problem," he situates the philosophy of history as a problem in media theory. Following on Marshall McLuhan, he argues for the similarity in the functions of media and the functions of history-writing: recording (overcoming of time), transmission (overcoming of space) and control (usage and interpretation). In suggesting direct corollaries between the two, Peters suggests that ways of thinking that have developed within communication can be fruitfully applied to the broader project of knowing the past.

Sociologist Paul Starr takes the conversation in the direction of democratic theory, when he asserts that democratic principles have long been the source of a normative standpoint for much writing on the history of modern communication. In "Democratic theory and the history of communications," Starr asserts that regardless of whether or not history has been told as a triumph, a tragedy, or a story of mixed implications, the basic question has been whether various aspects of the development of communication have advanced or conflicted with democratic ideals. Starr offers three debates to serve as examples of this disciplinary blending: the debate over the formation of the public sphere in the early-modern era; the debate over the relation of mass commercial media to democracy in the nineteenth and twentieth centuries; and the fate of democracy in the post-broadcast era. He thus argues that for better or worse, the political anxieties about the media today inevitably color our understanding of the past.

Cultural historian and media theorist James Curran concludes the conversation on the most broadly-scoped engagement between history and communication. In his essay "Narrating media history," Curran draws on British media history to identify contending themes for a contemporary history of the media in economically advanced liberal democracies. Tracking claims about the media and the people and their counter-narratives that have emerged over time, he argues that the differing accounts provide an agenda for developing a new comparative history of the media. That history both breaks free from the easy generalizations of technological determinism and attends to the convergences and divergences of societal development.

Audiences

A second engagement between communication and history involves audiences and their alternate conceptualization by each discipline. How and for which reasons have history and communication conceptualized audiences? Why are audiences important? What role do audiences play in the larger conceptual project? Does an emphasis on the audience facilitate an understanding of the linkage between communication and history, and if not, why not?

Leading this discussion is cultural and media historian Susan Douglas, who in her essay, "Does textual analysis tell us anything about past audiences?", asks how scholars capture audience meanings of media texts when audiences are gone. Douglas challenges one of the long-standing canons of the communication field – that one cannot infer audience responses from the text itself – and she maps the multiple structures of meanings in texts to the multiple structures of meanings in viewers and readers. Douglas calls for a recognition of textual analysis as an historical tool in understanding media audiences and provides examples of how historical context, remnants of audience responses and media texts can be combined in productive, historically accurate ways.

Media historian Richard Butsch, in "The citizen audience: Crowds, publics and individuals," takes the discussion in the direction of political action, where he argues that although audiences have been seldom regarded as a political category, history reveals that they have been consistently represented in politically significant terms. Focusing on three representations of audiences – movie audiences in the 1910s and 1920s, radio audiences in the 1930s and

1940s, and television audiences in the 1950s and 1960s – Butsch tracks the differing notions of audience that have figured over time and the ways in which they have been enmeshed in political discourses, even when the political nature of the representation was not explicit.

Finally, anthropologist S. Elizabeth Bird considers how scholarship on media audiences has moved away from studies of direct engagement with texts and towards a consideration of the multiple articulations with media in everyday life. In "Seeking the historical audience: Interdisciplinary lessons in the recovery of media practices," Bird traces the change to the (re)discovery of practice as a guiding concept in theorizing the diffuse nature of the media audience in the twenty-first century. She demonstrates how communication history can be enriched by using scholarship on mediated practices deriving from cultural history and literary studies. Moving beyond the question of "reader response," such scholarship has applied ethnographically-inspired methods to show continuities (as well as differences) among media practices over time.

Technology

A third engagement between communication and history is that of technology. In thinking about how history and communication address technology, the impact wielded by the traditional historical approach to technology on the scholarly understanding of technology itself underlies many of the questions that arise: What have been the strengths and limitations of historical approaches to technology? Has technology advanced or obscured the linkage between history and communication?

Literary scholar Peter Stallybrass opens this discussion, addressing the technological constraints and possibilities inherent in "Printing and the writing revolution." Stallybrass argues that the single most important aspect of printing has been the incitement to write by hand and the related dissemination of blank forms. Tackling widely-held misconceptions about writing, printing and the relation between them, Stallybrass shows that the communication revolutions of the last five hundred years have depended on a revolution in manuscript.

In "Governing by television," cultural and film studies theorist Anna McCarthy turns the conversation toward television history, where she argues for an approach to television history that understands public service programming as a flexible discursive position. Such a position would encompass a range of possible relationships between audiences, sponsors and broadcasters. Focusing attention on the diverse strategies that sponsors have used to gain access to the arena of broadcasting where viewers are addressed as citizens renders visible, in all of its complexity, the contentious history of ideas about how to transform TV into a tool of liberal governance.

Finally, communication historian John Nerone takes up the historical construction of communication technology by looking at specific technologies as they have intersected over time with tensions in changing work relations and routines. In "Newswork, technology, and cultural form: 1837–1920," Nerone offsets the longstanding regard for the history of communication technology as seen through a technological prism. Instead, discussing the telegraph, picture technology, printing technology and newsroom technology, Nerone shows how the impact of technology has varied by workplace structures, market pressures and ideological or cultural factors.

Journalism

The fourth relevant intersection between communication and history is that of journalism. Beyond a fundamental tension over whether historical record-keeping has been conducted for professional or scholarly purposes, this section addresses the ways in which history and communication have differently conceptualized journalism as a focus for scholarly endeavor. Have existing approaches to journalism history succeeded and/or missed the boat? And how has the input from communication and history helped us understand journalism differently?

Leading the discussion is journalism historian David Paul Nord, whose essay, "The history of journalism and the history of the book," examines the indifferent relationship between journalism history and the history of the book. Arguing that such indifference stems from a rooting in different scholarly disciplines, Nord explores the origins of the two fields and the sense of distinctiveness that has grown from a core theoretical difference: while journalism history has been concerned with institutions, book history has been concerned with texts. Nord suggests that an understanding of that difference could lead to a sharing of research strategies, which would be profitable to both fields.

In "Public spheres, imagined communities, and the underdeveloped historical understanding of journalism," sociologist and communication scholar Michael Schudson takes the discussion in the direction of imagined and constructed collectivities. Considering the coexistence of Habermas' "public sphere" and Anderson's "imagined community," Schudson argues that both concepts help release the historical study of journalism from the assumption that the only thing to look for is progress or retreat from the liberty of the press. Schudson calls for a more critical perspective among scholars toward both concepts, arguing that they should act as no more than guiding metaphors in the face of the historical specificity and complexity that arises in journalism's historical study.

Finally, political economist Robert W. McChesney rounds out the discussion in his essay, "How to think about journalism: looking backward, going forward." Tracing a key tenet of the political economy of communication – that media systems are not "natural" or the province of a "free market" but result from explicit and often enormous government policies and subsidies –

McChesney addresses a number of critical historical moments in which the range of debate has been relatively broad, leaving society to go in numerous directions with its media policies and subsidies. McChesney considers the implications of such critical junctures for the field.

Back to the future

Not long ago, communication historian John Nerone spoke to many of the ideas implicit in this volume, noting that while communication has always looked to the future, its moorings have always been mired in the past.[8] Today that past covers an uneven territory of interdisciplinary ramblings with no specific audience in mind. Histories of literacy, histories of the public sphere, histories of journalism, and histories of technology are all situated across continua that differently stress form versus content, broad concept versus concrete detail, history for professional aims versus history for scholarly ones. This book attempts to discern what we are to make of this territory in creating a coherent state of affairs for the public, our students and ultimately ourselves. In that the question of matching method to concept, of choosing the right tool to excavate the right idea, has always rested at the underside of how one structures one's academic projects, it is undeniable that not enough has been done to clarify what we mean when we say we "do" communication history.

And so we come back to the future. The aim of this book is both to navigate the terrain connecting communication and history as well as raise meta-questions about its shaping. The essays in this volume elaborate our understanding of what communication and history have to give each other, how they build off of each other's strengths and often subvert each other's weaknesses. Looking back in time, then, is an exercise that has forward looking dimensions in its impact, its relevance and ultimately its pedagogic appeal. Looking backward will hopefully take us forward, teaching us about what has been but also about what our future might look like.

Notes

1 C.P. Snow, *Two Cultures and the Scientific Revolution* (Cambridge: Cambridge University Press, 1960).
2 See Zeus Leonardo, "Editor's Introduction: Theme Issue – Disciplinary Knowledge and Quality Education," *Educational Research* (June/July 2004): 4.
3 Thomas Kuhn, *The Structure of Scientific Revolutions* (Chicago, IL: University of Chicago Press, 1964). Also see Barbie Zelizer, *Taking Journalism Seriously: News and the Academy* (Thousand Oaks, CA: Sage, 2004).
4 Peter Berger and Thomas Luckmann, *The Social Construction of Reality* (Garden City, NJ: Anchor Books, 1966); Emile Durkheim, *The Elementary Forms of the Religious Life* (New York: Free Press, 1965 [1915]); Michel Foucault, *The Archaeology of Knowledge* (London: Tavistock, 1972); Nelson Goodman, *Ways of Worldmaking* (Indianapolis, IN: Hackett Publishing Company, 1978); G. Nigel Gilbert and Michael Mulkay, *Opening Pandora's Box: A Sociological Analysis of*

Scientific Discourse (Cambridge: Cambridge University Press, 1984); Mary Douglas, *How Institutions Think* (Syracuse, NY: Syracuse University Press, 1986).

5 Stanley Fish, *Is There a Text in This Class?* (Cambridge, MA: Harvard University Press, 1980); Barbie Zelizer, "Journalists as Interpretive Communities," *Critical Studies in Mass Communication* 10, no. 3 (1993): 219–37.

6 See, for example, Tony Becher and Paul Trowler, *Academic Tribes and Territories*. (Buckingham: Open University Press, 1989); Ken Hyland, "Academic Attribution: Citation and the Construction of Disciplinary Knowledge," *Applied Linguistics* 20/3 (1999): 341–67; Leonardo, "Editor's Introduction: Theme Issue," 3–5.

7 This group included Barbie Zelizer, Director of The Scholars Program at the University of Pennsylvania's Annenberg School for Communication, and members of the Annenberg Graduate Working Group in Communication and History. The conference was entitled *Back to the Future: Explorations in Communication and History*, run by then graduate students Josh Lauer, Deborah Lubken, Jennifer Ruth Horner, and Nicole Maurantonio and convened on December 1, 2006.

8 John Nerone, "The Future of Communciation History," *Critical Studies in Media Communication* 23, no. 3 (August 2006): 254–62.

Part I

Overview

Communication and history

Introduction

Communication and history

Josh Lauer

Historical inquiry is a decidedly modern and tragically human enterprise. The idea of the past as a vast repository of evidence to be discovered, reconstructed, and cumulatively archived is only several centuries old, and its impetus in the dream of perfect knowledge belies the existential anxiety of modernity. The damned project of historical representation is well illustrated by Jorge Luis Borges, the Argentine fabulist who understood the paradoxes of memory and perception perhaps better than anyone. In one of his many brilliant fictive fragments he recounts the work of ancient cartographers who, seeking to produce a perfectly accurate map of their empire, construct a map that corresponds to the exact dimensions of the empire itself. The absurdity of this undertaking exposes the limits of human comprehension. The whole truth – lived reality in its material, temporal, and experiential entirety – corresponds to the full dimensions of reality itself. Mere mortals must content themselves with something far less, or succumb to the cartographers' folly.

These three essays provide the groundwork for thinking about the limits and possibilities of communication history. Each regards the history of communication as one of many possible histories, and each demonstrates how the communication histories we have are shaped by the interests and very historicity of their authors. Together Peters, Starr and Curran draw pointed attention to the *biases* of communication history. Historical inquiry is by necessity selective, reductive, incomplete, partial – in a word, biased. The concept of communication bias derives from Harold Innis, the Canadian economic historian whose media-centric interpretation of world civilization is now classic. Yet "bias" has an unfortunate pejorative ring; it bears an association with error, and in particular error borne of human fallibility in the context of dispassionate scientific inquiry. Bias, in this light, refers to the investigator's failure to probe the object of study with proper neutrality; it is a misinterpretation, a false-reading as a result of mishandled evidence or instrumentation. But as Peters, Starr and Curran suggest, bias is not only inevitable in all domains of human inquiry (including the scientific), it may also be productive. To note that history – and communication history specifically – is biased is not to disparage the significance of the past, but to acknowledge its dynamism.

Peters offers a rich historiography of communication that not only explodes conventional notions of media history but, bounding past Innis, places the history of media at the center of historical inquiry itself. Peters observes that the problem of historical inquiry bears striking resemblance to the problem of communication in that, at a fundamental level, the historian's task is to conjure the conditions for perfect communication with distant others – namely the dead. The historian's medium is the record of the past, the body of evidence that he or she painstakingly disinters, assembles, and interprets, and through which the dead are re-presented. Evidence, however, is characterized by a curious ontology. Records of the past (as well as telling lacunae) are continually coming into being as a result of new technologies, methodologies, and historical interests that make them intelligible. Paradoxically, Peter notes, technological advances may be only nominally futuristic. Recent developments in DNA analysis, for example, permit dead men (and women) to speak again. The temporal direction of progress, after all, may be backward, toward the revivification of the past. Peters' radical insight reveals the parallel concerns of communication and history, as found in their shared concepts of recording, transmission, and interpretation.

While Peters argues for a more expansive and imaginative conceptualization of media, Starr draws close attention to the political stakes of communication history. Noting that historians are all too eager to elide questions of political theory in their studies of the past, Starr asserts that media history is deeply implicated in the ongoing struggle over democracy in the United States. Communication history is not simply a chronicle of technological change and cultural experience, but also a history of the idea of communication as a political right. Starr identifies three vying theories of democracy – minimalist, radical, and deliberative – and illustrates how their respective understanding of key moments in American media history informs their divergent visions of government, citizenship, and the circulation of information in a democratic society. The debate over contemporary media policy – whether media conglomerations are a legitimate result of market forces or a pernicious aberration – is thus contingent on one's interpretation of the past, even when many important "facts" are generally agreed upon by all involved. Starr's analysis reminds us that no history, media history included, is innocent. To recount the past is to interpret it. In this way history and historiography are two sides of the same coin. One's theoretical perspective dictates the selection (and exclusion) of evidence and the conclusions one draws from its interpretation.

Curran, like Peters and Starr, is keenly attentive to the biases of communication history. Noting the increasingly global perspective of mainstream communication studies, Curran observes that Anglo-American media history remains hidebound in its conventional focus on a single communication technology – newspapers, radio, or film, for example – in isolated national contexts. The blindness of such "national introversion," he argues, is compounded by a proliferation of media subspecialties, from book history to television history, that further encourage insularity and inhibit comparative or synthetic histories of media across time and geography. Moreover, Curran observes, where media historians have failed to address large-scale, transnational developments in communication history, the work of world-historical explanation has fallen into the hands of technological determinists. If the limitations of media micro-history are glaring, they pale in comparison to the biases of technological determinism at their worst, which Curran enumerates and summarily dismantles. The real poverty of "techno-history," however, is not to be found in the work of erudite determinists such as Marshall McLuhan, Elizabeth Eisenstein, and Neil Postman, but in the pronouncements of over-zealous new media scholars who champion the latest technology – notably the internet – as an agent of revolutionary human change. The central problem of technological determinism, Curran shrewdly notes, is not simply its mono-causal interpretation of the past but its naïve extrapolations into the future. If historians have learned anything from positivist critique (or Marx, for that matter), it is that they tread into the future at their own peril.

Each author foregrounds selection as a determining factor in historical inquiry and underscores its significance for communication history. Finite existence demands parsimony; for historians this is achieved through decisions about which evidence to use and which to put aside. In effect, selection is as much a form of willed ignorance as it is a display of mastery in one's chosen specialization. (Ignorance, like bias, also bears an unfortunate negative connation that mistakes the fertility of the unknown for barrenness.) All history is a history of this and *not* that. The problem of selection is central to Curran's criticism of contemporary media history. As he notes, the choices one makes in terms of which media to study, where, when, and in what location have profound implications. The experiences of entire regions and huge populations may be invisible to the history of communication if they happen to exist in places that are *not* North American and *not* Europe. Likewise, in advocating for deliberative democracy Starr illustrates how partisans at opposite ends of the political continuum select (or ignore) different elements of American media history to legitimize their respective policy agendas. The rise of commercial media may be viewed as a Whiggish story of mass enlightenment or a dystopic story of mass control. Neither version is entirely false, yet the truth is in the telling. The problem of selection, as Peters notes, carries weighty ethical baggage. By framing the past as "otherness," human otherness in particular, he argues against the extremes of historical relativism and its cynical amorality.

Historical inquiry, as these authors attest, reveals as much about the present as it does about the past. There is no single unified past to be discovered, but many pasts, each informed by the questions that are asked and the evidence that is both available and deemed meaningful. Though the history of communication is inherently interdisciplinary – the field of communication has no special purchase on the subject – interest in the study of media past has special urgency for communication scholars. Together these three essays cast a bright light on one of the most grievous features of contemporary communication studies: its presentism. The field of communication, in all of its disparate and confusing splendor, suffers from a myopic preoccupation with the here and now. Those who seek to understand the theoretical principles, processes, effects, institutions, and technologies of communication do not look backward often enough. Time is a powerful variable, and the material culture, social structures, and *mentalities* of the past offer useful comparative lenses through which to view the world we happen to inhabit at the moment. The study of communication history, as Peters, Starr and Curran show us, offers deep insight into the conditions of life and in its infinite variety in contexts ranging from the local to the global and, indeed, the cosmological.

Chapter 1

History as a communication problem

John Durham Peters

The study of communication history is itself historically recent. Until the late nineteenth century, no one thought of communication as an entity unto itself that was distinct from domains such as transportation, publishing, exchange, language, or speech. The idea that there was such a thing as communication and that it had a history emerged in nineteenth-century history and political economy among figures such as Tocqueville and Guizot in France, Mill in England, and Knies and Schäffle in Germany. Two representative figures who consolidated this work sociologically in the early twentieth century were Charles Horton Cooley in the United States and Werner Sombart in Germany. Cooley's dictum that "transportation is physical, communication is psychical" was one stop in the long journey of the concept of communication from material to metaphysical modes of carriage.[1] By the 1930s, outlines for a history of communication were taking shape in thinkers such as Lewis Mumford, John Dewey, Edward Sapir, Walter Benjamin and his fellow-travelers in the Frankfurt School, but the key figure is probably the Canadian political economic historian, Harold Adams Innis (1894–1952), who devoted the last years of his cancer-shortened life to preparing a series of essays, books, and a massive incomplete manuscript on the history of communication. Starting his career with the study of staples and ending it with the study of media, Innis's subject was always the crucial role played by networks and materials of exchange. He too did his bit to push the concept of communication in a more symbolic direction.

Many of his colleagues seemed to have thought Innis a bit mad to place media of communication alongside such traditional drivers of world history as politics, markets, war, demography, and culture. To be sure, Innis could sound a bit monomaniacal about his new key to the rise and fall of civilizations. Read uncharitably, Innis's discovery that the oral tradition, stone, clay, papyrus, parchment, and paper would each produce a different social and political life and kind of historical record might seem banal. Read generously, Innis was more than simply adding another topic to the historian's repertoire. Once admitted into the study of history, communication was a theme that threatened – or promised – to revolutionize the entire enterprise. As he wrote in 1949, "Our knowledge of other civilizations depends in large part on the character of the media used by each civilization insofar as it is capable of being preserved or of being made accessible by discovery."[2] Our knowledge of the past is a question of media. Innis not only invented the history of media; he also discovered the media of history.

For Innis, history is a problem of communication over time and space, and every medium selectively transmits, records, and makes accessible to discovery. Each medium of history – documents, ruins, household artifacts, bones, DNA, or whatever else has survived the journey from past to present – has inherent biases. Historians who study long temporal spans, Innis noted, usually over-emphasize religion and neglect bureaucracy because the documents that endure are typically designed by time-conserving agents like sages and priests rather than space-controlling agents like lawyers and merchants. The choice of topic and method a priori swerves the record. Interpreting the past means not only reading the content of the historical record but studying the constitution of the record itself. "Bias" implied not only potential threats to objectivity: Innis had in mind the textile metaphor of a slant cut. Historians necessarily read along the diagonal. Inasmuch as they reflect on the conditions of their own practice, historians are necessarily media scholars.

Communication scholars have hardly sounded our deep resonances with the task of history-writing. Both fields face the methodological problem of how to interpret under conditions of remoteness and estrangement. They share a strikingly common vocabulary of sources, records, meanings, and transmissions. Though media studies in particular has typically focused more on diffusion over space, media also enable duration over time. Transmission and recording, the overcoming of space and of time, are central themes to both fields. Recording is the act of inscribing something in enduring form; transmission is the act of sending a record across some kind of distance, whether space or time; and interpretation is the act of receiving transmitted records and putting them to work in the present. Historical research is always a matter of triangulating record, transmission, and interpretation. In this essay, I propose to explore the convergence of the philosophy of history and communication theory with the hope not only of enlarging our vision of what communication history might be, but also of aiding recognition of how central problems of communication are to the study of history. Communication history is not only a supplement to historical inquiry; it is a challenge to how we approach history itself.

Historians already have an acute sensitivity to questions of mediation. Their business is to evaluate documents in terms of their date, provenance, author, authenticity, tradition, and so on. A historian's first question of a document is not, What does it say?, but rather, How did it come to be?, or perhaps even more, How did it end up here? The very fact that it (still) exists at all may be the most telling fact. All historians are media scholars in the sense that they read texts and artifacts in terms of their processes of production and dis-tribution. The past is constellated by the gap between past and present and is shaped by the very historical processes we are trying to understand.

Historians, in other words, are highly sensitive to conditions of encoding and decoding. Cultural historian Carlo Ginzburg speaks of the semiotics of clues and the philosopher Paul Ricoeur speaks of the hermeneutics of testimony. Both styles of interpretation have the habit of focusing on incidentals and contingencies. One watches the extras, not the stars; one listens not to the speech, but to the slips of the tongue. Ginzburg and Ricoeur point to a forensic habit that treasures circumstantial evidence and symptoms. For an art historian, the tell-tale sign that a painting is a forgery is found in the rendering of ears or hands, not of faces. For a judge, the clinching evidence that determines what really happened in a crime can be found in the details that authenticate the veracity of a witness's testimony. As in the Sherlock Holmes story, sometimes the most significant thing is that the dog didn't bark.[3] Art scholars, judges, and detectives share with historians the habit of reading records sideways. A historian getting a first look at old documents will not go straight to the "contents"; he or she will look at the source, the bundle, the order items are gathered, the creases, etc. Historians of printing can find a book's binding more interesting than its words just as a historian of cholera outbreaks in Europe might be more interested in sniffing documents for the smell of vinegar (used as a disinfectant against the disease) than in reading them in the traditional sense.[4] The medium is the message in history too.

The historical record

It is the unusual that gets documented. This is the cognitive bias beloved of journalists: Man bites dog. Records are inherently fallible and partial preservations of events. Even in everyday talk, which can be considered as a kind of oral documentation of actions and thoughts, the ratio of what is unstated-but-understood to what is actually stated is huge. Only a minimum of shared understanding is ever articulated into speech. All documents rest against an unnoticed background.

Harold Garfinkel applies this insight to institutional practices of record-keeping. Documents such as medical records, for instance, are not made with the point of making a full and complete account suitable for an historicist. What might seem like flawed documents to an outsider can serve institutional routines splendidly. As he titles one of his studies, there are "'good' organizational reasons for 'bad' clinic records." Psychiatric records do not reveal the ordinary modes of social interaction in a clinic; rather, they presuppose (and thus hide) them. Considered as verisimilar mirrors, the records might seem distorted; for insider use, they do their job.[5] The most vital bits of information are often precisely not recorded. There is a cognitive economics, politics and sociology of documentation. The historical record was rarely if ever written for historians, who are usually in the position of eavesdroppers (as most of us are in communication). This situation is familiar from hermeneutics: we read texts that were never addressed to us.[6]

Records vary with transcription protocols. Once a colleague walked into my office, brandishing a "special offer" that had come in the mail. With a cynical grin on his face, he announced a new video of "the greatest moments in sports history." It took me a minute to get the point: If it's a video, it thereby rules out all sports history before the movie camera existed, and all of sports history that took place away from the presence of a camera. "Sports history" had suddenly shrunk to the period from 1895 to the present. But note how I just made a subtler mistake: letting in the dream that there is such a thing as a continuous "sports history" unaffected by the media that record it. In the most literal sense, the choice of medium determines the historical record.

A more subtle case is the archaeological record of prehistoric humans. The record is biased towards axes, daggers, arrowheads and objects that endure. These tend to be what Lewis Mumford calls "power technologies" rather than "container technologies" such as baskets, food storage, language, families, reservoirs, and rituals, which leave relatively few traces. Tools survive better than words, deeds, thoughts, or childrearing practices. This differential survival, Mumford complains, gives us a distorted and rather masculinist view of humans as tool-using animals – rather than, say, as dreaming or language-using animals.[7] Reading what time has done to the record along with the record may free us from enslaving ideologies.

Records are descriptions, and it is the nature of descriptions to be inexhaustible. Potential communication about an event is never complete. There is always something more to say; a record, by definition, is never finished. Every speaker of a language has the astonishing capacity to produce completely intelligible sentences that have never been uttered before in history, and every speaker pulls off this enormous stunt several times each day. This generativity is equally true for documentation and description. No record is ever the final word. This is not, of course, to say that some records are not richer than others. We can be grateful to Samuel Pepys and Margaret Ballard for providing vistas into their worlds, but no one would claim their diaries said everything about seventeenth-century London or eighteenth-century Maine.[8] We never know when another record will arise that will complicate, destroy, or confirm what we already know. Russia, as the old saying goes, has an unpredictable past. New old documents rewrite old new ones. Discovery of the Dead Sea Scrolls in 1947 utterly revolutionized understanding of the Bible. Like any object of description, the past is emergent.

The past is radically incomplete because the historical record is itself historical. Scholars interested in the social history of ordinary women have had to work around the "lack of evidence" that was once held to block such history.[9] Historians of labor, childhood, slavery, diet, mentalities, everyday life, privacy, and disease have similarly set about uncovering what now seems an almost absurdly fecund historical record. Before 1900, few dreamed that something as ephemeral as the weather had a knowable history. Thanks to dendrochronology (using tree rings as indicators of annual temperature) and the drilling of core samples in the polar ice to tap small bubbles of atmospheric air trapped centuries ago among other techniques, the lively field of climate history now offers a growing understanding of the history of earth's weather – something of immediate relevance given the global warming crisis. Evidence emerges in response to sensitization (women's history) or instrumentation (climate history), but perhaps they are ultimately the same thing. Martha Ballard's diary wouldn't be half as telling without such an able reader as Ulrich. Changing sensitivities change the record: where would French social history be for the past five decades without all its police transcripts and local court records, documents that skilful reading has made so eloquent? Just as there is no such thing as an a priori limit on what can be a message – you cannot not communicate – so there is no end to the potential richness of the past.

The past emerges in the future. An Italian anthropologist who took part in the recent exhumation of two Renaissance humanists explained:

> Bodies are an archive of information surrounding the life and death of a person. With today's technology, we can clear up various doubts that have been passed down for centuries and we can provide answers that could not [have] been discovered years ago.[10]

Pico della Mirandola has been dead since 1494, but for most of those five centuries, his body was just a rotting cadaver; only recently did it become an "archive." The scientists planned a DNA analysis of the bodies, and DNA of course is the preeminent figure by which bodies have become readable texts of late. New forensic methods have called a new historical record into being – or is it an old historical record? The old is as emergent as the new. Geoffrey Winthrop-Young smartly notes the name for the sudden reemergence of something long lost or buried: trauma.[11]

The historian is in the same position as the witness: neither can know what will be the crucial evidence while events are unfolding. Evidence, both in court and in history, only appears as evidence post facto.[12] What is refuse today may be priceless tomorrow.[13] In noting the Buddhist scriptures preserved on stone by over a thousand years of careful labor by monks in the Yunju monastery in China, Stewart Brand adds:

> probably we would value the stones more if the monks had simply recorded the weather and what they were eating. Better still would have been a reverently preserved sequential archive of dried monk poop, which would yield no end of data on diet, agriculture, climate, health, and racial and family lineage.[14]

In his preference for feces over holy writ, Brand points to the unpredictable market value of historical traces – and like Garfinkel, he notes the deletion of the ordinary in documentation. (It is probably too unsavory a thought to ponder what a treasure for some future historian we destroy every time we flush the toilet.) Fortunately, attrition is the precondition of historical intelligibility. Who knows if we would value the writings of the ancients as much if the library of Alexandria had survived. Perhaps we would esteem Sophocles less great a playwright if more of his plays were extant. The historical record, like all goods, is precious when scarce.

My discussion of "history" as a general philosophical abstraction is dangerous since such a conception is itself a product of a particular historical moment. And even this insight – that the past emerges in the future – is itself historical. Only in modernity, with its dynamic swelling of the past thanks to geology, critical–historical methods, evolutionary biology, cosmology, and archaeology could such an acute consciousness of the dynamism of the historical record exist. Thanks to the graphic revolution of the nineteenth century, in which photography, phonography, myography, cinematography, spectrography, and many other techniques burst apart writing's long-held monopoly on cultural storage, we have an exploded notion of records. Thanks to such automatic inscriptions, we can now "read what was never written." Analog media allow us to capture nonintentional tracings whose significance does not depend upon the symbolic preprocessing of language.[15] The most modern thing about modernity may well be our vision of antiquity, all the way back to the first second of the Big Bang; and the best site to see temporal rupture may not be medicine and technology but the constant remaking of the past. We live with the awareness that there may yet emerge media of witnessing that will make the most insignificant bits of our world into precious nuggets of historical information. The historical record does not only degrade over time; it can also become more articulate. We never know when some new (or rather old) jawbone will rewrite the history of the human family. That old things can be new is the secret to the dynamic historical record.

Historical transmission

"Communication theory" was first Claude Shannon's study of how to filter and make intelligible signals sent over a distance. Without the mathematics, history-writing has a similar concern. The winners may write the history, but they depend on the fortunes of nature and the good will of posterity for knowledge of their victory to survive. "Look on my Works, ye Mighty, and despair!" boasts the great Ozymandias in Shelley's poem. The king meant those words to taunt his rivals, who are to despair at ever matching his grandeur; the modern reader, in contrast, despairs upon finding those words in deserted wreckage. Moth and rust can be unkind to memory. So can human beings. The remembrance of events depends upon the labor and favor of anonymous scribes. As recent research has shown, institutions of cultural transmission – monasteries, libraries, universities, museums, and archives – have all kinds of interests, political and otherwise.[16] So much depends on an auction catalog or a royal archivist. Both history and media have gatekeepers.

Culture and nature both shape transmission of the historical record. As of this writing, the Bush White House is fighting in court for the right to delete e-mails.[17] A sign of a disfavor (and likely execution) in Stalin's Soviet Union was to be removed from historical photographs. Such *abolitio memoriae* can occur in less calculated ways. How accessible will our historical record be in fifty years when CDs are already starting to degrade, terabytes of data stored on floppy disks now languish in techno-limbo, and vinyl LPs and VHS tapes fill the shelves unplayed? Much of the film stock of early cinema has already disintegrated. Sibelius torched his eighth symphony some time in the 1940s – around the same time Bakhtin was smoking away his legendary magnum opus, using the manuscript pages to roll his own cigarettes during the wartime shortage. (This may have also been a good way to explain away a horrid case of writer's block. We'll never know.) The most famous example is the oft-lamented burning of the ancient library of Alexandria. Before this train of wreckage calls up too much melancholy, we should note that the preservation of Linear B, a language crucial for our knowledge of early writing systems, owes to a fire that destroyed the palace in Knossos but baked the clay tablets on which the script was written. The same is true for Ugaritic.[18] Vesuvius's hot ash killed Pompeii's lives but preserved its life.

Communication scholars study slant coverage in news, and something similar is found about the past. The critical study of Homer (among other Greek classics) and the Bible was at the heart of the historicist revolution around 1800, and modern scholarship on both has put enormous effort into studying the transmission of those texts. In antiquity already such eminences as Cicero and Josephus noted the unusual composition and transmission of Homer. The mark of modernity is the sense of an irretrievable loss of the source. As the late eighteenth-century German philologist Heyne wrote, "We will not regain the Iliad, as it came from Homer's mind and lips – that is clear; no more than the books of Moses and the Prophets can be restored as they came from the authors' hands."[19] Having given up on the hope of an oral or originary fullness, scholars devoted their lives to the study of manuscript variants and the establishment of the best text. Sometimes they have even imagined source texts, such as the famous "Q" (from the German *Quelle*, source) that is conjectured to lie behind the three synoptic Gospels of Mark, Matthew, and Luke. New Testament scholars, in tracing the sayings of Jesus, try to determine their circulation: "If the report is communicated through different people over a period of time before it achieves written form (as is the case with the gospels), revision can occur at every human link in the chain of transmission."[20] The book that was once thought to be dictated to "the secretaries of the Holy Ghost" started to look like a historical patchwork.

Transmission is never just an empty channel. Media are not pipes for content any more than time is a homogeneous and empty medium that carries the past along. F. A. Wolf, the coiner of the term "philology" and the great eighteenth-century Homer scholar who was central in the rise of modern historical–critical methods, argued that later manuscripts can be more authentic than older ones. He believed he had better manuscripts of Homer in 1794 than the scholars in Alexandria who edited Homer two millennia earlier. (He knew that the past could emerge in asynchronous ways.) Some scholars find apparent distortions in transmission to be of enormous historical value – especially since the idea of word-perfect textual transmission is itself historical. The distinction between scribe and author was rare in the middle ages, and perhaps the printing press launched the notion of a "uniform and repeatable text" in the first place.[21] Scribal "'errors' – misspellings, grammatical faults, transpositions, even apparent omissions – can be significant historical evidence, occasionally about the politics that informed the creation of the particular text and always about the literary technology of the age."[22] The vernacular scholia in the Hebrew texts of the great eleventh-century biblical commentator Rashi had been long ignored by Jewish scholars as scribbles until they were discovered to be a treasure trove of unattested forms of medieval French.[23]

Analysis of the delivery of evidence is always a key part in any systematic study. All inquiry, perhaps, is communication inquiry. Such is clear in evolutionary biology and cosmology, two fields that study the deep past and make processes of transmission into interpretive keys. Darwin's chapter "On the Imperfection of the Geological Record" in *The Origin of Species* in 1859 confronts the scant evidence of transitional links between species. These missing links are unattested in the fossil record not because they did not occur, he argues, but because the record is mutilated and abbreviated. The record of life's history is subject to all the obliterating processes of earth history, from erosion to volcanism. Like Garfinkel, Darwin reads records by reference to the processes that formed them. To uphold his uniformitarian assumptions in the face of a catastrophic record Darwin argued gaps in the transmission of the past, not in the past per se. If the transmission had been more complete, he claims, we would have better evidence of the transitional forms he conjectures. Looking for evidence of links between species in the geological record would in Darwin's view be like trying to find the ancient Olympics on the video of the greatest moments in sports history.

In cosmology, potential disturbances in transmission are actually key data for the history of the universe. When we look deep into space, we are actually looking far back into time. The light that hits our retinas when we look into space began its journey from its source potentially eons ago. Since we live in an expanding universe, light that travels the farthest also undergoes the most extreme disturbance. Following the Doppler effect – waves moving away from a fixed observer are stretched into greater lengths (and thus lower frequencies) – light from distant sources in space is shifted toward the red (lower frequency) part of the spectrum. The redshift is a measure of the velocity of such sources, and thus indirectly of their age. The earlier a light transmission began in the history of the universe, the faster it will be receding, since the greatest speeds of expansion were presumably found at the beginning of the Big Bang. The farther we see into space, the earlier we look into time, and the redder the light is the farther we look. The universe is inside out: its distant edges constitute its youngest parts. (But they are oldest to us.) Instead of discarding redshifts as distorted transmissions, astronomers like Edwin Hubble realized that such distortions could be read as evidence of the history of the universe. He learned to read the bias of the transmission as an index of the past. Redshifts are now routinely used as measures of age for distant celestial transmissions. This is the same interpretive strategy as mining the scholia in Rashi's commentaries.[24]

History and communication share the nineteenth-century dreams of full or perfect transmission. Putting it too schematically, historicism, the ruling doctrine of history-writing since the nineteenth century, has the ideal of time-travel, of achieving a historical reconstruction so perfect that the historian could be fully immersed in the old world. In spiritualism, which has shaped popular ideas of communication in the same period, the dream is that of telepathy, of achieving a mental communion so full that the breaches between minds would melt away. Both dreams turn on the longing for a perfect medium of communication that would transcend the gaps. Both dreams arise in response to ever-thickening apparatuses of history and communication. The critical method as it emerged in Germany around 1800 taught that documents, archives, and sources are precisely not transparent or neutral channels of communication. Modern historical research is always at some level a reflection on the conditions of its own (im)possibility. Source criticism is the hallmark of historicist method, and historians would be the first to say that the past is ultimately inaccessible. Modern men and women around 1900 had to engage in source criticism as they became used to communicating by telegram, phone, and fast mail. They had to learn to filter out medium effects (such as delays in delivery) from communicative choices (such as choosing not to answer). As electrical and other media tore open the space–time continuum, they both promised to span old distances and threatened to destroy old intimacies. Our ideas about history and communication reflect both the modern hope of transcendence and its despair of breakdown.[25]

It is all too easy to criticize these dreams, but transmission, in some form, is too important a category for historians and communication theorists to discard. Critical–cultural communication theorists regard the notion with suspicion. James Carey led the way in a famous essay, contrasting the transmission view of communication with the ritual view.[26] He pointed out that thinking about communication had been ruled by concerns for transmission, which he thought reflected a slightly diseased romance in American culture with dominion over space. Carey wanted, quite correctly, to nudge us from thinking about the accuracy of signals to the constitution of relationships. And yet something was lost in transmission: Carey's own thinking was subtler than the binary of transmission and ritual – he always showed that transmission has rituals, and rituals must be transmitted.[27] Those who want to argue for the importance of transmission, as I do, sometimes have an uphill push against doxa. To some, the concept sounds mechanical, administrative, and professing a false neutrality. And yet none of us can do without it. It is a multi-trillion dollar industry annually. When we speak on the phone, turn on the cable TV, fax a document, overnight a letter, or surf the internet, we expect transmission processes to work. Even more when we catch a plane or train. Transmission is an essential language game in our world. When the doctor or car mechanic gives their diagnosis, we want it to be accurate. We want voting machines to count votes properly. Those who reject transmission as a chief aspect of communication fail to reflect deeply on the conditions of their existence (something that Carey never failed to do).

An interest in transmission does not commit us to a simple-minded positivism. Events are never pure or full; and no story is ever adequate. And yet facts matter and events have their own integrity. Because the past and other minds can never be fully sounded does not mean that we are free to romp in the postmodernist playground. The question shifts from epistemology to ethics. (1) Historians construct stories about the past. (2) Some stories fit the evidence better. These two statements are not incompatible. The French term *histoire* and the German *Geschichte* do not differentiate between story and history. Does this mean that history is only a literary genre? Tragedy, comedy, apocalypse, lyric, and history are all distinct genres of literature, but they are also names for distinct worldviews. A genre is a web of obligations and contracts. To write history is to enter into a kind of covenant with the reader to do one's best to honor the past in its autonomy. Justice depends on the discovery of what really happened in legal – and historical – investigations. Establishing the detailed reality of the past cannot leave us indifferent in questions of crime, war, or love. Care for the past need not commit us to a notion of it as fully "there" and "final." Though we can never know the past perfectly, we can certainly eliminate false claims about it. That we cannot travel in time doesn't mean that we can't avoid anachronisms. "The possibility of error" is an anchor of the universe's intelligible order, claimed the great, forgotten Josiah Royce.[28] Interest in correct transmission is sooner an ethical stance of respect for the otherness of history than an epistemic quest for purity of access or fullness of presence. Denying the Holocaust is not only stupid; it is immoral. It is not so much a defect of cognition as of justice.

Interpretation

Many moments in history have faced the apoplexy of too much information – there is nothing new here. But we live in a moment of an acute archival sensibility, thanks in part to the internet. Historians face what Michael Pollan has called, in another context, "the omnivore's dilemma."[29] Any inquiry is potentially bottomless. Fractal geometry shows that the level of magnification is a contingent choice. The length of the coast of Britain will be a function of the length of your measuring stick.[30] It is the despair of the doctoral student contemplating a historical dissertation that any sentence could be an entire dissertation, and that your own dissertation will be a single sentence in someone else's. What got recorded is a minute fraction of what happened, and what got transmitted is a fraction of that, but the choices we make in interpretation may be the most selective of all. (Of course selection is not only diminution; recording, transmission, and interpretation can also massively augment "what happened.") We have no choice but to choose because our attention is finite and our lives are mortal. We can write big histories of small things – like cod, salt, or the signature – or small histories of big things – like time or the first second of the Big Bang – but no author in a single lifetime can write a universal history. Sampling is not only a procedural question of determining how to access a body of data; it is also an existential one of deciding where to spend your time. Interpretation is in part a logistical concern of how to budget time, space, and energy.

History-writing is one of the most historical of all human things. Our own situatedness in history shapes the way we write it in a more radical way than we usually suspect. The "anthropic principle" in cosmology underscores just this link of position and insight. The principle suggests that only a certain kind of universe could support us as knowers. The universe would have to be old enough and cool enough to have produced the complex chemicals that are the necessary ingredients to sustain intelligent life as we know it. The very possibility of our knowing the universe requires the kind of universe in which we could exist. By the time the universe is mature enough to support life-forms that are able, in some measure, to understand it, it will necessarily be a cold, empty, and dark place (assuming an organic basis for intelligent life). "What we can expect to observe must be restricted by the condition necessary for our presence as observers."[31] The anthropic principle points to the convergence of our existential situation and our epistemological capacity. As historians of the universe, we are subjects of that history. Only at a certain point in the history of the universe can we start to be its historians. Our receptivity to transmissions from deep-space/deep-time owes to our point in space and time. Our ability to read such messages is co-constituted by the historical processes that made such messages. Historians have access to that realm of history that history allows them to have. Within those limits, they have to make hard choices.

The positivist dream of matching the past in its fullness tried to evade this demand. Respecting the past's autonomy and recognizing the inevitability of one's own role as a teller of tales puts the historian in a tight squeeze. The boundary between the fictional and the factual is ethical as much as empirical. We generally assume that fictional narratives about the past are thinner in their relations to the world than factual ones. Conan Doyle never detailed the books on the walls in Sherlock Holmes's flat.[32] The text leaves that patch of reality eternally open. If a thermometer were dropped into a chapter of George Eliot's *Middlemarch*, we would never get a precise reading of the ambient temperature, while a thermometer teleported back to a given hour in 1830s provincial England would presumably provide a precise reading. The clouds mentioned in *Hamlet* let him toy with Polonius but no one expects to get their design or shape from the text. Reality is held to be rich in incidentals and fiction to be poor once we turn away from center stage. An author has no need to fill in the extraneous details that would exist as ignorable background in a fully fledged world. We usually take this vagueness of the circumstantial context to be a chief distinguishing feature of fiction from fact.

Audiovisual media reverse this supposition. They are susceptible to witnessing – that is, to documenting metonymic details.[33] Conan Doyle's text can be indifferent about background details, but a movie version of Holmes cannot. Media that recreate history such as films and museums cannot escape the burden of supplying extraneous evidence, due to their relatively high mimetic "resolution" as we might call it. A film only has one chance to get it right: it is forced to commit on incidentals that the literary text is free forever to leave indefinite.[34] A text can inspire a huge abundance of interpretations without losing its power or meaning. To portray a face, a photographer or painter must use a lot of pixels or oil. An author need only mention a person, and the assumption that they have a face follows. A word implies myriads of other bits of information a priori. Language may be empty in particulars compared with a portrait but it is open by virtue of a semiotic system that can be perpetually refreshed. Vagueness is not only a deficit; it is a resource of meaning. The Bible is drastically minimal in its descriptions, and yet how richly it is "fraught with background."[35] The Gospel narratives say nothing about Jesus' or Mary's appearance, yet they inspired two thousand years of imaging. A film-maker would have to decide if he is a blonde or brunette, whether she has brown or blue eyes; the text's silence on such points makes it richer. A word is worth a thousand pictures.

We presume that fictions are poor and facts are rich, but the vague character of fiction also applies to fact. What we take to be a documentation problem might be a reality problem. Events can be inherently indefinite. Take the case of the assassination of Abraham Lincoln. This event, like the assassination a century later of John F. Kennedy, has sustained microscopic inquiry. When did the Lincolns arrive at the theater? Around 8:30 p.m., during the first act of the play, *Our American Cousin*. When was Lincoln shot? Despite varying testimony, it seems around 10:30 p.m. How far did John Wilkes Booth jump from the presidential theater box to the stage? Ford's Theater was gutted in 1866 and witnesses put the distance loosely between nine and fifteen feet and, so the answer remained unclear until the architectural plans of the original theater were found, providing the precise detail of ten feet, six inches. Did Booth break his leg in the jump? The only contemporary witness is Booth's back-dated diary, a source that has been shown to be unreliable on a number of counts. Eyewitnesses saw him "rush" or "run" across the stage. What did Booth shout? The witnesses largely agree it was "Sic Semper Tyrannis" though other options heard include "The South shall be free," "Revenge for the South," "The South is avenged," "I have done it," and "Freedom." For his part, Booth, in a diary entry written some time between the assassination and his death in a shoot-out twelve days later, claimed only to have said "Sic Semper."[36]

A final mystery with Lincoln's death is what Edwin Stanton, Lincoln's secretary of war, uttered at his bedside upon Lincoln's last breath. "Now he belongs to the ages" was long the undisputed benediction. Recently "now he belongs to the angels" has been advanced as an alternative. The dispute involves two readings of Lincoln: as a Christian–romantic (angels) or as an ancient Stoic (ages). In a thoughtful essay, Adam Gopnik shows that the "ages" quote, which was taken as historical fact for a century, was not recorded until 25 years later in a 1890 biography of Lincoln by two of his secretaries. The "angels" interpolation is more recent, and politically motivated by an interest in reading Lincoln as a Christian figure, but there are at least some plausible historical reasons for it. In the end, we don't know what Stanton said, or even if Stanton knew what he said. If a tape recorder had been in the crowded, chaotic room – a room filled with a changing cast of grieving people – at the moment it might not have resolved anything. As Gopnik concludes, "The past is so often unknowable not because it is befogged now but because it was befogged then, too, back when it was the present."[37]

The uncertainty of the past comes not only from the limitations of our vision; it comes from the indefiniteness of what happens. We might fantasize that a more perfect machinery of documentation would catch the motion of every molecule – but such would only show us the bounciness at the heart of things. As one Vienna circle philosopher said with a bit too much zeal: "The doctrine of the exact location of physical events in space and time is metaphysical, and therefore meaningless."[38] We should not hold our breath waiting for methods of documentation that will finally settle what really happened. That things are often fuzzier the better they are documented is a lesson from quantum physics. Reality may be as vague as texts, and texts may be as richly unfathomable as reality. Description may be inexhaustible not only because language is generative but also because the universe is incomplete. Just as we often do not know what we mean when we speak, so the universe itself might not be sure about itself.

Only a few carbon dateable relativists will see this conclusion as an excuse for wild abandon. There could be no more exacting mandate for historical interpretation than to recognize that we act in history by attempting to communicate with it. The past is open-ended because it was made in part by human beings, and human beings are worthy of respect and remembrance. The dead must not be allowed to die again. Nothing less is at stake in history. Doing violence against history is in some deep way also violence against human beings. As students of the past, we are dealing with the most essential and most delicate of all communicative relationships: that between the living and the dead.[39] The historian's job is to not kill the dead. It is to see that they are born again and again in memory and to see that the world is ever replenished with new old things. This is the deep ethic that unites the study of history and communication.

Postscript

Inasmuch as history, viewed reflexively, is communication history, we have much work left to do. One axis for expansion is time itself. Innis has been cited more than imitated in his interest in comparative civilizations, ancient and modern. Prehistory offers a rich field that was long the lone province of anthropologists: the domestication of fire, the institution of kinship, bodily and vocal techniques, the arts of speech and of writing. The domestication of plants and animals, cooking and child-rearing, techniques of navigation and time-keeping, ritual and the arts of memory are essential parts of the long history of communication. The accumulated archive of the human race – religious, philosophical, legal, literary, and artistic – is a rich repository of media practices. There are histories of communication outside of Europe and North America that await their historians. The globalization of scholarly communication in the contemporary world might help stimulate a more global past. The push toward interdisciplinary studies might help us move beyond the bridge between the humanities and social sciences toward the history of science and of technology. Metaphysics, said Peirce, is the ape of mathematics, and physics and mathematics is the secret history in many ways of communication. Finally, to follow Innis, we should expand our definition of media.[40] To name a few: astrolabe, bell, coin, dial, elevator, fork, glass, horn, island, journal, keyboard, lens, metronome, name, observatory, point, quantum, reed, signature, tower, ultrasound, vowel, wax, yoctosecond, x-ray, zero. The future of the history of communication is nothing if not abundant.[41]

Notes

1 For a brief parsing of that history, see my "Communication, History of the Idea," in *International Encyclopedia of Communication*, ed. Wolfgang Donsbach (Oxford: Blackwell, 2008).

2 Harold Adams Innis, "The Bias of Communication," in *The Bias of Communication* (Toronto: University of Toronto Press, 1991), 33.

3 Carlo Ginzburg, "Clues: Roots of an Evidential Paradigm," in *Myths, Emblems, Clues*, trans. John and Anne C. Tedeschi (London: Hutchinson Radius, 1990), 96–125, 200–214; Paul Ricoeur, "The Hermeneutics of Testimony," in *Essays in Biblical Interpretation*, ed. Lewis S. Mudge (London: SPCK, 1981).

4 Both examples are taken from Anthony Grafton, "Dreams of a Universal Library," *The New Yorker*, 5 November 2007, 50–54.

5 Harold Garfinkel, *Studies in Ethnomethodology* (Englewood Cliffs, NJ: Prentice-Hall, 1967), esp. chapters 2, 3, and 6.

6 Paul Ricoeur, *Hermeneutics and the Human Sciences*, collected and edited John B. Thompson (Cambridge: Cambridge University Press, 1981).

7 Lewis Mumford, *Technics and Human Development* (New York: Harcourt, Brace, and World, 1967), 141–42. See also Zoe Sophia, "Container Technologies," *Hypatia* 15 (2000): 181–201. Mumford might be pleased to learn that female scholars armed with DNA analysis have broken the long-standing archaeological assumption that any body found buried with weapons was necessarily male.

8 Laurel Thatcher Ulrich, *A Midwife's Tale: The Life of Martha Ballard, Based on Her Diary, 1785–1812* (New York: Knopf, 1990).

9 Laurel Thatcher Ulrich, *Well-Behaved Women Seldom Make History* (New York: Knopf, 2007), xxii, 42–43, 208–20, passim.

10 "Researchers Exhume 2 Renaissance Writers," Associated Press, 27 July 2007. Accessed at www.yahoo.com, 28 July 2007.

11 Geoffrey Winthrop-Young, "Memories of the Nile: Egyptian Traumas and Communication Technologies in Jan Assmann's Theory of Cultural Memory," *New German Critique*, no. 96 (Fall 2005): 103–33.

12 John Durham Peters, "Witnessing," *Media, Culture and Society* 23 (2001): 707–24.

13 Michael Thompson, *Rubbish Theory: The Creation and Destruction of Value* (Oxford: Oxford University Press, 1979).

14 Steward Brand, *The Clock of the Long Now* (New York: Basic Books, 1999), 103.

15 Friedrich A. Kittler, *Gramophone, Film, Typewriter*, trans. Geoffrey Winthrop-Young and Michael Wutz (Stanford, CA: Stanford University Press, 1999).

16 For a recent survey, see Wolfgang Ernst, *Das Rumoren der Archive* (Berlin: Merve, 2002).

17 One shudders to ponder that mass of malfeasance.

18 Barry B. Powell, *Writing and the Origins of Greek Literature* (Cambridge: Cambridge University Press, 2002), 105.

19 Quoted in Anthony Grafton, Glenn W. Most and James E. G. Zetzel, (eds and trans.) "Introduction" to Friedrich A. Wolf's *Prolegomena to Homer* (Princeton, NJ: Princeton University Press, 1985), 13.

20 Paula Fredriksen, *From Jesus to Christ: The Origins of the New Testament Images of Jesus* (New Haven, CT: Yale University Press, 1988), 5.

21 Marshall McLuhan, *The Gutenberg Galaxy* (Toronto: University of Toronto Press, 1962), 134.

22 Martha Howell and Walter Prevenier, *From Reliable Sources: An Introduction to Historical Methods* (Ithaca, NY: Cornell University Press, 2001), 62.

23 David S. Blondheim, *Les Gloses Françaises dans les Commentaires Talmudiques de Raschi*, vol. 2 (Baltimore, MD: Johns Hopkins, 1937).

24 I develop this argument in "Space, Time, and Communication Theory," *Canadian Journal of Communication* 28 (2003): 397–411, a companion piece to this one.

25 Here I reprise my *Speaking into the Air* (Chicago, IL: University of Chicago Press, 1999).

26 James W. Carey, "A Cultural Approach to Communication," in *Communication as Culture* (Boston, MA: Unwin Hyman, 1989), 13–36.

27 Kenneth Cmiel, "Review of James Carey's *Communication as Culture*," *Theory and Society* 21 (1992): 285–90.

28 Josiah Royce, *The Religious Aspect of Philosophy* (1885; Gloucester, MA: Peter Smith, 1965).

29 Michael Pollan, *The Omnivore's Dilemma: A Natural History of Four Meals* (New York: Penguin, 2006).

30 Benoit Mandelbrot, "How Long is the Coast of Britain: Statistical Self-Similarity and Fractional Dimension," *Science* 156 (1967): 636–38.

31 John D. Barrow, *The Constants of Nature* (New York: Pantheon, 2002), 160–76; quotation from Brandon Carter on p. 162.

32 Slavoj Žižek, *The Ticklish Subject* (London: Verso, 1999), 56.

33 John Ellis, *Seeing Things: Television in The Age of Uncertainty* (London: I.B. Tauris, 2000).

34 Philip Rosen, *Change Mummified: Cinema, Historicity, Theory* (Minneapolis, MN: University of Minnesota Press, 2001).

35 Erich Auerbach, *Mimesis*, trans. Willard Trask (Princeton, NJ: Princeton University Press, 1953), 15.

36 All information taken from Timothy S. Good, *We Saw Lincoln Shot: One Hundred Eyewitness Accounts* (Jackson, MS: University Press of Mississippi, 1995).

37 Adam Gopnik, "Angels and Ages," *New Yorker*, 28 May 2007.

38 Hans Hahn, "The Crisis of Intuition" (1933), in his *Empiricism, Logic, and Mathematics: Philosophical Papers*, ed. Brian McGuinness (Dordrecht: Reide, 1980), 76.

39 Walter Benjamin, "Theses on the Philosophy of History," in *Illuminations*, trans. Harry Zohn (New York: Schocken, 1968 [1940]).

40 I develop this claim in "Strange Sympathies: Horizons of German and American Media Theory," in *American Studies as Media Studies*, eds Frank Kelleter and Daniel Stein (Heidelberg: Winter, 2008).

41 I am grateful for very helpful commentary and corrections to Samuel McCormick, Benjamin Peters, Peter Simonson, and Geoffrey Winthrop-Young.

Chapter 2

Democratic theory and the history of communications

Paul Starr

To argue about the media today is almost inevitably to argue about politics. Similarly, at a deeper level, conflicting views of the history of communications often reflect disagreements about democracy and its possibilities. Much of the foundational thought about communications – from the writings of Walter Lippmann and John Dewey in the 1920s and 1930s to the work of Jürgen Habermas and others in recent decades – has held wide intellectual interest because of its implications for democratic theory and politics. Has the media's development advanced or devastated democratic hopes? Is the public a mere "phantom," in Lippmann's phrase, or can it be an active force in popular self-government if the media furnish the necessary information and means of criticism and debate?[1] Many of us who study the history of communications do so because of its relevance to the bigger, unfinished political story about the origins of democracy, the struggles over its extension, and the continuing efforts to realize aspirations for a more vital democratic politics. Like journalists, however, historians are often loath to address questions of political theory, and some may believe that just as it is better to travel light, so it is better to do history without any theoretical baggage. But whether or not historians and other analysts of the media make any use of theory, their understanding of democracy influences what they make of the past.

Democratic theory comes in many varieties, but here I want only to distinguish three general perspectives, each of which represents not a single position, but a composite of related ideas. None of these perspectives rejects the framework of representative government and rights of free speech and a free press that are embodied in the Constitution and the Bill of Rights. In that sense, all belong to the tradition of liberal, constitutional democracy, though they interpret the tradition differently.

Three conceptions of democracy

The first of the three perspectives – let us call it "minimalist" – conceives of democracy, in Joseph Schumpeter's famous definition, as an institutional arrangement in which individuals acquire the power to make political decisions "by means of a competitive struggle for the people's vote."[2] In this view, the key criterion for democracy is free competitive elections, which serve as a means of adding up voters' preferences and holding officials accountable for their performance. The minimalist view may therefore be described as aggregative, adversarial, and majoritarian. In conceptualizing democracy as a contest for individual voting preferences, this version of democratic theory sees politics as analogous to a market. Just as competition in an industry takes place among firms, so competition in the political marketplace takes place among elite groups. The minimalist view does not demand extensive popular engagement in politics; according to the theory of rational ignorance, voters typically do not pay close attention to the details of public policy because they have scant likelihood of influencing the outcome and can maximize their utility by attending to their own private lives and livelihoods. At election time, however, they are able to use party labels and other signals to make voting choices that satisfactorily reflect their preferences.

In regard to communications, the minimalist view calls for freedom of speech and the press in the sense of non-interference by the state – that is, negative liberty – to allow for an open contest for electoral support and to prevent those in office from perpetuating their own rule. By analogy, if democracy is a competitive struggle for the people's vote, so a democratic media system is properly conceived as a competitive struggle for readers, listeners, viewers, and internet traffic – in short, for ratings. The minimalist democrat is not greatly disturbed if competition in a media market drives out hard news and public affairs programs in favor of entertainment. That is a reflection of individual free choice and rational ignorance. Just as voters delegate decisions to elected officials in a representative system, so they leave public policy to experts. High concentrations of media ownership in particular industries also do not necessarily upset the minimalist. According to a line of economic analysis also descended from Schumpeter, the threat from a new technology or from invasion of a market by rivals in an adjacent industry is typically sufficient to keep would-be monopolists in line. The key criterion in deciding whether ownership concentration is excessive is not whether a market has active competition but whether it is potentially "contestable." And, happily enough, most markets usually are.

At the opposite end of the theoretical spectrum is a conception of democracy that calls for the active engagement of citizens in public affairs and an equal distribution of power in society. According to exponents of radical, participatory, or "strong" democracy, the aggregative and adversarial model offers too "thin" an ideal and too passive a model of citizenship. For there to be genuine popular rule, there must be more than a contest among elites for popular favor. In this view, democratic principles ought to apply not simply to elections, but also between elections to the process of government and to other economic and social institutions. Only in this thorough-going way can political inequality be overcome.[3]

In regard to communications, the radical democrat sees the market as a corrupting influence that degrades political discussion and reinforces what used to be described as the cultural hegemony of the capitalist class and is now usually just characterized as the dominance or "monopoly" of big media corporations. If the public is inattentive to public affairs, it is because the political system and the media have failed to engage them. As the old radical maxim goes, the cure for the ailments of democracy is more democracy. While the minimalist sees the First Amendment as demanding non-interference by the government in the press, the radical democrat sees the same rights as demanding plenty of interference to break up media monopolies, counteract commercialism, and create an informed citizenry. In the radical view, the rights assured by the First Amendment are not the rights of the companies that own the press or other media to be free of governmental interference; rather, in the words of Robert McChesney and Ben Scott, the First Amendment guarantees "a social right shared equally by all citizens in a democracy ... to be exposed to a wide range of uncensored, informed analysis of social affairs."[4]

Between these two antithetical theories of democracy and conceptions of constitutional rights lies a third perspective, with different implications for communications. According to this view, democracy is a system of "government by discussion," which requires that all those interested in influencing political decisions offer reasons justifying their positions in terms of generally accepted values. Instead of simply aggregating preferences, therefore, democratic politics also serves as a means of eliciting and weighing public arguments, and instead of merely pitting elites against each other in an adversarial contest, democracy calls for mutual respect between those on opposing sides and seeks to create a basis for cooperation that transcends particular moral and political disagreements. In the language of Amy Guttmann and Dennis Thompson as well as other political philosophers, this is a "deliberative" rather than "aggregative" model of democracy or, to use the terms that Ronald Dworkin has recently proposed, it is a "partnership" model of democracy rather than a purely "majoritarian" conception.[5] The deliberative or partnership approach does not presuppose that power must be equally distributed among citizens, nor does it count on high levels of everyday popular engagement in public affairs. These goals, while admirable, are so removed from the realities of modern society that they cannot be conditions for political legitimacy. Even without equal power and a general political awakening, however, public deliberation can serve critical purposes: to focus attention on the public good rather than private and partial interests, to bring failures and mistakes to light and thereby lead to the discovery of more effective policies, to promote equality of respect in public life, and to make political decisions more legitimate by subjecting them to scrutiny and counterargument.

The lineage of the deliberative ideal is traceable to liberal and republican thought in the eighteenth and nineteenth centuries, above all to John Stuart

Mill, though Mill's conception of government by discussion still limited it largely to a political elite. As Gutmann and Thompson point out, it was with Dewey and others in the early twentieth century, and later with Habermas, that the deliberative ideal acquired a more democratic cast. Many radical democrats also invoke the values of deliberation, but there is a tension between the participatory and deliberative ideals. Deliberation requires listening to arguments on all sides, but according to empirical research on face-to-face communication, many people are willing to participate only in like-minded groups.[6] The liberal deliberative perspective, unlike the radical one, also does not regard big profit-making corporations as irredeemable but instead holds that with the proper legal rules and incentives, public policy can harness the creativity and dynamism of the market for public purposes.

The liberal deliberative view has direct implications for communications. Because the quality of public discussion matters for deliberative democracy, there is reason to be concerned if market forces drive out public-affairs programming and serious journalism. Rather than overturning the market and commercialism, however, the deliberative liberal is concerned with getting incentives right through reforms of the legal framework of the media and with fostering independent efforts in civil society. The liberal deliberative view does not accept the proposition that the media flourish only when the government observes a rule of non-interference in the market; in myriad ways – postal policies, broadcast licensing decisions, intellectual property laws, laws governing libel, and much else – the state has always intervened, and these interventions have been vital for the growth of well-functioning markets. But the deliberative liberal also does not share the radical view that the First Amendment guarantees citizens a right to be exposed to diverse viewpoints and that this right trumps that of the press and other media to be free of government regulation. Rather, within the bounds of the First Amendment, the Congress may decide, as a matter of good policy, to promote a diversity of sources of opinion and information, as it has through postal policies and subsidies to public broadcasting. And, with the same concerns in mind, the government may constitutionally make provisions for the financing of political campaigns to encourage fair and sustained debate between political candidates. If democracy is not only about the aggregation of preferences on election day, but also about the communicative process for arriving at decisions by voters and their representatives – if the aim is not simply an adversarial contest, but also an effort to discover deeper grounds of cooperation and agreement – then communication policy, in the broadest sense, is integral to the health of a democracy.

The historiographic implications of democratic theory

A potential objection at this point might be that while these different theories of democracy may lead to different evaluations of developments past and present, they ought not to affect the ascertainment of historical facts. And, indeed, historians with different conceptions of democracy should be able to agree not only on specific facts, but also on how to characterize many broader developments. None of these perspectives, as I said earlier, rejects representative government or the Bill of Rights. Neither would they necessarily lead to disagreement about whether, for example, the expansion of the franchise, the growth of literacy, the rise of a popular press, and the creation of ubiquitous communication networks have led to a more democratic society. The differing implications of these perspectives on democracy become apparent, however, in the interpretation of developments critical to the basic narrative line of communications history in three broad periods – what might be called the "founding era" in the eighteenth century, the age of mass media in the nineteenth and twentieth centuries, and the rise of a post-broadcast, networked public sphere that we are living through today.

The minimalist theory of democracy tends, on the whole, toward a narrative of progress – of increasing democratization of culture and politics. From this perspective, the great watershed of communications history in the founding era in England and America was the achievement of negative liberty – the end of state censorship and the establishment of freedom of the press – along with the institutionalization of electoral competition. In the minimalist democrat's view, the growth of a popular commercial press in the nineteenth century represented a further extension of democracy. Indeed, in the analysis of the economist James Hamilton, new technology and market forces in the second half of the nineteenth century led to the development of independent, nonpartisan journalism. Seeking the widest possible circulation to spread high fixed costs and to boost advertising revenues, newspaper publishers rationally abandoned partisan identities that limited their readership.[7] (Hamilton characteristically neglects the political side of the story, never asking why political parties and government officials first sponsored their own newspapers and later stopped channeling subsidies to them.) From the minimalist viewpoint, the later rise of mass media such as radio and television confirmed the overarching tendency toward the multiplication of sources of information and opinion, whatever the limits within particular industries. Changes in the postbroadcast era, moreover, have overcome many of these earlier limits, such as the restricted number of television channels, creating an even more open media system, which complements and supports the electoral competition that is democracy's decisive feature. From a Schumpeterian perspective, the "gales of creative destruction" set in motion by the rise of the internet may well bring about the collapse or retrenchment of obsolete forms of media, such as the daily printed newspaper. But effects of this kind are to be expected and, amid the new information cornucopia, they ought not to occasion remorse, much less new forms of government intervention.

The radical democratic interpretation of these developments is dramatically different. If the minimalist tends toward a narrative of progress, the radical offers a narrative of struggle and betrayal. Like the minimalist, the radical democrat also stakes a claim to the legacy of the founding era in the eighteenth century. In the Habermas version of the story, the public sphere of the eighteenth century, though dominated by the bourgeoisie, provided a genuine means by which private individuals could come together as a public to confront the state with the force of reason, as opposed to the later sham public sphere of the commercial mass media.[8] Or as McChesney interprets the First Amendment and America's early newspaper subsidies, which supported numerous local publications, the founding fathers didn't intend to create a system of media monopolies.[9] With this backdrop, the radical democratic interpretation views the rise of commercial mass media under the control of large corporations as a betrayal of the original promise of the public sphere and a free press. The emphasis of the radical interpretation is on the suppression of alternatives: suppression, first of all, of the voices of marginalized groups and dissident journalists and, secondly, of alternative policies that might have limited the dominance of the corporate media. For example, instead of favoring the rise of a few powerful radio networks, the early licensing decisions in the 1920s and 1930s could have fostered a strong nonprofit or public broadcasting sector from the start. In the radical narrative, the long-term trend of media markets is toward monopoly, where the term "monopoly" is being used, not in the strict economic sense of control over a market by a single firm, but rather to refer to control by a single type of firm – the profit-making corporation. And, against the view that technological change in the post-broadcast era, particularly the rise of the internet, has created a more open media system, the radical narrative stresses the growing scale of the biggest media corporations and emphasizes their extensive ownership of radio stations, continued command of the prime-time TV audience, and dominance even of internet traffic. Still, amid these dire trends, the radical democrat spies rays of hope in occasional bursts of public protest over the power of the big media.

Whenever writers present a series of three viewpoints of which the first two represent polar opposites, one can usually count on the third position to be offered as the most sensible of all. I will not disappoint, though I want first to offer some words in praise of the first two interpretations. The minimalist, Schumpeterian conception of democracy has conspicuous advantages for comparative political and social research. As the term "minimalist" suggests, it identifies a lower-bound criterion for democracy (whether or not there are free competitive elections), and as a result it is relatively easy to determine whether any particular country at a given time satisfies the threshold conditions for democracy and to create either a dichotomous classification of governments or a scale measuring electoral competition and the protection of supporting rights such as freedom of the press.[10] In contrast, the radical conception of democracy, with its emphasis on active citizenship and equal power, is based on aspirational criteria that are not only hard to measure but nowhere satisfied on a national scale. The radical conception has its advantages not in comparative research but as a critical standpoint in understanding the limits of democracy where democracy has flourished most. It reminds us of alternatives – roads not taken and not likely to be taken – that are important not just for historical analysis, but if we are to make the most of the political possibilities that we have.

While the minimalist and radical theories make legitimate contributions, the liberal deliberative view has a particular value for the historical study of communications. Like the other two perspectives, this version of democratic theory also stakes a claim to the legacy of the founding era. The establishment of rights of free speech and a free press was indeed critical, but the political framework of communications in Britain and America involved more than negative liberty. As I have tried to show in my own work, a wide array of constitutive choices influenced the long-term developmental path of communications. In the case of the early American republic, these choices created a vibrant, at time vituperative, sphere of political debate that was closely tied to vigorous electoral competition.[11] The line of work derived from Habermas's *The Structural Transformation of the Public Sphere* – which in turn goes back to Dewey and was directly influenced by C. Wright Mills[12] – has illuminated that process. Habermas may idealize London coffeehouses, exaggerate the freedom of the English press of the eighteenth century, and misjudge the class character of the early reading public. Nonetheless, by framing the critical change in the early modern era not simply as a release from censorship, but as the formation of a field for rational public argument – the public sphere – Habermas puts the deliberative conception of democracy at the center of the history of communications. If we do not romanticize the eighteenth-century public sphere, however, we also do not need to interpret the rise of the commercial mass media in the nineteenth and twentieth century as a story of degradation. Like his mentors in the Frankfurt School, Habermas has the typical continental European intellectual's disdain for popular culture; he combines that disdain with a nostalgic and historically false image of an earlier pure, precommercial public sphere to produce a narrative of cultural decline, a theme with deep roots in German political and intellectual life.[13] But none of this ought to be convincing to us today. Popular culture has been a rich source of innovation, and much of it has depended on the impetus of profit.

In the interpretation of democracy that I favor, the development of the mass commercial media has had a mixed, though on the whole positive, character. Here I would like to quote from the conclusion to my book *The Creation of the Media*:

> ...[M]arkets, however much reviled, make vital contributions to a democratic public sphere that are unlikely to be made any other way. The production of original books, movies, music, and television is inherently

risky: No one knows for sure whether an audience for any new work exists beforehand. Public tastes are fickle; precisely what distinguishes a hit from a dud may be unpredictable. These uncertainties give strategic importance to those who put capital at risk. As publishers and other producers of cultural goods search for new works on which to place their bets, they are continually testing the popular appeal of new genres, styles, and subjects. This entrepreneurial activity expands the scale and scope of the public sphere, extending its known frontiers.

Sometimes even a single influential work—a book, a movie, a song— can give a latent public its voice and bring it into full awareness of itself. The discovery of a new market may thereby trigger public (and private) self-discovery and alter what politics is about. While most writers and publishers and others involved in making such choices mostly stick to familiar terrain, the industry's hunger for new products is a spur to cultural as well as economic risk-taking. More amply capitalized organizations are better able to assume that kind of risk—and are far more likely to do so in a legal environment that protects free expression. Moreover, the growth of markets does not extinguish noncommercial interests in culture and public life. The market, even when its products are distasteful, is a continual stimulus to innovation outside the market and in reaction to it. In a dynamic sense, markets in liberal societies enrich the public sphere far more than they impoverish it. If, however, all were left to the market—if government had not promoted communications networks, the press, education, and innovation while attempting to check tendencies toward excessive concentrations of power—the public sphere would be poor indeed. Our public life is a hybrid of capitalism and democracy, and we are better off for it, as long as the democratic side is able to keep the balance.

There is even a case to be made for the big media that have born the brunt of the radical democratic critique. During the 1950s and 1960s, at the height of the broadcast networks' power, Mills, Habermas, and others deplored the political effects of mass culture. But there is now strong evidence that network television in that era had a positive impact on the public's knowledge of politics and news. According to research by Markus Prior, when Americans typically could watch just three television stations, all of which broadcast their network's national evening news at the same time, many viewers who would have preferred entertainment watched the news because that was all there was and, in the process, became better informed and more interested in politics than they would otherwise have been. As more television channels became available, however, this group of viewers turned to such shows as *The Simpsons*. As a result, greater freedom of media choice led to a diminished audience for the news, less political knowledge, and lower civic engagement.[14]

A similar process may be taking place over a longer period among newspaper readers. The daily newspaper brings together a multiplicity of different interests, and many readers who may pick up a paper for the classified ads or for the cartoons nonetheless scan the front page and thereby become better informed about politics. The long-term loss of readership with the rise of television – and then with the changes in television that came with the increasing number of channels – may also help to account for diminishing levels of civic engagement. This process may not yet have run its full course. As the various elements that make up the general-interest newspaper become disaggregated on the internet, readers interested in sports, entertainment, and so on may no longer inadvertently encounter as much political news as they used to.

Moreover, as the classifieds and other advertising migrate to other media, newspapers are losing the ability to cross-subsidize the more expensive kinds of journalism, such as an international and investigative reporting, which have never paid their own way. The disappearance of journalism from radio, except for public radio, may signal a process that is likely to become far more widespread. As cross-subsidies in commercial media dry up, some of the journalism that has long been supported commercially may need new sources of nonprofit support if it is to survive at all.

At the same time, the internet is clearly enriching the public sphere in other ways. While it may not yet support the more costly forms of journalism, it offers a vast range of opinion, reduces the barriers to entry for individual writers and new publications, and facilitates the growth of collaborative, nonmarket production online, as exemplified by such phenomena as open-source software and Wiki publications. These new forms of social production have already begun to serve some of the classic watchdog functions of the press. As Yochai Benkler has argued, the network information economy offers a platform for the public sphere that is in many respects superior to the platform created by the mass media. By reducing the cost of becoming a speaker, the internet has enabled far greater numbers of people to enter the public debate. Furthermore, instead of simply becoming a cacophonous Babel or a series of echo chambers of fragmented and polarized views, the Web has developed a variety of peer-produced mechanisms for filtering and evaluating facts and opinions and organizing public discussion at higher levels. The promise of new political and cultural creativity is extraordinary, but technology alone does not guarantee that the potential will be realized. Some of the new developments are deeply threatening to established interests, which may use their political influence to bend law and regulation to their own advantage.[15]

This is a more ambiguous story than the radical narrative. Increased freedom of choice, rather than the greedy media, may be eroding civic engagement and threatening high-quality journalism, even as alternative forms of public knowledge and discussion are emerging in the networked public sphere. To realize the democratic possibilities of that new environment, however, will require not simply the government's non-interference, but a variety of critical political decisions about such areas of law as intellectual property, campaign finance, and the subsidy of underproduced public goods. The lesson of history is that just as in the past we have used government successfully to foster public debate and enrich the diversity of voices in the public sphere, so we could again. The historical narrative we need is neither one of ever brighter progress, nor one of darkening descent into the grip of monopoly capital, but a balanced account of achievements and setbacks and unfolding challenges and opportunities that can help us build a democracy where we can talk through our disagreements and where the public can be, not just a phantom of our imagination, but the real force in government that the democratic tradition has said it should be.

Notes

1 Walter Lippmann, *Public Opinion* (New York: Harcourt, Brace and Company, 1922); idem, *The Phantom Public* (New York: Harcourt, Brace and Company, 1925); and John Dewey, *The Public and Its Problems* (1927; Athens, OH: Swallow Press, 1991).
2 Joseph Schumpeter, *Capitalism, Socialism, and Democracy*, 3rd edn (1942; New York: Harper & Row, 1950), 269; Adam Przeworski, "Minimalist Conception of Democracy: A Defense," in Ian Shapiro and Casiano Hacker Cordón, eds, *Democracy's Value* (New York: Cambridge University Press, 1999), 23–55.
3 For an example, see Benjamin R. Barber, *Strong Democracy: Participatory Politics for a New Age* (Berkeley, CA: University of California Press, 1984).
4 Robert W. McChesney and Ben Scott, eds, *Our Unfree Press: 100 Years of Radical Media Criticism* (New York: New Press, 2004), 7.
5 Amy Gutmann and Dennis Thompson, *Why Deliberative Democracy?* (Princeton, NJ: Princeton University Press, 2004); Ronald Dworkin, *Is Democracy Possible Here? Principles for a New Political Debate* (Princeton, NJ: Princeton University Press, 2006).
6 Diana C. Mutz, *Hearing the Other Side: Deliberative versus Participatory Democracy* (New York: Cambridge University Press, 2006).
7 James Hamilton, *All the News That's Fit to Sell* (Princeton, NJ: Princeton University Press, 2004).
8 Jürgen Habermas, *The Structural Transformation of the Public Sphere* (Cambridge, MA: MIT Press, 1989).
9 Robert W. McChesney, *The Problem of the Media: U.S. Communication Politics in the Twenty-first Century* (New York: Monthly Review Press, 2004).
10 See, for example, Adam Przeworski *et al.*, *Democracy and Development: Political Institutions and Material Well-being in the World, 1950–1990* (New York: Cambridge University Press, 2000). Among media researchers, Pippa Norris draws on a Schumpeterian conception; see *A Virtuous Circle: Political Communications in Postindustrial Societies* (New York: Cambridge University Press, 2000).
11 *The Creation of the Media: Political Origins of Modern Communications* (New York: Basic Books, 2004).
12 See Chapter 13, "The Mass Society," in C. Wright Mills, *The Power Elite* (New York: Oxford University Press, 1956).
13 Mass culture, Habermas writes, is successful because it meets "the need for relaxation and entertainment on the part of consumer strata with relatively little education, rather than through the guidance of an enlarged public toward the appreciation of a culture undamaged in its substance." *Structural Transformation of the Public Sphere*, 168.

14 Markus Prior, *Post-Broadcast Democracy: How Media Choice Increases Inequality in Political Involvement and Polarizes Elections* (New York: Cambridge University Press, 2007); idem, "News vs. Entertainment: How Increasing Media Choice Widens Gaps in Political Knowledge and Turnout," *American Journal of Political Science* 49 (July 2005): 577–92. Prior's account modifies the argument by Robert Putnam in *Bowling Alone* (New York: Simon and Schuster, 2000) that the shift from newspaper reading to television watching reduced civic engagement. From the start, TV may well have promoted the further privatization of leisure time (which had begun with the phonograph and radio) and thereby depressed participation in civic groups. This would agree with the evidence Putnam cites from the research on the introduction of TV in remote Canadian communities (*Bowling Alone*, 2000, 235–36). But if Prior is correct, TV in its early stages had a positive effect on political knowledge and voter turnout, and it was the later proliferation of TV channels that led to the full, long-term effect on civic engagement that Putnam observes.

15 Yochai Benkler, *The Wealth of Networks: How Social Production Transforms Markets and Freedom* (New Haven, CT: Yale University Press, 2006).

Chapter 3

Communication and history

James Curran

The biggest single change in communications research during the last twenty years is that it has become more international.[1] A spate of comparative and international media studies – usefully reviewed in separate pieces by Oliver Boyd-Barrett and Daya Thussu – have been published in recent years.[2] A rapidly expanding, academic cottage industry is investigating globalization and culture.[3] Perhaps most important of all, communications researchers now more often take account of research outside their own country than was formely the case. This is exemplified by Michael Schudson's celebrated overview of the sociology of news production. When his essay was first published in 1989, it focused mainly on American news media. By contrast, its fifth version, published in 2005, draws extensively on evidence and examples drawn from around the world.[4]

This intellectual reorientation is partly a response to the worldwide expansion of communications studies. Communications research is now undertaken on a substantial scale in numerous countries, from Korea to South Africa, where there was little work a generation ago. The rise of English as a universal language of scholarship has also made available a growing body of work in a form that can be widely understood. Chinese, Korean, Japanese, Swedish, Dutch, Egyptian, Malaysian, Argentine, Brazilian and Iranian media academics – among many others – now present their work partly in English in order to reach an international audience. The expansion of the field, in a common language, has broadened horizons.

Adaptation has also been spurred by criticism. It has been argued repeatedly that it is inherently absurd to generalize in a universalistic way about the media – about what influences the media, about their role in society, and about their power or lack of it – on the basis of evidence drawn from a tiny sample of rich countries, usually featuring America and Britain. This selective sampling weakens this work's validity as social science and leads to tendentious theorizing based on unrepresentative or undifferentiated experience.[5]

The development of a more international and comparative perspective has also come about as a consequence of external change. National autonomy has diminished, as a consequence of global climate change, rapid changes in the international division of labor, and the increasing influence of global financial markets, transnational corporations and international regulation. The world's media system has also been affected by globalizing influences. Leading media corporations, and their partners, girdle the globe; the internet has come into its own as a global medium of communication; and television has become more international due to the rise of satellite broadcasting, and the rapid growth in the volume of program exports. Globalizing tendencies now penetrate the pores of national life in ways that are impossible to ignore.

In short, an historic shift is taking place in mainstream communications research in response to the worldwide expansion of the field, critical self-reflection and external change. This has given rise to greater diversity in the discipline's intellectual range. The United States remains the headquarters of social science-based, communications research; Latin America has developed a strong tradition of radical media political economy; and Europe has established an influential tradition of cultural studies, drawing on the humanities and critical social theory. New arrivals will generate different research agendas, paradigms and traditions. Whatever reservations one may have about specific local developments, the field as a whole seems set to become bigger, more varied, more multidisciplinary and more international.

Nation-bound media history

By contrast, media history has been little affected by these developments. Perhaps, globalizing tendencies in the contemporary world have less resonance for historical research. Perhaps also, the expectation that historians should be fluent in several languages has weakened the pressure for English to emerge as the universal language of media history. Media historians also tend to think of themselves primarily as historians rather than as communications scholars, limiting their exposure to pressures for change from the communications field.

Whatever the reasons, media history remains nation-bound. Thus, *all* the standard general histories of British journalism are centered exclusively on Britain.[6] Histories of the media in other countries display a similar national introversion, as in the case of France and America.[7]

This national orientation has become so engrained that it can defeat heroic attempts to rise above it. Thus, John Nerone's recent commentary on media history encompasses different countries, and engages with broad, transnational themes.[8] Yet, close examination reveals that Nerone's ostensibly international overview is really a view from America. Over three quarters of the publications he cites are authored or edited by Americans: only very distinguished outsiders – such as E.P. Thompson, Raymond Williams, Jurgen Habermas and Lucien Febvre – are admitted to this American academy (and they are nearly all Europeans). Although countries other than the United States feature, their communications histories are presented largely in terms of American work.

Nerone's survey resembles an early sixteenth century European map, in which the home country is at the center of the universe and the periphery is charted through "overseas missions."

Yet, his overview is insightful and eloquent, and my criticism is written from a glass house. My own co-authored general history of British media is trapped inside a national template, save for a belated and limited shift in its sixth edition.[9] The overwhelming majority of media historians – with rare exceptions – are implicated in perpetuating the nation-bound nature of media history.[10]

What makes this restrictive focus still more problematic is that it is often combined with a strong miniaturizing tendency. National media histories tend to be subdivided into *medium* histories: newspaper history, magazine history, film history, radio history, television history and book history (and various offshoots such as library history). These divisions are reinforced by divergences of tradition: for example, newspaper historians tend to be interested in institutions, while film historians generally focus on content. And of course there are the usual further temporal subdivisions, in which media historians – already separated by nation, segregated by medium, and differentiated by custom – focus their attention on particular historical periods. Exploring conventional media history can be a bit like opening a Russian doll, to find a smaller doll, in which nestles a still smaller doll.

Seductive alternative

The nation-bound, and miniaturizing, orientation of conventional media history has created a vacuum filled by a seductive alternative: technological determinist interpretations of the development of communications initiated by Harold Innis.[11] These have captured the imagination of the field, and indeed displace all conventional media history in some media textbooks.[12] This tradition has also gained extensive public attention. The two best known exponents of technological determinism – Marshall McLuhan and Neil Postman – are revered by some to this day as media gurus, and their books continue to be devoured long after their deaths.[13]

There are obvious reasons why this techno-tradition – written largely by non-historians – is so popular. While mainstream media history remains locked inside national borders, techno-histories soar across territorial frontiers. Whereas conventional media history tends to be concerned with micro issues (such as the genealogy of television dramatic genres), the techno-tradition offers arresting interpretations of how the development of communications has changed the world.

Techno-history's first claim is that new media are inherently subversive because they undermine established control over the production and dissemination of information. Thus, the mass printing of vernacular Bibles eroded the Catholic Church's monopolization of religious knowledge, and fuelled the Protestant Reformation.[14] This argument has a clear affinity to similar claims made in relation to other media, some coming from outside the technological determinist tradition. "Small media" (notably the combination of telephone, audiocassette and loud speakers) aided, according to Sreberny-Mohammadi and Mohammadi, the overthrow of the Shah in Iran in 1979 by breaching the regime's control over the media.[15] Likewise, the audiocassette, video and fax bypassed state domination of mass communications in Soviet Russia, and weakened Communist control.[16] Satellite television (and DVDs) now allegedly pose a challenge to authoritarian, patriarchal regimes in the Middle East by providing liberating access to Hollywood feminism.[17]

Second, it is argued that new technologies of communication have expanded social and cultural horizons. Print preserved and extended knowledge of the past and also fostered a sense of national identity within traditional, localist societies.[18] By contrast, the global media of the telegraph, satellite broadcasting and the internet encouraged increased awareness of the wider world and promoted a more cosmopolitan outlook.

Third, it is alleged that new media changed social relationships. In particular, Joshua Meyrowitz argues that the print era reinforced the separateness of the social spheres occupied by men and women, adults and children, leaders and led, because each tended to read different things. It was followed by the mass television era, with only a limited number of channels. The ubiquity of television as a shared experience tended to bring men and women closer together, and to demystify adults in the eyes of their children. Television also rendered leaders of society less shrouded in august mystery, and consequently less vested with authority.[19] However, some writers (mostly with a non-techno-determinist orientation) conclude that the expansion in the number of television channels and also of television sets in the home is fragmenting the mass viewing audience. This, they argue, is eroding a shared sense of togetherness, and weakening communication between social groups.[20]

The fourth main claim of the technological determinist tradition is that new media have modified the conceptual and sensory equipment of human kind. Whereas print promoted linear, logical thought, electronic media brought into being an associative, syncretic culture by simultaneously engaging more than one sense.[21] An alternative, dystopian variant of this position argues that print-based media, in their heyday, fostered sequential, propositional thought. However, they were overtaken by television which elicited applause rather than reflection, and encouraged an attention-deficit culture averse to complexity.[22]

The first three claims contain shafts of insight, and are undeniably interesting. It is easy to understand why writers in the techno-tradition occupy the sunlight, while conventional media historians mostly labor in the shadows. However, technological determinism suffers from major flaws which weaken its value. It tends to portray each new medium as being autonomous, and defined solely by its technology. This ignores the varied influences, embedded in society, which shape the historical evolution of new media – a point well made by a number of notable studies.[23]

The techno-tradition is also wrong to see new communications technology as inherently subversive. In some contexts, print was harnessed to sustain the social order, while in others print played a part in challenging it. What mattered, above all else, was the wider context which strongly influenced print's content and reception.[24]

Techno-histories also tend to offer mono-track accounts that focus on a new medium as agent of change, while ignoring or downplaying other influences contributing to the change in question. This can be illustrated by looking again at a central claim made by Elizabeth Eisenstein, perhaps the best exponent of the technological determinist tradition. Eisenstein describes how the mass production of printed vernacular bibles undermined the corporate authority of the Catholic Church by bringing into being a "priesthood of all believers", and goes on to retell how Protestant dissenters used the printing press as an instrument of mass propaganda. This account is balanced by her contention that the Post-Tridentine Catholic Church both harnessed and controlled the power of print in order to resist the advance of Protestantism, and that print had earlier contributed to the renewal of Catholicism. Her narrative of religious conflict is thus defined in terms of a battle of ideas and beliefs in which the printing press was central.[25] But what this overlooks is that the Protestant Reformation had major political, economic and social causes, as did the relative success of the Counter-Reformation. Indeed, it has become almost a truism among modern historians to observe that religious conflict, and the course of its development, in early modern Europe was, in reality, only partly about religion.[26]

In short, the basic underlying shortcoming of the technological determinist tradition is that it attributes too much influence to technology, too little to society, and fails to engage adequately with their complex interrelationships.[27] The intellectual space opened up by the limitations of conventional media history has been filled by an inadequate substitute.

New techno-narrative

Instead of re-treading old ground by critically scrutinizing standard works of techno-determinist history, it is more useful to illustrate the limitations of this tradition by looking at its latest manifestation. A new narrative has emerged, centered on the internet. It is written by diverse hands – not only by academics, but also by politicians, journalists, civil servants, think tank commentators, investment analysts, computer scientists and others. However, it uses a common code: the internet is always spelt with a capital "I," just as awed and credulous Victorians spelt the press with a capital "P." And it has a common theme: the internet is fundamentally changing the world. The internet, we are told, is "blowing to bits" traditional business strategy; it is rejuvenating democracy; empowering the people; inaugurating a new era of global enlightenment; transforming human sensibility; creating new communities; giving rise to a new self-expressive culture; and, with interactive television, undermining established media empires.[28]

These claims are based primarily on extrapolations from the technology of the internet (though sometimes backed with thin evidence). It is reasoned that the internet is transforming the economy because it has the technical capacity to displace retail outlets; it is rejuvenating democracy because its technology allows grassroots voices to be heard, provides access to alternative information that is reconnecting people to politics, and facilitates "e-government"; it is weakening nationalism because the internet is a global system of communication; it is empowering people because the internet transcends physical space and so allegedly cannot be controlled; it is renewing community because its interactivity and reach enables new forms of relationship based on real affinity rather than human proximity; it is liberating human sensibility because its anonymity allows for communication free of the external markers of gender, ethnicity and age; it is forging a self-expressive culture because its technology enables non-professional, or marginalized, authors, artists and musicians to connect to audiences; and it is undermining giant media corporations by enabling people to select from a cornucopia of choice.

All of these claims make the same mistake. They inflate the internet's impact by making inferences derived from the *potential* of its technology, while discounting the ways in which the net's content and use, and consequently its influence, is powerfully constrained by the structures, culture and social processes of society. Put very simply, the offline world exerts more influence on the online world than the other way around.

This contention will be supported by looking more closely at four familiar claims made about the internet's impact. We will begin by considering the internet's supposed rejuvenating effect on American democracy. There are some indications of positive effects: blogging has generated a legion of citizen watchdog journalists, with a demonstrable impact on politics, while the internet has made it easier for outsider candidates to raise money and mobilize support in ways that are promoting competition and choice.[29] But the regenerative impact of the net is still powerfully constrained by the fact that most Americans are not very interested in politics. This leads most Americans to use the web primarily for entertainment and useful information for everyday living rather than to engage with the political process.[30] The Pew Internet and American Public Life 2004 survey found that just 8 per cent of the population used blogs as a political source.[31]

During 1995–2004, a time of increased net adoption, news use across the media spectrum (including the internet) actually declined in the United States.[32] The decline was greatest among young adults, the most wired age cohort.[33] Indeed, 18–25-year-old Americans were least likely to vote or to register, least interested in politics, and knew least about political issues, despite being the age group most inclined to turn to the internet for political news.[34] If we look not only at America but also beyond, the evidence suggests that internet-based political participation experiments usually engage activist and elite actors rather than the general public.[35] E-government has generally entailed little more than publicizing government services online, partly because governments have been reluctant to give away power but partly also because participation is a minority interest.[36] In short, while the internet is making a difference, its capacity to *transform* democracy is limited by widespread public disconnection from the world of politics. Existing public predispositions shape the use of the net rather than the net reshaping citizens.

Reservations of a slightly different sort apply to the claim that the internet is bringing into being a new era of global enlightenment. The internet is a cheap, fast, international and interactive medium of communication with the capacity to bring different groups of people, around the world, into closer communication with each other. This has facilitated the co-ordination and mobilization of international social movements; forged closer links between likeminded people, not least members of the "gay global village"; and enabled worthwhile experiments in global journalism.[37] In these and other ways, the internet is contributing to the building of an international civil society. But the wider context of massive global inequality – in the late 1990s, the richest fifth of the world possessed 86 per cent of the world's GDP, while the poorest fifth possessed just 1 per cent[38] – distorts who gets to speak, respond and be understood in cyberspace. There are enormous disparities of internet access between rich and poor countries. There are also big geographical differences in content production: London, for example, produced more websites than the entire continent of Africa in 2000.[39] And since wealth is linked to cultural power, inequality also distorts in other ways. To judge from the latest available estimate, 69 per cent of all online communications are in English (i.e. American), a language that most of the world does not understand.[40] Thus, the global communion advanced in cyberspace is greatly distorted by the unequal relationships of the real world.

Likewise, the bursting of the dotcom bubble in 2000 illuminates the distance that can open up between what a technology can do in principle and what it does in practice. It was widely thought that the rapid growth of home internet access in the 1990s would provide a cheap alternative to the retail shop. Indeed, the net did become a significant retailer of some products and services such as books, concerts, travel and insurance. But the net did not dislodge the retail store due to consumer resistance. It turned out that many people enjoyed the experience of shopping in a traditional way; wanted to see or try out a product before they bought it; expected to own it immediately on purchase; had in some cases security or technical anxieties about buying online; or did not have ready online access. Similarly, experience confounded the forecast that flexible "network enterprise" would compete, with growing success, against "Fordist" companies because online market feedback would enable the former to respond more quickly to changing demand. In the event, this prediction did not take adequately into account the enormous cost advantages of large-scale production. Thus, the culture of society limited the way in which the internet was used as a retail agency, while the economics of production limited the internet's impact on business organization.

Yet, large numbers of people bought – literally – into inflated expectations of the economic impact of the internet. The extravagance of this collective delusion is epitomized by a dotcom financial company commercial, shown during a Superbowl Game, which featured a football player being carried off on a stretcher to hospital because dollars were pouring uncontrollably out of his "wazoo".[41] The image captures the "irrational exuberance" of popular belief in the invincible power of technology to transform society – the shared meta-narrative of modernity. The perspective that informs technological determinist history is deeply embedded in our culture.

In reality, the impact of technology is filtered through the structures and processes of society. However, this does not mean that the external environment functions necessarily as a "drag," limiting change. The reverse can also be the case (both now and in the past), a point illustrated by our next example comparing the role of the internet in two countries.

In Singapore, the internet has been politically tamed because of the context in which it operates. The People's Action Party (PAP) has ruled Singapore since 1965, and has exercised control partly through a restrictive National Security Act, manipulative defamation law, and the annual registration of civil society organizations. But it has also ruled by consent as a consequence of rising economic prosperity, and the prevailing national ideology that stresses Asian values, public morality and the need for ethnic harmony. One-party dominance has resulted in the local internet being co-opted in support of the regime through largely non-coercive means.[42] Even critical websites directed at the local population from outside the city state's jurisdiction are relatively moderate in tone, reflecting the consensual support that the regime has successfully engineered.[43]

By contrast, Barisan Nasional (BN), the dominant political coalition in Malaysia, is more fractured and divided than PAP. It has also been beset by allegations of crony capitalism, and rides uneasily the tiger of Islamic fundamentalism. The much greater degree of political division and opposition within Malaysia, by comparison with Singapore, was accentuated when Anwar Ibrahim, the deputy prime minister, was imprisoned in 1997 for unsubstantiated charges of corruption and homosexuality. Growing dissent found expression in online newspapers and magazines critical of the regime, which gained a large audience in the late 1990s when a substantial number of people distrusted the mainstream press and television.[44] This dissident online journalism is still important, though less so than it was because of the release of Anwar (now in exile), the revival of the Malaysian economy, and BN's electoral recovery in 2004. Even so, different political contexts encouraged the development of the net as an agency of dissent in Malaysia, but of co-option and control in Singapore.

Rejecting extremes

But if the external environment, as here, is important in "regulating" the impact of the internet, the nature of its technology also matters. The technical attributes of the net and the world wide web – their global reach, low cost, speed, interactivity, hypertextuality, and prodigious storage capacity – are central to understanding why they are having a cumulative effect on the politics, economy, culture and everyday life of society.

It is also misleading to view communications technology as being, in a simple sense, "constructed" by society. The internet provides a case in point. The by-product of America's Cold War defense program, it was shaped in its early days by the values of academic science, American counter-culture and European public service. Academic science bequeathed the decentralized, open and difficult-to-control architecture of the net; American counter-culture helped to turn the net into a sub-cultural playground, a legacy that left an enduring influence on net use; and the tradition of European public service gave rise to the free, connective nature of the world wide web. Other influences subsequently shaped the web. Authoritarian governments found ways of censoring the internet through internet service providers (ISPs), and of using surveillance technology developed for commercial use to track online dissidents.[45] Leading media corporations re-positioned themselves as dominant online news providers,[46] while major institutions also developed a significant online presence. There was also an intensive drive to make money from the web, though advertising and charging fees. However, public and computer worker resistance prevented cyberspace from being balkanized into fees-only enclosures reached only through proprietary software.[47] "Society" has not created the net and the web: rather a variety of different, and sometimes contending, forces within society have left their mark.

In brief, the rise of a new techno-narrative about the internet illustrates the pitfalls that arise from reading off the effects of a new medium from its technology. But this should not lead to a contrarian rebuttal that portrays each new medium as a mere extension of society reproducing, in a closed and unchanging loop, its culture and social relations. What is needed is a nuanced account which rejects not only technological determinism, but also its polar opposite of social determinism.

Back to the future

However the popular historical interpretations of the impact of new media, advanced by pundits like McLuhan and Postman, are the expression of a simplifying, technological determinist tradition. The lasting success of their work is a consequence of the limitations of conventional media history, as well as of the power of modernist mythology.

One response to the enduring influence of technological determinist history should be to revise it. To borrow a term from British dry cleaners, we should set out to "retexturize" the old garments of this tradition, and offer a more sophisticated, contextualized historical exploration of new media influence.[48]

Another response should be to develop a more international tradition of media history that matches in its grandeur of vision and intellectual ambition the technological determinist approach. This is of course an enormously difficult thing to do, given where we are at now: namely, dependent on national, subdivided media histories published in diverse languages, without a strong comparative research tradition or knowledge base.

The difficulties involved are highlighted by a pioneering international media history written by Asa Briggs and Peter Burke.[49] They are among Britain's best historians. Yet, their book – though heroic in its scope – is uneven. The most successful part is the early section, concerned with print in early modern Europe. This section is aligned to a strong comparative tradition of social and cultural research (concerned with religious conflict and the Enlightenment). It is good, in other words, because it is building on good research. But when the book moves forward in time, and outward across the world, its analytical focus becomes blurred. The book drowns in information (overwhelmingly sourced in English) culled from different countries, ranging from Russia and Japan to America and France. Its weaknesses are the product of an underdeveloped tradition of world history, and very little comparative historical examination of modern media.[50]

In the present circumstances, almost anything that contributes to the development of international and comparative media history is welcome. But perhaps the best way to develop an internationalizing project is to do the exact opposite of most national media history. Instead of centering media history on the development of individual media, it might be more productive to identify major changes that have taken place in extensive parts of the world, and then consider how the media's evolution connected to these changes.

My six nominated mega-trends (though doubtless others can nominate a better list) are:

1 Nation-building.
2 Development of liberal democracy.
3 Decline of landed elite.
4 Advance of women.
5 Growth of consumer society.
6 Rise of secularism (and resistance to it).

These trends are more pervasive than they might seem,[51] although they clearly do not correspond to the experience of some countries. They offer a thematic spine for developing a comparative understanding of the part played by the media in the "making" of modern society, alert to convergences and divergences of national experience.[52]

By way of illustration, let me indicate what a conventional British historical entry might be under each of these headings.[53] The media assisted a relatively new nation – the United Kingdom – to imagine itself as a single entity, and to re-imagine itself in different ways over time. The media became free of government and empowered the people (incidentally a simplifying argument). Part of the media system contributed to the decline of aristocratic rule, and the media subsequently formed ambivalent links to the evolving power structure that replaced it. The media shifted from being an agency of male domination to assisting, in part, the advance of women. The rise of consumerism encouraged the increasing commercialization of the British media, with both positive and negative results. The increasing de-Christianization of Britain weakened media support for moral traditionalism.

There are of course good reasons why much media history will continue to be national.[54] But the nation should no longer be the automatic starting point, and marker of intellectual boundaries, for the writing of media history. Indeed, there are telling, pragmatic reasons for partly breaking free from media history's national embrace. A comparative perspective can open up new questions; de-familiarize the familiar; and throw into sharp relief the central features of different media systems, and of their different positioning within society. It can supply the critical distance that will enable more media historians to identify and explore big intellectual themes – something that is very much needed. It will also mean that media history will no longer lag behind the growing internationalization of communications studies.

Notes

1 This shift was prefigured by the development of research on media and development that emerged in the 1960s. This "media and modernization" tradition came under sustained attack for very good reasons, causing it to founder. But at least it addressed large questions about the role of the media in economic growth, social change and political development in diverse contexts that were – and remain – important. Something like this tradition's broad intellectual scope, though not its prescriptive approach and exclusive focus on developing countries, ought to be revived in comparative historical research.
2 Oliver Boyd-Barrett, "Publishing, Research and the Communications Curriculum under Globalization," in K. Leung, J. Kenny and P. Lee, eds, *Global Trends in Communication Education and Research* (Cresskill, NJ: Hampton Press, 2006); Daya Thussu, ed., *Media on the Move: Global Flow and Contra-Flow* (London: Routledge, 2007).
3 See, for example, John Tomlinson, *Globalization and Culture* (London: Routledge, 1999); David Morley, *Home Territories* (London: Routledge, 2000); R. Kaur and A. Sinha, eds, *Bollywood: Popular Indian Cinema Through a Transnational Lens* (London: Sage, 2005); N. Gentz and S. Kramer, eds, *Globalization, Cultural Identities and Media Representations* (Albany, NY: State University of New York Press, 2006).
4 See Michael Schudson, "The Sociology of News Production," *Media, Culture and Society* 11, no. 3, (1989): 263–82; Michael Schudson, "The Sociology of News

Production Revisited," in James Curran and Michael Gurevitch, eds, *Mass Media and Society*, 2nd edn (London: Arnold, 1996); Michael Schudson, "Four Approaches to the Sociology of News," in James Curran and Michael Gurevitch, eds, *Mass Media and Society*, 4th edn, (London: Hodder Arnold, 2005).

5 See, for example, Schudson, "The Sociology of News Production Revisited;" John Downing, *Internationalizing Media Theory* (London: Sage, 1996); James Curran and M.-Y. Park, "Beyond Globalization Theory," in James Curran and M.-Y. Park, eds, *De-Westernizing Media Studies* (London: Routledge, 2000).

6 Mark Hampton, *Visions of the Press in Britain, 1850–1950* (Champaign, IL: University of Illinois Press, 2004); Martin Conboy, *Journalism: A Critical History* (London: Sage, 2004); S. Koss, *The Rise and Fall of the Political Press in Britain*, 2 vols (London: Hamish Hamilton, 1984).

7 Paul Starr's important history of American media is unusual in that it takes account of developments elsewhere, in the form of intermittent sideways glances towards Europe. See Paul Starr, *The Creation of the Media* (New York: Basic Books, 2004). On France, see D. de la Motte and J. Przyblyski, eds, *Making the News: Modernity and the Mass Press in Nineteenth-Century France* (Amherst, MA: University of Massachusetts Press, 1999); J.-M. Charon, *La Presse en France de 1945 a Nos Jours*, (Paris: Seuil, 1991); P. Albert, *Histoire Generale de la Presse Francaise: de 1871 a 1940*, vol. 111 (Paris: Presses Universitaires de France, 1972). On America, see Michael Emery, E. Emery and N. Roberts, *The Press and America* (Boston, MA: Allyn and Bacon, 2000); Thomas Leonard, *The Power of the Press* (New York: Oxford University Press, 1986); Eric Barnouw, *A History of Broadcasting in the United States, 1933–1953* (New York: Oxford University Press, 1985).

8 John Nerone, "The Future of Communication History," *Critical Studies in Media Communication* 23, no. 3 (2006): 254–62.

9 James Curran and Jean Seaton, *Power Without Responsibility*, 6th edn (London: Routledge, 2003).

10 Exceptions include B. Harris, *Politics and the Rise of the Press* (London: Routledge, 1996); K. Ward, *Mass Communication and the Modern World* (London: Macmillan, 1989); D. Finkelstein and A. McCleery, eds, *The Book History Reader*, (London: Routledge, 2006).

11 Harold Innis, *Empire and Communication* (Oxford: Clarendon Press, 1950); Harold Innis, *The Bias of Communication* (Toronto: Toronto University Press, 1951).

12 Lawrence Grossberg, Ellen Wartella and D. Charles Whitney, *MediaMaking*, 2nd edn (Thousand Oaks, CA: Sage, 1998).

13 See Marshall McLuhan, *Understanding Media* (London: Sphere Books, 1967 [1964]); Marshall McLuhan, *The Gutenberg Galaxy* (New York: Signet Books, 1969 [1962]); Neil Postman, *Amusing Ourselves to Death* (New York: Penguin, 1986).

14 Elizabeth Eisenstein, *The Printing Press as an Agent of Change* (Cambridge: Cambridge University Press, 1980).

15 Annabelle Sreberny-Mohammadi and Ali Mohammadi, *Small Media, Big Revolution* (Minneapolis, MN: University of Minnesota Press, 1994).

16 Terhi Rantanen, *The Global and the National* (Lanham, MD: Rowman and Littlefield, 2002).

17 Annabelle Sreberny, "Television, Gender and Democratization in the Middle East," in James Curran and M.-Y. Park, eds, *De-westernizing Media Studies* (London: Routledge, 2000).

18 See McLuhan, *Understanding Media*; Benedict Anderson, *Imagined Communities* (London: Verso, 1983).

19 Joshua Meyrowitz, *No Sense of Place* (New York: Oxford University Press, 1985).

20 Elihu Katz, "And Deliver us from Segmentation," *Annals of the American Academy of Political and Social Science* (1996): 546; Joseph Turow, *Breaking Up America* (Chicago, IL: Chicago University Press, 1997).

21 See McLuhan, *Understanding Media*.

22 Postman, *Amusing Ourselves to Death*.

23 Carolyn Marvin, *When Old Technologies Were New* (New York: Oxford University Press, 1990); Brian Winston, *Media Technology and Society* (London: Routledge, 1998); J. Abbate, *Inventing the Internet* (Cambridge, MA: MIT Press, 2000); P. Flichy, "New Media History," in Leah Lievrouw and Sonia Livingstone, eds, *The Handbook of New Media* (London: Sage, 2002); Fred Turner, *From Counterculture to Cyberculture* (Chicago, IL: University of Chicago Press, 2006).

24 James Curran, *Media and Power* (London: Routledge, 2002).

25 Eisenstein, *The Printing Press as an Agent of Change*, 310.

26 See E. Cameron, *The European Reformation* (Oxford: Oxford University Press, 1991); D. MacCulloch, *The Reformation* (London: Penguin, 2004).

27 It is worth noting recent, more sophisticated attempts to rehabilitate the technological determinist tradition, represented by Sarah Kember, "Doing Technoscience as ('New') Media," in James Curran and David Morley, eds, *Media and Cultural Theory*, (London: Routledge, 2005); M. Lister *et al.*, *New Media* (London: Routledge, 2003); and Lev Manovich, *The Language of New Media* (Cambridge, MA: MIT Press, 2001). The questions they raise are perhaps best resolved by agreeing that both technological and societal influences shape the impact of new media; but that how important these are in relative terms, and how they interact, depends on time and place.

28 See P. Evans and T. Wurster, *Blown to Bits* (Cambridge, MA: Harvard University Press, 2000); R. Tsagarousianou, D. Tambini and C. Bryan, eds, *Cyberdemocracy* (London: Routledge, 1998); Mark Poster, *The Second Media Age* (Cambridge: Polity, 1995); Jon Stratton, "Cyberspace and the Globalization of Culture," in D. Porter, ed., *Internet Culture* (New York: Routledge, 1997); Sherry Turkle, *Life on the Screen* (New York: Simon and Schuster, 1997); Howard Rheingold, *The Virtual Community*, revised edition (Cambridge, MA: MIT Press, 2000); C. Anderson, *The Long Tail* (New York: Random House Business Books, 2006); N. Negroponte, *Being Digital* (London: Hodder and Stoughton, 1996).

29 E. Scott, "'Big Media' Meets the 'Bloggers': Coverage of Trent Lott's Remarks at Strom Thurmond's Birthday Party" (Cambridge, MA: Kennedy School of Government Case Program, Harvard University, 2004), available from www.ksgcase.harvard.edu; A. Chadwick, *Internet Politics* (Oxford: Oxford University Press, 2006).

30 James Hamilton, *All the News That's Fit to Sell* (Princeton, NJ: Princeton University Press, 2004); K. Hill and J. Hughes, *Cyberpolitics*, Lanham, MD: Rowman and Littlefield, 1998).

31 *Trends 2006*, http://pewresearch.org/assets/files/trends2005-media.pdf. Accessed 6/11/2006

32 *Trends 2006*, http://pewresearch.org/assets/files/trends2005-media.pdf. Accessed 6/11/2006

33 http://people-press.org/reports/display.php3/Report1d-282. Accessed 6/11/2006

34 Michael Delli Carpini, "Gen.Com: Youth, Civic Engagement and the New Information Environment," *Political Communication* 17 (2000): 341–49.

35 Sonia Livingstone, "Critical Debates in Internet Studies: Reflections on an Emerging Field," in James Curran and Michael Gurevitch, eds, *Mass Media and Society*, 4th edn (London: Hodder Arnold, 2005).

36 Manuel Castells, *Internet Galaxy* (Oxford: Oxford University Press, 2001); F. de Cindio, "The Role of Community Networks in Shaping the Network Society: Enabling People to Develop Their Own Projects," in D. Schuler and P. Day, eds, *Shaping the Network Society* (Cambridge, MA: MIT Press, 2003).

37 G. Meikle, *Future Active* (New York: Routledge, 2002); W. Van de Donk *et al.*, eds, *Cyberprotest* (London: Routledge, 2004); Larry Gross, "The Gay Global Village in Cyberspace," in Nick Couldry and James Curran, eds, *Contesting Media Power*, Lanham, MD: Rowman and Littlefield, 2003); James Curran, "Global Journalism: A Case Study of the Internet," in Nick Couldry and James Curran, eds, *Contesting Media Power* (Lanham, MD: Rowman and Littlefield, 2003).

38 UNDP [United Nations Development Programme], "Patterns of Global Inequality" [Human Development Report] in David Held and A. McGrew, eds, *The Global Transformation Reader*, 2nd edn (Cambridge: Cambridge University Press, 2003).

39 Castells, *Internet Galaxy*, 264.

40 Shashi Tharoor, "The Information Revolution: Where Do We Go From Here?" 15th Annenberg Distinguished Lecture in Communication, University of Pennsylvania, 2006.

41 "It Traded on a Dime.............. or $2Trillion," *San Jose Mercury News*, 10 March 2005, 1.

42 G. Rodan, *Transparency and Authoritarian Rule in Southeast Asia* (London: RoutledgeCurzon, 2004).

43 Y. Ibrahim, "The Role of Regulations and Social Norms in Mediating Online Political Discourse," Unpub. PhD Dissertation, University of London (LSE), 2006.

44 G. Rodan, *Transparency and Authoritarian Rule in Southeast Asia*; C. George, "The Internet's Political Impact and the Penetration/Participation Paradox in Malaysia and Singapore," *Media, Culture and Society* 27, no. 6 (2005): 903–20.

45 C. Hughes and G. Wacker, eds, *China and the Internet* (London: RoutledgeCurzon, 2003).

46 Hamilton, *All the News that's Fit to Sell*; Curran and Seaton, *Power Without Responsability*.

47 S. Weber, *The Success of Open Source* (Cambridge, MA: Harvard University Press, 2004); L. Lessig, *Free Culture* (New York: Penguin, 2005).

48 Elihu Katz and Paddy Scannell are currently masterminding such a project in relation to television.

49 Asa Briggs and Peter Burke, *A Social History of the Media*, 2nd edn (Cambridge: Polity, 2005).

50 Briggs and Burke now have a rival in J. Chapman, *Comparative Media History* (Cambridge: Polity, 2005), a welcome addition to this emerging field.

51 To take just two examples, the theme of secularization and resistance fits the recent history of Iran (R. Varzi, *Warring Souls* [Durham, NC: Duke University Press, 2006]), and that of the media as a nation-building agent fits the recent history of Egypt (L. Abu-Lughod, *Dramas of Nationhood* [Chicago, IL: Chicago University Press 2004]).

52 After having edited fifteen books, I have made a resolution never to edit another one. Someone else ought to develop this project since it would make for a good edited volume (or possibly two volumes).

53 A fifty page review of rival interpretations of British media history is offered in James Curran, *Media and Power* (London: Routledge, 2002); reappraised in James Curran, "Narratives of Media History Revised" in Michael Bailey, ed., *Narrating Media History* (London: Routledge, 2009).

54 In modern history, the nation is the core unit of government, the locus of military power, the site where democracies were developed, and an increasingly important focus of social identity – all good reasons why much media history will continue to be national. What is being proposed is the development of a tradition that supplements, not displaces, national media history.

Part 2

Audiences

Introduction

Audiences, communication and history

Jennifer Ruth Horner

The problem of audiences in communication research has generated strong methodological adaptations and a good deal of scrutiny. Although a view of the passive mass audience continues to haunt our work, theory and research on the uses of industrial and post-industrial consumer media have incorporated notions of audiences as active interpreters and co-creators of meaning. The active audience framework, catalyzed by Stuart Hall's 1980 essay "Encoding / Decoding," has inspired ethnographic studies of a range of popular media products and the multiple interpretations and practices brought by media use. Interpretation, enjoyment, and use of media requires creativity on the part of audiences, but it also reflects cultural constraints on the range of possibilities for what can be understood. Audience research from a cultural studies perspective strives to understand how culture constrains yet makes possible the meanings brought to and drawn from mass media content.

Cultural constraints are not necessarily enduring and constant; they can change over time in a mutually constituting relationship with communication technologies and media content. To understand the historical development of contemporary interpretive frameworks, we must engage the history of ideas and make problematic the power dynamics engendered by certain ways of seeing. Similarly, historians need methods for conceptualizing the audience in studies of past uses of media and communication. Historians cannot use participant observation, interviews, and surveys to assess the social role of media products in aggregating attention, facilitating interaction, and mobilizing meaning in the everyday lives of people who are long gone. Conversely, as Peters reminds us in this volume, we should keep in mind that audiences of the present are every bit as ephemeral as audiences of the past. Empirical researchers of either persuasion do well to shift from a positivist to a pragmatic approach to evidence. To this end, essays by Richard Butsch, Susan Douglas and S. Elizabeth Bird address the uncertainties of absolute historical knowledge (or, in Peters' terms, the dream of perfect communication between present and past) while urging creativity in the use of historical methods and sources to triangulate research across media industries, textual content, and the practices of everyday life.

Susan Douglas takes issue with the notion that audiences cannot be understood through the textual analysis of images, stories, and materials with which they engaged. In defense of the role of the historian in construing informed yet imaginative contexts for media reception, Douglas suggests strategies for validating these meanings through evidence including letters, reviews, editorials, and, above all, the forms and images concurrent in various other media venues. By moving across media and genres, the critical historian gains an understanding of the regularities as well as disjunctures in the social concerns of audiences as they resonated with popular genres of the day. As media historians, we are urged to "reclaim the legitimacy of our own hermeneutic talents and duties," through cautious, informed, empathetic engagement with images, recordings, and texts of the past.

Richard Butsch argues that the articulation of the ideal of the citizen-audience in historical and cultural context is itself a useful source of evidence for an informed analysis of our mediated past. Audiences were inscribed in the practices used to assemble and address the public, and, in turn, were described in terms of the strengths and weaknesses of certain publics assembled through particular media in particular eras. As Anderson has pointed out, our default understanding of an audience follows classical notions of physically proximate assemblages of individuals, for example, a theater audience.[1] Butsch addresses the interplay between the physical and virtual audiences, and argues that the ideal of the responsible public was reflected in expert commentary on the effects and capabilities of early audiences for film, radio, and television. This commentary subsequently informed government and business policies for media regulation and use. Thus, the idea of the "citizen audience" was strategically deployed for political as well as economic purposes.

S. Elizabeth Bird addresses the problem of reception by merging insights from contemporary audience ethnography with historical studies of media practices. Cultural historians have focused on accounts of social practices around the media of news, gossip, etiquette, and politics, and found significant overlap between these seemingly disparate realms of experience. Working within the tradition of what John Nerone has called "the history of the book," literary historians have investigated practices around various genres of literature, including the growth of communities of readers – what we might call fan communities – and the development of institutional mechanisms for linking production and consumption in the creation of meaning.[2] Perhaps most importantly, Bird brings her anthropologist's sensibility to the study of particular media, pointing out that like ourselves, the media users of the past were "not fixed groups paying attention to 'the news,' or 'soap opera,' or whatever, but individuals moving among media and articulating with them in a large variety of ways."

Audience history, or the history of social engagement with communication media, plays an important role in critical scholarship. Guy Debord, writing on the meanings monopolized by the mass media *spectacle,* argues that representations favoring the interests of power foster the illusion that their meanings have always been obvious. In his view, a lack of historical perspective strengthens the spectacle's "ability to cover its own tracks – to conceal the very progress of its recent world conquest. Its power already seems familiar, as if it had always been there. All usurpers have shared this aim: to make us forget that *they have only just arrived.*"[3]

Critical media studies require a historical sensibility in order to question certain "common sense" assumptions about power and authority in the present day.[4] By the same token, histories of media remain incomplete without critical perspectives on the social groupings – the audiences – through whom media are constituted as communication. In advocating more nuanced understandings of historical media audiences, Butsch, Douglas and Bird plot paths toward more productive cultural histories.

Notes

1 James A. Anderson, "The Pragmatics of Audience in Research and Theory," in James Hay, Lawrence Grossberg and Ellen Wartella, eds, *The Audience and its Landscape* (Boulder, CO: Westview Press, 1996), 75–93.

2 John Nerone, "The Future of Communication History," *Critical Studies in Media Communication* 23, no. 3 (August 2006): 254–62.

3 Guy Debord, *Comments on the Society of the Spectacle* (London and New York: Verso, 1990), 15–16.

4 Sonia Livingstone, Jessica Allen and Robert Reiner, "Audiences for Crime Media 1946–91: A Historical Approach to Reception Studies," *The Communication Review* 4, no. 2 (1991): 165–92.

Chapter 4

Does textual analysis tell us anything about past audiences?

Susan J. Douglas

How do we capture what meanings audiences make of the media texts laid before them? More impossibly, how do we do this for past audiences who are gone and may have left scant traces behind? These are central dilemmas that have vexed communications studies scholars as we seek to understand the cultural and political work that a host of media texts – films, advertisements, radio shows, television, the web – have done in constituting us as individuals and as groups, and in constituting our society and culture.

This essay considers the various sources media historians seek out as we try to piece together what past media texts meant to audiences now long gone. I propose to take direct issue with one of the long-standing canons in our field: that one cannot, and most certainly should not, infer audience responses and meaning-making from the text itself. Various of us have obviously ignored this canon, while then permitting it to burrow into our confidence about whether we've remotely gotten things right. This methodological prohibition stems, in part, from the concern that media historians would mechanistically attribute whatever appeared to be the obvious, dominant, preferred meaning of the media text onto the responses of audiences in a kind of ex post facto hypodermic needle fashion. We can only infer the intentions of the producers, but not the meanings made by recipients of media texts, or so the conventional wisdom has gone. The prohibition also stems from the fact that it is very hard to teach textual analysis. Unlike conducting an effects experiment, learning how to run regressions, or mastering the protocols of the focus group, textual analysis has so far had limited models for how to train people to do it. When I was in grad school, for example, one learned it by osmosis, by reading primarily the historical or literary interpretations of others. So how can a method be a legitimate method if there are not even good protocols for teaching it? And if it's not legitimate, how can it possibly help us resurrect the meanings made by past audiences from past eras?

These positions fail to recognize how much more theoretically and methodologically sophisticated textual analysis has become in recent years, in no small part because of the role cultural studies has played in making our understanding of audiences, past and present, more nuanced. We have come to appreciate that there are interpretive communities who do different readings of texts (although here we have to be careful not to cast them as monolithic) and we also understand that people develop layered and multiple interpretive repertoires that they bring to bear on media texts. These repertoires may be further inflected by gender, race, class, age, sexuality and geography.

Indeed, there have been dramatic changes over the past thirty years in how historians have thought about past audiences and why textual analysis has become more subtle and careful. First we must begin with the acknowledgment that, within the humanities, until the late 1970s there was an elitist bias against studying the mass media at all, past or present. Echoing the German émigrés Theodor Adorno's and Max Horkheimer's assertion that the "culture industries" produced recycled, low culture drivel that made consumers "fall helpless victims of what is offered them", leading American intellectuals sneered at the mass media, and by inference any analysis of it.[1] As the prominent critic Dwight Macdonald wrote in the 1950s, popular culture is

> a debased, trivial culture that voids both the deep realities (sex, death, failure, tragedy) and the simple, spontaneous pleasures. The masses, debauched by several generations of this sort of thing, in turn come to demand trivial and comfortable cultural products.[2]

Historians were supposed to study political elites, like presidents, or huge trends, like immigration. But the mass media? Why study something that was evanescent, banal, "trivial"?

A new generation of scholars, the first television generation, who, in addition to being reared on banal fare like *Mr. Ed*, also saw the Civil Rights, anti-war and women's liberation movements unfold on their television screens. Radio, first AM and then FM, helped constitute baby boomers as a distinct youth culture; newspapers like *The New York Times* and *The Washington Post* defied the Nixon administration and helped bring it down. For these young scholars, the media mattered and their influence on culture and society screamed out to be studied.

As this new field of media history developed in the 1970s and 1980s, humanities scholars had to think differently about media audiences. New historical work that dug through newspaper and other first-hand accounts, city and state reports, surveys of workers and the like contradicted stereotypes about audiences as passive recipients of whatever had been laid before them. Stuart Hall, in his seminal article "Encoding/Decoding," dispatched the notion of some monolithic audience, and instead posited that consumers of media texts fell into one of three broad categories: those who bought into the preferred, intended meaning of the text, those who consciously resisted that meaning, and those who produced a negotiated reading.[3] Hall was not suggesting that the structure and content of the preferred messages were not powerful, but under certain circumstances viewers talked back to them. These insights coincided with an appreciation for "fragmented subjectivity," which jettisoned the conception of a unified, coherent self and instead conceived of people as inhabiting multiple, contradictory subject positions, many of them inter-pellated in part by their engagement with the mass media. People were "dis-placed across a range of discourses," hailed in different ways by the media, sometimes at exactly the same time. So it wasn't just that a woman, for example, could inhabit the role of daughter in the morning, supervisor in the afternoon, girlfriend in the evening and the like (while she was, of course, always all of these things). She could be hailed by feminist discourses one minute and anti-feminist ones the next, and recognize herself in both. Scholars saw media texts as incoherent despite a surface smoothness; the news media could promote social justice and corporate capitalism; crime dramas could both deplore and promote violence as a solution to complex problems.

These insights required that textual analysis be more sensitive and rigorous, but also made it more daunting. How could, say, a white, heterosexual male academic analyze advertising images from the 1920s and be able to capture the multiple ways they might have been read and made sense of? We now know that the reception and meaning-making of media texts are complex social, psychological and cultural processes in which individuals and groups make sense of media representations while they do – or do not – intertwine those representations with their world views and, indeed, ongoing identity con-struction. As John Thompson says in *Media and Modernity*, "It is simply not possible to infer the varied features of reception processes from the character-istics of media messages considered by themselves." Calling this the "fallacy of internalism," Thompson warns that it is too mechanistic and simplistic "to infer ... what the consequences of media messages are likely to be for the individuals who receive them" and that inferences of this kind "must be trea-ted with skepticism." Thompson, pointing to Herb Schiller's work on cultural imperialism, was especially concerned about imputing only the dominant, preferred, ideologically repressing meanings to audiences. Thompson further cites Tamar Liebes and Elihu Katz's classic study of the reception of *Dallas*, which showed that

> different groups found different ways of making sense of the programme, different ways of negotiating its symbolic content. The process of recep-tion ... was a creative encounter between ... the symbolic form and ... individuals who belong to particular groups and who bring certain resources and assumptions to bear on the activity of interpretation.[4]

Well, Amen. And this is particularly relevant when considering one individual media text on its own. But in this reverential attitude towards, and, at times, over-mystification of the hermeneutic processes of others, we are supposed to demote, even devalue, our own hermeneutic skills. Suspicion about the reliability and representativeness of textual interpretation increased further during the high

Fiskean moment of the late 1980s when we were urged to see polysemic ruptures everywhere, a thousand appropriations and oppositional readings blooming.

Other research suggests, however, and not surprisingly, that if multiple media texts, from the same or different media outlets, represent certain kinds of narratives, heroes and villains repeatedly, favor and even magnify certain media frames over and over, there is likely to be some correspondence between these media representations and many peoples' attitudes and beliefs. This is especially true when the issue or person being represented is remote to us and the media outlets are prestigious. Work on thinness ideals in the media and young girls' self-esteem and body image, on racial stereotypes in the media and racial attitudes, on coverage of politicians and their poll ratings, among others, affirm that the dominant, preferred meanings of multiple, overlapping media texts are often the same meanings many audience members assume as well. And while cultivation analysis – made famous by George Gerbner – has taken its licks over the years, especially for the possibility of confounding correlations with causality, the findings about certain dominant discourses in the world of TV, and heavy viewers' worldviews corresponding to the ideologies of those discourses remain persuasive. In this view of the media as reinforcer of ideology, it is not necessarily that the media create these meanings out of whole cloth and impose them on the population, but rather that the ongoing iteration and intertextuality of such meanings, which draw from and magnify certain socially held worldviews over others, find widespread purchase because they come to seem like the culture's "common sense." It is the job of media historians to identify what the common sense was in past media environments, what the dominant sensibilities were, and which co-existing discourses challenged that common sense.

And once we appreciate – as cultural studies has insisted we do – that media texts are often contradictory, even incoherent, and hail us differentially, even evoking contradictory responses within the same individuals, we can begin to try to map the multiple structures of meanings in texts to the multiple structures of meanings in viewers and readers. We can begin to retrieve audience responses to past media through the texts themselves, as long as we also triangulate this work with the broader historical context of the period under study and whatever shards of audience response exist. In other words, in our perfectly legitimate efforts to avoid the "fallacy of internalism," I don't think textual analysis as a method has been given its due as an historical tool in understanding media audiences. And indeed, as cultural studies work has tended to favor textual analysis over reception studies, and to have produced some unfortunate and unpersuasive readings of individual media texts, textual analysis has been further denigrated as self-indulgent, unverifiable and not representative of broader meaning-making.

Social scientists, through surveys and experiments, can get access to some of the effects of contemporary media content, as can humanists conducting focus groups and in-depth interviews. But even here, self-reports are not always reliable, surveys don't typically capture the process of meaning-making, and people may not have access themselves to the kind of work the media do in constituting them as historical subjects. For those of us interested in past audiences and past media reception, these tools are rarely at our disposal. We sometimes get lucky, and have letters to producers, networks, newspapers or magazines, old polls and studies and ratings. But often these sources are sketchy, incomplete or non-existent – do we just give up?

In fact, some of our social science colleagues, by pairing content analysis with public opinion data, have documented that when media texts present one preferred, dominant representation over others, public opinion changes in response. In *Why Americans Hate Welfare*, Martin Gilens showed that when the news media changed how they illustrated stories about poor people and welfare in the 1960s from picturing poor, rural whites to picturing poor, inner city blacks, the stories also contained more criticisms of government anti-poverty programs.[5] The visual racialization of these texts coupled with their new framing devices mattered; public support among whites for anti-poverty programs eroded. In *Cracked Coverage*, Richard Campbell and Jimmie Reeves documented that when the news media followed Ronald Reagan's agenda setting "War on Drugs" initiative, they produced multiple texts, including cover stories in the major news magazines, reproducing the administration's preferred take on the alleged crisis. The result? Within several months, surveys showed that Americans identified drugs as one of the top problems confronting the country, even though in reality drug use had actually declined.[6] So of course we, as media historians, must do what we can to retrieve whatever records we can of audiences' responses to past media texts. But such studies also suggest that with careful readings, one would hardly be reckless in identifying dominant discourses presented to people in the past and suggesting that they had an impact on people's meaning-making.

In arguing for the legitimacy of textual analysis, there are several caveats. First, such work must pay attention to the broader historical, political, and economic context within which such texts were produced and received. Second, we must also examine the media context: how was the media landscape changing during the period under study? What was new, and emergent, what was residual? What new genres, or technological forms, or modes of advertising became popular and what can they tell us about reception? Third, textual analysis must track the repetition, ubiquity and intertextuality of representations. Some images, metaphors, and narratives are repeated, within and across texts, and without finding such repetition, making certain claims about preferred meanings are very difficult. Fourth, we must pay careful attention to the contradictions within or against dominant representations. We may want or expect to see one thing from past media texts – unremitting racism or sexism, for example – but the record may not always be that neat and clean, even when racism and sexism were widely accepted in society and obviously present in the texts. Fifth, it is indeed very dangerous and

historically irresponsible to do "a" reading of one media text in isolation –
Buffy, for example, a recent industry unto its own of textual analyses run
amok – and think you have much to say either about the text, its times or its
significance. Sixth, we must be skeptical of all these texts, of whose views and
responses are included and whose are not. And seventh, we must also be
empathetic and try to get into the mindset of previous audiences, to embrace
the pastness of the past. It is context, repetition, intertexuality, contradiction,
skepticism and empathy that must shape and guide this work. Models of such
work are Roland Marchand's *Advertising the American Dream*, Richard
Ohmann's *Selling Culture* and Carolyn Marvin's *When Old Technologies
Were New*, to name a few.[7]

Marchand's *Advertising the American Dream* remains a classic of the genre
because of his astute and empathetic readings of ads from the 1920s and 1930s
coupled with his exhaustive archival research into the papers, directives and
memoranda of the ad agencies themselves. Marchand does not read the body
of ads he discusses out of context; he places them within the increased mobi-
lity of Americans which undercut community ties; within post-World War I
self-conceptions about modernity; within the changing status of women; and
within the tensions all of this posed between tradition and modernity. Nor
does he study just a few ads or ad campaigns in isolation. Through his archival
work, Marchand reveals the class and urban biases of most ad men (and they
were mostly men) and shows how they came out in the ad copy and illustrations. Thus, when Marchand lays out his readings of 1920s ads and offers his
schematization of the prevailing "social tableaux" and instructional, normative
"great parables" about proper, successful behavior embedded in them, he is
very convincing. We are persuaded that the dominant, preferred messages in
these ads – while they may indeed have been resisted or negotiated by various
individual or interpretive communities – were also the meanings and lessons
many Americans absorbed.

Another example from my own work.[8] When looking at the representations
of women in the early 1960s – still the height of the feminine mystique – one
can not miss that we started seeing on television quite a few women with
magical powers that men begged them not to use. The media historian needs
to gets past the dismissal of such shows as kitsch, and ask "why these kinds of
shows with these kinds of contradictory messages about female power at this
time?" Of course in television there is widespread copying of a formula that
works, so once *Bewitched* soared to number two in the ratings in 1964, changing the fortunes of ABC, it's not surprising that *I Dream of Jeannie*, *The
Flying Nun*, *Nanny and the Professor* and *The Girl With Something Extra*
might follow.

But such industrial imperatives alone do not account for the reception,
popularity, and longevity of certain of these shows. (*Bewitched* and *I Dream of
Jeannie* were in syndication for decades.) To account for that, we must look at
the rumblings of pre-feminism throughout the culture in the early 1960s; the

way these texts engaged with those rumblings; the contradictions in the texts about the pleasures and dangers of female power; the messages these texts repeated that resonated with messages in other texts; and their enormous popularity – and then you start to have something. The Kennedy Commission on the Status of Women published its report, *American Women*, in 1963, documenting that women were economically and politically second-class citizens. Helen Gurley Brown's 1962 bestseller *Sex and the Single Girl*, hardly a feminist tract, nonetheless urged young women to postpone marriage and childbirth, have a career, travel, and defy the double standard. Then came *The Feminist Mystique*, Betty Friedan's blockbuster that was the number one bestselling paperback in the country in 1964. Teenage girls were knocking down police barricades, defying male authority, so they could touch Ringo's hair. It is within this historical moment in which women were still expected to be wives and mothers, confined to the domestic sphere, yet clearly hungering for something more, that we must embed a textual analysis of such TV programs. Then *Bewitched* and *I Dream of Jeannie* do not appear only as banal media texts, but as television shows that opened up metaphorically, managed and resolved major cultural anxieties about the changing status and aspirations of women in 1960s America.

Likewise, when I was trying to make sense of why there was, and remains, such powerful nostalgia for radio, from the "golden age" through to underground, progressive rock,[9] I did indeed conduct focus groups with people old enough to have listened to such shows; go through all the Office of Radio Research and Bureau of Applied Social Research studies; read letters to the editor of old radio magazines; reviewed contemporary accounts of people's early experiences with radio; read what polling data existed; and the like. But I also had to listen, really listen, to a lot of old radio, to the different forms and genres, to the modes of address, to the humor, to the sound effects – I had to try as best I could to be an empathetic subject. Empathy has become underrated as too idiosyncratic, not generalizable, verging on auto-ethnography or solipsism. But without it, we can't do good media history, and we can't begin to retrieve how those media hailed and constituted past audiences.

For example, when listening to Depression era comedy on the radio, from *Amos 'n' Andy* to Jack Benny, and Burns and Allen, one is struck by the centrality of linguistic slapstick and, indeed, verbal aggression and jousting from the likes of Joe Penner, Will Rogers, Ed Wynn, Burns and Allen, Jack Benny, and Abbot and Costello. Their comedy elevated the wisecrack, the witty comeback, the put-down to an art. "[B]ecause of radio," noted *Literary Digest*, America was becoming "a nation of wisecrackers." Now, commentators noted, the air was filled with puns, malapropisms, insults, quips, and non sequiturs. Obviously, in this non-visual medium, that denied sight to its audience, words, tone of voice, and sound effects carried all the freight. But what remains striking is the nature of the linguistic acrobatics that went on over the airwaves in the 1930s, the centrality of verbal dueling, which suggests that radio comedy was enacting much larger dramas about competition, authority, fairness, and hope during the greatest crisis of American capitalism.

Through this word play, we are also struck by the anxieties about masculine authority that are repeatedly staged in these shows. Let's remember that from 1929 to 1933, GNP dropped by 29 per cent, construction by 78 per cent, and investment by 98 per cent. Unemployment rose from 3.2 per cent to a staggering 24.9 per cent.[10] Just one look at the enormously popular Shirley Temple films of the period, with their lost daddies, dead daddies, or blind daddies, drives home the enormous anxiety about the threatened collapse of patriarchy. Individual reaction to this catastrophe ranged from acquiescence, self-recrimination and a sense of personal failure to outrage and a determination to find scapegoats and restructure society. In 1934 alone – the same year that radio comedy, with all its insults and linguistic battles, established its primacy over the air waves – nearly 1.5 million workers participated in 1800 strikes.

Successful male comics like Jack Benny set themselves up as self-inflated egoists in desperate need of deflation, often by women and ethnic minorities, but also by their white, male straight men. Other men like Ed Wynn or Joe Penner squealed and whinnied in their high-pitched voices, their vocal cross-dressing central to their jokes and their on-air personalities. Still others like George Burns had wives who refused to speak the official (male) language properly, and used the double-jointedness of the English language to slip out of official linguistic handcuffs and to render their husbands helpless. Gracie Allen may have played the airheaded ditz, but it was George who, week in and week out, was the benighted chump, trapped in a web of "illogical logic" by a woman.

I would hardly suggest that listeners were saying to themselves – oh, I'm anxious about the near collapse of patriarchal capitalism and so I think I'll listen to stingy, vain, self-deluded and imperious Jack Benny get deflated by "the gang" again this week. But the media historian's hermeneutical responsibility is to seek to make explicit what is implicit, something that viewers rarely do, even in in-depth interviews or focus groups. That doesn't mean that we are positing **the** meaning or **the only** meaning, but that we struggle to link text with context with audience response to ascertain what kind of cultural, ideological work was going on. And this can't be done by analyzing one text in isolation, but by considering many together. We must track and observe the weight of the patterns and repetitions in these texts.

My own hobbyhorse, especially but not exclusively with radio, is that different media favor different senses and cognitive, emotional engagements, and this too we must struggle to retrieve about past audiences. So I am not arguing that media technology reconfigure our sensory equipment. But each medium favors certain senses, and the privileging of one sense over another does have consequences for how the medium is used and how it inflects culture and society. Just as millions listened to *Amos'n'Andy* or the Fireside chats or Joe Louis boxing matches at the same time and thus had water cooler content to share the next day, they were also engaging in a very similar cognitive activity of listening and imagining, and this cognitive activity, the knowledge (again, however unacknowledged and unstated) that millions of others were doing this kind of cognitive work at exactly the same time also profoundly constituted the identities and meaning-making of radio audiences.

Cultural studies has also emphasized the importance of intertextuality: reading texts in relation to others with which they circulated, and considering how meanings, a prevailing "common sense," might accumulate across and through these multiple texts. So another of our responsibilities, especially when analyzing the past, is to try to retrieve which texts might indeed have been in conversation with each other. This may not always be obvious. How many of us, until Michael Denning's *The Cultural Front* came out,[11] understood the infamous "War of the Worlds" broadcast as embedded in broader anti-fascist discourses, and some also produced by Orson Welles? "War of the Worlds" had been so often ripped out of its historical moment as an example of a media panic, that its intertextual resonance with other radio programs (and not just coverage of the Munich Crisis) was lost until Denning restored it.

Likewise, when examining the images of motherhood in the media in the 1980s and early 1990s, one is struck by the dominance of two icons in two very different kinds of media outlets. Celebrity mothers and their "miracle babies," nearly all white, rich, privileged and beautiful, began to colonize the covers of a variety of women's magazines. The stories inside featured increasingly normative (and fantasized) accounts of proper upper-middle-class child rearing. Welfare mothers dominated in the news, first as the objects of attack from the right and then as objects of attack from Bill Clinton, who promised, if elected, "to end welfare as we know it." These women – represented predominantly as poor, black, irresponsible, and promiscuous – never appeared in women's magazines. But, these two maternal icons did circulate together in the media, and thus in the American imaginary, and were in a binary and dialogic relationship to each other that defined "good" and "bad" mothering and contributed powerfully to the rise of the new norm of intensive mothering. Everyday Americans might not have consciously been comparing the two; the media historian needs to retrieve and juxtapose such seemingly disparate representations and examine how they worked together.[12]

We also have new tools and texts to help us teach textual analysis. *Representation: Cultural Representations and Signifying Practices*, edited by Stuart Hall, contains several essays that walk students through this method.[13] Peter Hamilton's "Representing the Social: France and Frenchness in Post-War Humanist Photography" considers how iconic black and white photographs – we all know Robert Doisneau's 1950 "The Kiss Outside the Town Hall" – helped redefine French national identity during the ravages of postwar recovery.[14] First Hamilton identifies French "humanist photography," pictures of the everyday life of ordinary people, as a dominant representational paradigm of the era. Frenchness, he argues, had to be redefined and reconstructed in the wake of the political rending of the country under Nazi control. These political divisions – collaborator, resistor, nationalist – were accompanied by serious economic inequality and demographic changes. Here Hamilton is less interested in intent than in how these photographs, which circulated in *Paris-Match* and the rest of the illustrated press, created images of a "more inclusive" France in which "division or strife were excluded." He begins by explaining what constitutes a dominant paradigm in photography, and discusses how documentary photography had come to signify both an "objective" truth and a subjective, personal point of view: the combination of the two had great representational power at the time. Hamilton then reviews the pre-war and wartime historical context in France and the significant class, regional and political divisions that reigned during this time. After the war, politicians and the press began extolling the importance of values such as equality, communality, and solidarity. Having established the salient cultural concerns of the moment, Hamilton then identifies the recurring images of these humanist photographs. They repeatedly featured images of young love, of everyday life in the streets, of people not expensively dressed, of children at play, of Paris and its sights, and of fairs and celebrations. Hamilton then moves from this very literal accounting of the images in the photographs to what, when taken together, they conveyed: the universality of human emotions; the historicity of France at the time; an empathy with everyday, ordinary people; and the commonality of human experience. Here students can see how one moves from a methodical and systematic recording of textual elements to identifying themes, and developing an analytical framework about the broader ideological valence of the photographs.

Likewise, Stuart Hall's own piece in the collection, "The Spectacle of the 'Other,'" uses images of black athletes to emphasize how their representations in the media "can carry several, quite different, sometimes diametrically opposite meanings." One photo "can be a picture of disgrace or of triumph, or both."[15] While Hall emphasizes the importance of understanding binary oppositions in the construction and reading of texts, he also wants students to appreciate that the visual and rhetorical construction of difference is often ambivalent: difference can be both "positive" and "negative" at the same time, and people of color in particular are often represented simultaneously as good/bad, primitive/civilized. Those of us doing textual analysis must be sensitive to the ways in which meaning floats, and how alternative readings can occur, while at the same time not being overly cautious about identifying dominant discourses and visual and textual tropes.

So, while textual analysis alone can not tell us all we want to know about past audiences, I believe that if we follow our caveats, and reclaim the legitimacy of our own hermeneutic talents and duties, we can learn and posit much more than critics of this method might allow. We cannot forget the importance of triangulation, of putting together in productive, historically accurate ways all these factors: historical context, remnants of audience responses, changes in media forms and technologies, repetition and contradictions in the texts themselves, and intertextuality among texts. The dominant discourses of past media texts – including and especially about the media – remind us how persistent and historically anchored are current media discourses that shape our lives and common sense today.

Notes

1 Theodor Adorno and Max Horkheimer, *The Dialectic of Enlightenment* (New York: Herder and Herder, 1972), 133.
2 See Bernard Rosenberg and David Manning White, *Mass Culture: The Popular Arts in America* (New York: The Free Press, 1957), 72.
3 Stuart Hall, "Encoding / Decoding," *Culture, Media, Language: Working Papers in Cultural Studies* (London: Hutchinson, 1980).
4 John Thompson, *The Media and Modernity: A Social Theory of the Media* (Stanford, CA: Stanford University Press, 1995), 171–2.
5 Martin Gilens, *Why Americans Hate Welfare: Race, Media and the Politics of Antipoverty Policy* (Chicago, IL: University of Chicago Press, 1999).
6 Richard Campbell and Jimmie L. Reeves, *Cracked Coverage: Television News, The Anti-Cocaine Crusade, and the Reagan Legacy* (Durham, NC: Duke University Press, 1994).
7 Roland Marchand, *Advertising the American Dream* (Berkeley, CA: University of California Press, 1986); Richard Ohmann, *Selling Culture: Magazines, Markets and Class at the Turn of the Century* (New York: Verso, 1996); Carolyn Marvin, *When Old Technologies Were New: Thinking About Electric Communication in the Late Nineteenth Century* (New York: Oxford University Press, 1988).
8 Susan J. Douglas, *Where the Girls Are: Growing Up Female with the Mass Media* (New York: Times Books, 1994).
9 Susan J. Douglas, *Listening In: Radio and the American Imagination* (New York: Times Books, 1999).
10 Robert S. McElvaine, *The Great Depression* (New York: Times Books, 1984), 75, 81, 171.
11 Michael Denning, *The Cultural Front* (New York: Verso, 1996).
12 Susan J. Douglas and Meredith Michaels, *The Mommy Myth: The Idealization of Motherhood and How It Has Undermined Women* (New York: Free Press, 2004).
13 Stuart Hall, ed., *Representation: Cultural Representations and Signifying Practices* (Thousand Oaks, CA: Sage Publications, 1997).
14 Peter Hamilton, "Representing the Social: France and Frenchness in Post-War Humanist Photography." In Stuart Hall, ed., *Representation: Cultural Representations and Signifying Practices* (Thousand Oaks, CA: Sage Publications, 1997).
15 Stuart Hall, "The Spectacle of the 'Other,'" in Stuart Hall, ed., *Representation: Cultural Representations and Signifying Practices* (Thousand Oaks, CA: Sage Publications, 1997), 228; Stuart Hall, "The Rediscovery of 'Ideology:' Return of the Repressed in Media Studies," in Michael Gurevitch, ed., *Culture, Society and the Media* (New York: Methuen, 1982).

Chapter 5

The citizen audience

Crowds, publics and individuals

Richard Butsch

Americans have talked a lot about media audiences over the past century. This chapter discusses how that talk often casts audiences as political actors. More specifically it looks at discourses that are critical of audiences and/or propose an ideal for audiences. There are three images that usefully distill the ways audiences have been characterized: the bad crowd, the good public, and the weak and isolated individual. These characterizations have influenced public policy and the actions of audiences themselves.

These images judge audiences using a standard that I have come to call the Citizen Audience. The good public constructs an image of audiences as people who exhibit attributes of the informed citizen. But this reference to the citizen also seems to haunt the two negative images of audiences, which exhibit attributes diametrically opposite to the ideal citizen. Media criticism in all three instances seems to imagine audiences as citizens: crowds or isolated individuals who fail as citizens, or publics who succeed.

Here, I give only a simplified sketch;[1] the full picture is much more complicated. But I hope that this will give some idea of what the picture looks like. To illustrate my thesis I offer three brief examples: movie audiences as bad crowds in the 1910s and 1920s; radio listeners as good publics in the 1930s and 1940s; and television viewers as isolated and weak individuals in the 1950s.

All three mirror the Citizen Audience, as an audience with civic responsibility. This kind of citizenship arose with the rise of the middle class in the nineteenth century, came to predominance in the Progressive era, and prevailed as an ideal during the decades I am discussing. It was a citizenship of "intelligence rather than passionate intensity" as Michael Schudson put it in *The Good Citizen*. It emphasized independent individualism rather than sectarian loyalty. It was a citizen who would use media for information, education and discussion. This citizen needed to be cultivated, i.e. educated and of good character, to fulfill his responsibilities.[2] Lastly, this was a middle-class, white male citizen. These examples reveal an underlying class politics that identifies subordinate groups' media habits as poor citizenship. The three examples take this model of the informed citizen as the standard for judging audiences and media for how well they serve the republic and democracy.

Crowds – Crowd psychology

In the nineteenth century, the image of crowds became antithetical to the idea citizenship. The middle-class ideal of citizenship had become by the end of the nineteenth century a knowledgeable person of an independent mind and good character who would rationally and critically evaluate information to decide what was best for the community.[3] By contrast, audiences of low-brow entertainments, such as blood and thunder melodrama, small-time vaudeville, and even matinee romance dramas, composed mostly of under-classes or women, were being characterized as dangerously suggestible crowds, easily led into crime or other impulsive or dissolute behavior by the wrong stimulus. They responded to emotional appeal rather than reasoned judgment, and acted rashly rather than considering consequences.

The history of audiences as crowds requires some preliminary historical background. Unruly crowd behavior among audiences was acceptable in theaters of the Early Republic. Audiences were expected to speak out. Calling for tunes or encores, calling performers and managers before the curtain, and even rioting were seen as part of the rights of audiences. Often the issue was not simply a performance but some partisan political matter, such as whether a Federalist or Republican tune was played. This tradition was rooted in the European crowd traditions of carnival and what British historian E. P. Thomson called a moral economy, which defined crowd action as a form of political expression by lower strata.[4] In moments and places where these traditions reigned, such as theaters, crowds held traditional rights to speak and act out. These traditions were part of societies in which the lower strata were subjects and did not have the rights of citizens to judge authorities. The traditions allowed lower strata of societies to voice concerns without questioning the social order. These traditional means to seek redress for wrongful use of power had been employed in the overture to the Revolution. They had helped the Revolution to succeed and so, after the Revolution it appeared unpatriotic to criticize such crowd actions.[5] At the same time, the Revolution asserted a new relation to government, that of citizenship, and enshrined the common man's rights and duties as a citizen to participate in public debate. The large public spaces of theaters were considered public sphere and audiences, particularly the common people in the pit, defined themselves as citizen publics, where they could exercise their rights and duties. Through the Jacksonian era, then, theater audiences were seen at once and uncritically as both crowd and public.

Gradually, however, elites and the growing middle class became increasingly intolerant of the older traditions of crowd actions, in and out of the theater. A major turning point occurred in 1849 when militia shot at a large crowd of working men protesting outside New York's exclusive Astor Place Opera House and killed over twenty people, with the full support of the middle and upper classes. After that, law and enforcement shifted toward quelling audiences in theaters. By the end of the century, audiences were tamed. The famous actor, Joseph Jefferson, exclaimed that audiences were "imprisoned" in a "helpless condition"; by 1921 the *New York Times* titled an article, "The Barkless Audience." Proper audiences, in these new terms, confined themselves to silence and self-cultivation – an important prerequisite to performing one's role as a citizen.[6]

Crowds were redefined as well. As crowd action in the theater was successfully contained, a remaining concern about crowds would be emphasized. With the arrival of movies early in the new century, crowds were conceived as dangerously susceptible to demagogues, in addition to their long-time identification with lower classes and mob violence.[7] This was a time when elites felt besieged by the nation's greatest immigration wave, considerable labor unrest, and the women's suffrage movement.[8] The new field of crowd psychology expressed this concern and, to a significant degree, was a study of audiences and was used to explain audiences. Gustave LeBon's influential *The Crowd*, first published in 1898, systematized widely shared ideas about crowds and colored them with scientific language. According to Le Bon, crowds form as people gather and focus, like an audience, on a shared object, be it an accident, a strike or a speaker. As the crowd forms, individuals surrender their independent thinking through a process of "emotional contagion." The crowd becomes of one mind, individuals lose their independent thinking and will and follow suggestions from others. This loss of individuality is the primary characteristic of crowds. It occurs as crowd leaders implant suggestions through emotional appeal. LeBon claimed that the impulsiveness and emotionality that cause suggestion were most pronounced in "inferior forms of evolution – women, savages and children," and that the upper classes, presumed of stronger character, were less susceptible to suggestion.[9]

The application of crowd psychology to audiences is illustrated in an American book, *The Psychology of the Aggregate Mind of an Audience* published in 1897, which reported the views of sixty-eight prominent American public speakers, including orators, lawyers, lecturers and preachers. Responding to queries from the author, their views were echoed in LeBon's yet-to-be-published book. They shared the view that audiences became of one mind, just as crowds did, and that the speaker did this using emotion rather than reason. For example, a teacher of rhetoric was quoted as saying that an orator uses sentiment and emotion to control the audience and make them obedient, and "turns a vast multitude into one man, giving to them one heart, one pulse, and one voice, and that an echo of the speaker's." Also like LeBon, the respondents imagined their audiences as inferior groups. One observed that the "popular" audience is easiest to fuse into one mind since they are "not sufficiently informed to be hypercritical." Others referred to the audience as a woman, "full of moods" who must be alternately persuaded, caressed or bullied.[10]

The same crowd psychology was applied to audiences in a 1912 article in the *American Journal of Sociology* by a future president of the American

Sociological Association, George Elliott Howard. His paper, "Social psychology of the spectator" claimed that theater audiences and sports spectators are crowds. Howard claimed that the spectator is "dominated by his feelings" and therefore highly suggestible. Crowding people together increased what he called the "bodily contagion" of suggestion. He also noted that inferior groups are more suggestible, including children, women, Southern and Eastern Europeans, striking workers, and the uneducated generally.[11]

Harvard psychologist Hugo Munsterberg described movies performing a function much like crowd leaders or speakers in this process of suggestion. In 1916 he claimed in his book, *The Photoplay*, that movies implanted ideas in the minds of audiences. In language reminiscent of LeBon, he wrote "The intensity with which the plays take hold of the audience cannot remain without social effects ... the mind is so completely given up to the moving pictures." He referred to "the millions ... daily under the spell" and exhorted reformers to use film to implant the *right* ideas in "the masses."[12]

Sociologist Robert Park, who became chair of the pioneering University of Chicago Department of Sociology, also was interested in issues of the crowd. His 1904 German dissertation adopted the popular crowd psychology and distinguished irrational crowds from rational publics. Park introduced crowd psychology to one of his most famous students, Herbert Blumer who soon applied it to movie audiences. In the 1920s, when a Cleveland philanthropy, the Payne Fund, sponsored an ambitious study of the effects of movies, Park helped recruit several University of Chicago faculty and graduate students, including Blumer, to carry out the studies. Blumer authored two of the eight book-length reports published by the Payne Fund. In both books he employed a concept he called "emotional possession" to describe the grip movies held on viewers, his version of "implanting" and "suggestion." Like others before him, Blumer also claimed that subordinate groups were more susceptible to suggestion.[13]

Writers across the political spectrum, including Progressives and eugenicists as well as academics, generally used crowd psychology to explain the effects of movies on children, women, the less educated, subordinate "races" such as eastern European immigrants and African Americans, or simply lower classes, emphasizing differences in emotionality and alleged suggestibility between the educated classes and subordinate groups.[14]

While this discourse did not claim that movie audiences might become violent mobs, they applied crowd psychology to argue that audiences of subordinate groups might be easily manipulated by the movies. Their concern was likely heightened by the era's most notable social change, the huge wave of poor immigrants from southern and eastern Europe. Much reporting of the time, in fact, equated movie nickelodeons with these immigrants.[15] Crowded together in tenement districts and harboring infections of socialism, they represented to elites a problem of socialization and social control. Conservatives hope to curtail their entry to the US and even to stop their propagation. But Progressives – and many of the advocates of crowd psychology were Progressives – and employers hoped to turn these immigrants into "good" citizens with Americanization campaigns.

Crowd psychology offered both caution and promise about the movies as a means to Americanize them. Since movies were believed to be so effective at suggestion, it was important to assure that movies suggested the right messages. Consequently, censorship campaigns quickly arose across the nation to attempt this. Approved movies would teach people American cultural values, e.g. to obey and respect the law, or depict literary classics instead of duplicating the dime novel. Censored subjects included unions, strikes and socialism, prohibited as un-American and fomenting social unrest.[16] Reformers hoped to turn audience crowds into well-behaved citizens through suggestion at the movies. Of course, as with other attempts at social control of working class leisure, they did not succeed, as commercial forces prevailed and offered more appealing alternatives to cultural uplift and civic lessons.[17]

Publics – Radio's *American Town Meeting of the Air*

Discourses about radio from the 1920s on had a distinctly difference trajectory than that about movies. Radio arrived just as the doors of immigration were closed by new US immigration laws. Also, radio listeners, dispersed as they were, lacked the visual feature of people "crowded" together. At the same time, Progressive ideas of civic community and public service were still influential. These circumstances provided the opportunity to frame radio in very different terms, as a tool for educating and incorporating Americans into civic participation.[18] In the 1930s the Roosevelt administration would build such goals into several New Deal programs, using many venues besides radio, to unite the nation during the Depression and then World War II.

Within this context, from the birth of commercial broadcasting in the 1920s, the US government defined the airwaves as public property licensed to private concerns, with the quid pro quo that license-holders must serve the public interest. This regulatory model of "publicly owned airways" and "serving the public interest" was a central part of broadcast discourse for six decades. In this model, the public's interest was to take precedent over the private, commercial interest of the licensee. While this was often interpreted or enforced to the advantage of commercial interests and to the detriment of educational broadcasting, it established a core principle in the law and regulation of radio and television that framed discourse, if not action.[19] License-holders at least had to pay lip service to and acknowledge the legitimacy of this principle. The founding premise of radio broadcast law and regulation imagined the audience as a public of citizens and radio as an institution of the public sphere. In other words, public discourse by government and private corporations presented radio as a public sphere and listeners as a public of citizens, even while they treated radio predominantly as a business and listeners as consumers.

News and public affairs programming was accepted by the FCC as fulfilling the public service requirement, and thus journalism became a regular part of broadcasting.[20] As a consequence, radio networks created over 50 public affairs programs from the 1930s through the 1950s.[21] Some of these lasted for many years. The most well known was *American Town Meeting of the Air*, which aired for 21 years, 1935–56. For each broadcast, a panel of experts spoke on either side of a public issue, such as whether social security was a good idea. After they spoke, people in the theater audience could ask questions or comment.

Town Meeting explicitly conceived of its audiences as publics, and made considerable efforts to encourage listeners to discuss issues and register their opinion with government and politicians. The creator of the program was George Denny, Jr. of the League of Political Education, an organization of the suffrage movement that continued to work for wider political participation after the passage of the Nineteenth Amendment. Denny envisioned his program as a means of recreating the popular democracy of the fabled New England town meeting. He wanted to put on the air the kind of programming the League had promoted at its Town Hall in New York City. When he proposed it to NBC in 1935, they agreed to broadcast the program on a sustaining basis, i.e. without advertisers. This was at the peak of unemployment, rapid growth of industrial unions, and controversial New Deal policies, in which citizens were intensely interested and often divided. The first broadcast was a debate on the topic, "Which way America – fascism, communism, socialism or democracy?"[22]

The program provided not only a public debate, but also considerable support and encouragement for groups around the country to listen collectively and then engage in their own discussions after the show concluded, to create town meetings all across the nation, linked to each broadcast. To support these groups, NBC and the League prepared and mailed out, at nominal costs, a wide range of printed material to aid in organizing groups and leading and participating in discussions. They published a book on how to lead group discussions. They sent a weekly announcement providing background and summarizing arguments for and against the issue in the upcoming broadcast and providing a reading list and topics for discussion to prepare listeners to understand the broadcast debate. For use after the broadcast they published the complete transcript of speeches, responses by speakers, and even the questions and comments from the studio audiences. To further encourage participation, they sponsored essay contests for adults and for children to write about an issue that would be the subject of a future broadcast in which the winners would participate. With the program's support, over a thousand groups varying in size from a handful to more than a hundred formed in the 1930s and participated in this exercise in publics.[23]

Such extensive efforts to support classic public discussion by citizens were not typical. Nevertheless, public service radio and television programs were constructed on the premise of the program as part of a public sphere and the audiences as publics. However, the regulatory foundation for these programs was dismantled, beginning in the 1980s. The FCC replaced the trustee model with a new marketplace model, presuming that consumers would regulate license-holders through their choices in the marketplace.[24] This new regulatory model redefined audiences as consumers rather than as publics, and eliminated the conception of broadcasting as a public sphere. From the point of view of the FCC nowadays, radio and television are no more than entertainment businesses.

The imagined citizen audiences that these programs hoped to serve or create exemplified middle class ideals. They were unlike the imagined crowds of suggestible subordinate groups at nickelodeons. The imagined audience was educated, high-brow upper-middle class, or aspiring self-educating middle brows, striving to improve themselves.[25] It was responsible, respectable and full of rectitude. George Denny, creator of *American Town Meeting of the Air*, stated that programs like his were primarily produced for people who were not wedded to one party or ideology, were leaders in the community, and had the capacity to deal with ideas.[26] They would choose *American Town Meeting of the Air* over *Major Bowes Amateur Hour*, would do the preparatory reading before the show and discuss the issues after.

Individuals – Mass man

The climate was different again when commercial television spread after World War Two and soon blanketed the country with *I Love Lucy* and other national nightly rituals. Television's arrival coincided with a robust postwar economy and a national craving for domestic tranquility after almost two decades of depression and war. This and Federal programs for urban renewal, highway construction, the GI bill and VA mortgages provided the desire and subsidies for massive suburbanization.[27]

The result, real or imagined, worried social commentators and cultural critics: that families might stay in their suburban homes glued to the television, displacing more worthwhile activities. Marketing surveys of early television purchasers reported that TV families were doing just that and socializing less. Movie ticket sales plummeted to one fourth their previous level. Mass culture critics and mass society theorists worried about a shriveling of community life and dramatic drops in civic participation.[28]

Critics were worried too about what people were watching. From the beginning, cultural critics pasted a low-brow label on television and railed at the consequence for our national intelligence and citizen education. In 1948 the *New Yorker* critic Philip Hamburger gave credit to television for informing citizens through full coverage of the United Nations founding conference in San Francisco, but lambasted it for the weekly slapstick comedy of Milton Berle. Television seemed to be the circus to the bread of postwar prosperity.

Moreover, the massive concentration of the television audience seemed more menacing than radio listeners ever did. Everyone seemed to be watching the same thing at the same time, delivering the entire population into the hands of programmers, advertisers and possibly demagogues. Almost a third of America listening to *Fibber McGee and Molly* on radio in 1946 did not disturb critics, but the similar numbers watching Lucy on television a decade later did. Political scientist William Kornhauser synthesized mass society theories of the era to argue that America was becoming a society of center and periphery with intermediate institutions shriveling. These theories argued that the highly centralized medium of television provided a means for elites, either for corporate advertising or political messages, to speak directly to the masses of the nation, bypassing local opinion leaders that were considered central to sustaining a process of thinking and digestion, and making mass demagoguery more effective. Ironically, print media were publicizing these concerns and probably making them a broader public concern in the 1950s than in the 1920s when elites debated these issues among themselves.[29]

A genre of anti-suburb books appeared, targeting especially the low-priced suburbs and young, first-time home buyers.[30] Common to these books was a criticism of the emptiness of suburban American life. Suburbs and television homogenized American life, so that every middle-class family lived in the same house and watched the same shows. The book, *The Crack in the Picture Window* phrased it, "Hell is homogenous"; and so did the song, *Little Boxes*, describing "Little boxes made out of ticky-tacky, and they all look just the same".

The fear of mass manipulation was captured in two widely discussed issues, brainwashing and subliminal advertising. Arising from the Korean War, there was much fear that communists were brainwashing captured American soldiers and replacing American values with communism, another theory of suggestion based on a confused mix of Behaviorism and Freudian theory. Some social critics began to claim that advertisers were doing the same thing to American television viewers through subliminal advertising, which flashed so quickly on the screen that viewers did not register it consciously and engage their critical faculties, but only unconsciously, so it would bypass any critical filters and implant directly in the mind a desire for the product. Muckraker Vance Packard's *The Hidden Persuaders* heightened fears of the power of advertisers more generally using mass media to master the minds of millions.[30] Hollywood director John Frankenheimer, cited both of these fears as the inspiration for his movie, *The Manchurian Candidate*, a paranoid fantasy that Russian and Chinese psychologists could program an American soldier to kill a candidate for president to make way for a candidate who would be a puppet president for these communist regimes. The audience in this discourse is the ultimate anti-citizen, appearing to carry on the role of electorate in a democracy when in fact they have been programmed to do the bidding of an all-powerful elite.

While much of this criticism and theory made no exceptions for the edu-cated in their susceptibility to such manipulation, it implicitly drew a distinc-tion between the manipulating elite and the manipulated masses. The less paranoid however did distinguish between the educated, upper-middle class and the working class and poor. Cultural critics especially emphasized the importance of cultivation and education. Educators and health professionals similarly cited the eroding effects of television in interfering in children's development of these, especially in working class households where adults provided insufficient supervision of their children's use of television and were themselves poor role models. The concern was the viewer who spent too much time with television, displacing more productive and worthwhile activities. Two market researchers, Ira Glick and Sidney Levy, drawing upon years of commercial data, in the 1950s published a book portraying the differences between responsible and irresponsible households when it came to television use. In their view, working-class viewers watched too much television, were indiscriminant in what they watched, and were irresponsible in letting their children do the same, including using the television as a baby-sitter. Middle and upper-middle class viewers on the other hand were selective in what they watched and consequently limited how much they and their children watched.

In the 1950s, academics, educators, health professionals, and cultural and social critics formed a chorus singing the sins of television and condemning the working class as television sinners for consuming too much, and doing too little to make themselves and their children into good citizens.

Conclusion

Despite the ebb and flow of liberal and conservative in American politics, what has endured through the twentieth century that these three examples span is an image of the informed citizen. This conception of citizenship actually has a longer heritage, well into the nineteenth century when the rising middle-class revulsion against the spectacle of party politics of the day began to breed a sanitized civic participation that would become the Progressive ideal. It was an ideal of the upper-middle class applied to the role of citizen, and was embo-died in Progressive electoral reforms. The informed citizen acted individually rather than as a person loyal to a party and was educated and continued self-education and self-cultivation, in order to make decisions about the commu-nity's governance in the public rather than private interest. Implicit in this was the differentiation between citizens who were capable of this and those who were not. The upper-middle class audience was more responsible, deserving and righteous than the uneducated, undisciplined masses. The images of audiences as crowds and as weak and isolated individuals were images of subordinate groups failing to fulfill their role as citizen.

These representations also provide a glimpse into how history can enhance our understanding of media and particularly the connection of media to the larger society and culture. Communication research traditionally has been present-oriented. One disadvantage of this is that it presumes that communication phenomena are changeless, not time-bound. By contrast, an historical approach foregrounds change and process. For example, histories of film text and the film industry have documented the evolution of styles and linked these to changes in the industry, from the nickelodeon to the Hollywood studio system to the blockbuster era. Similar histories of radio and television are now accumulating.

However, most media histories have focused on text, technology or the industry. Audience history has been slower to develop. This lag may have been because it is difficult to document audiences, who are ephemeral and leave behind few artifacts of their existence. Audience history also is late to develop because, compared to other aspects of media history, audiences had seemed trivial, the everyday familiar to us all, not the important stuff of culture, society and history, and thus not worth researching. This attitude is a residue of the prejudice from three decades ago, when scholars still dismissed popular culture as an unsuitable topic for scholars.

But audience history can offer an important and substantial new dimension to media and historical scholarship. The history of representations of audience, in particular, demonstrates connections of audiences to cultural, political and class history. This chapter, for example, indicates how audiences have been a major concern to contemporaries and how the consequent representations have been invested with the major issues of their day. The representations indicate that audiences after all were considered not trivial, but a matter of public concern for the nation, and demonstrate processes of cultural hegemony that justified supervision, manipulation and control of subordinate groups by elites. Audiences were and are deeply implicated in our culture, our politics and our inequality. Audience history can reveal how.

Notes

1 For a longer view see Richard Butsch, *The Citizen Audience: Crowds, Publics and Individuals* (London: Routledge, 2008).
2 Michael Schudson, *The Good Citizen* (Boston, MA: Harvard University Press, 1998), 182; Chantal Mouffe, "Citizenship" in Seymour M. Lipset, ed., *Political Philosophy: Theory, Thinkers, Concepts* (Washington, DC: Congresinal Quarterly Press, 2001), 291–95; Margaret Somers, "The Privatization of Citizenship," in Victoria Bonnel and Lynn Hunt, eds, *Beyond the Cultural Turn* (Berkeley, CA: University of California Press, 1999); Catherine Hall, Keith McClelland and Jane Rendall, "Introduction" in *Defining the Victorian Nation* (Cambridge: Cambridge University Press, 2000), esp. 56–70.
3 Schudson, *The Good Citizen*; James Kettner, *The Development of American Citizenship 1608–1870*, (Chapel Hill, NC: University of North Carolina Press, 1978); Rogers Smith, *Civic Ideals: Conflict Visions of Citizenship in US History* (New Haven, CT: Yale University Press, 1997); Glenn Altschuler and Stuart Blumin, *Rude Republic: Americans and Their Politics in the Nineteenth Century* (Princeton,

NJ: Princeton University Press, 2000). On the Anglo tradition see Chantal Mouffe, "Citizenship" in Lipset, ed., *Political Philosophy*; Margaret Somers, "The Privatization of Citizenship", in Bonnel and Lynn Hunt, eds, *Beyond the Cultural Turn*; Hall, McClellad and Rendall, "Introduction" in *Defining the Victorian Nation*, esp. 56–70.

4 On carnival see Natalie Davis, *Society and Culture in Early Modern France* (Stanford, CA: Stanford University Press, 1975); Michael Bristol, *Carnival and Theater: Plebian Culture and the Structure of Authority in Renaissance England* (London: Methuen, 1985); Peter Borsay, "'All the Town's a Stage': Urban Ritual and Ceremony, 1600–1800," in Peter Clark, ed., *The Transformation of the English Provincial Towns, 1600–1800* (London: Hutchinson, 1984), 228–58. On the moral economy see Edward P. Thompson, "The Moral Economy of the English Crowd in the Eighteenth Century," *Past and Present* no. 1 (February 1971): 76–136; Adrian Randall and Andrew Charlesworth, eds, *Moral Economy and Popular Protest: Crowds, Conflict and Authority* (New York: St. Martin's Press, 2000). Davis' description of carnival crowds using these opportunities to reign in their superiors who had violated traditional norms is reminiscent of E. P. Thomson's concept of moral economy.

5 American historian Edward Countryman argues that the colonial elite needed the actions of urban crowds to succeed. See "Moral Economy, Political Economy and the American Bourgeois Revolution," in Randall and Charlesworth, eds, *Moral Economy and Popular Protest*, 153–54, 156.

6 Richard Moody, *The Astor Place Riot* (Bloomington, IN: Indiana University Press, 1958); Peter Buckley, "To the Opera House: Culture and Society in New York City, 1820–60," PhD diss. (New Yourk: SUNY Stony Brook, 1984); Joseph Jefferson, *Autobiography* Alan Downer, ed., (Boston, MA: Harvard University Press, 1964), 319; "The Barkless Audience" *New York Times*, 3 December 1921, 12.

7 John McClelland, *The Crowd and the Mob: From Plato to Canetti* (London: Unwin Hyman, 1989), 1–7.

8 For reactions to immigrants, see John Tehranian, "Performing Whiteness: Natural Litigation and the Construction of Racial Identity in America," *Yale Law Journal* 109, no. 4, (January 2000): 817–48.

9 Gustave Le Bon, *The Crowd* (New York: Viking Press, 1960), 31–36, 39–40, 117–18, 158. Also see Robert Nye, *Origins of Crowd Psychology* (London: Sage, 1975); Erika King, *Crowd Theory as a Psychology of the Leader and the Led* (Lewiston, NY: Mellen, 1990), iii–v, 25–33, 56–68, 110–23.

10 Gideon Diall, *The Psychology of the Aggregate Mind of an Audience* (Terre Haute, IN: Island Publishing Co., 1897), 27, 15, 26.

11 George Elliott Howard, "Social Psychology of the Spectator," *American Journal of Sociology* (1912): 40.

12 Hugo Munsterberg, *The Photoplay: A Psychological Study* (New York: Dover, 1970), 95, 96, 98–99.

13 Robert Park, *The Crowd and the Public, and Other Essays* (Chicago, IL: University of Chicago Press, 1972); Leon Bramson, *The Political Context of Sociology* (Princeton, NJ: Princeton University Press, 1961), 61–67; Garth Jowett, Ian Jarvie and Katherine Fuller, *Children and the Movies: Media Influence and the Payne Fund Controversy* (Cambridge: Cambridge University Press, 1996). On Blumer, see Stanford M. Lyman and Arthur J. Vidich, *Selected Works of Herbert Blumer: A Public Philosophy for Mass Society* (Urbana, IL: University of Illinois Press, 2000), xv–xvi.

14 On rationality see Genevieve Fraisse, *Reason's Muse: Sexual Difference and the Birth of Democracy*, Jane Marie Todd, trans. (Chicago, IL: University of Chicago Press, 1994).

15 It is only since the establishment of film studies that this equation has been challenged. See Russell Merritt, "Nickelodeon Theaters, 1905–14: Building an Audience for the Movies" in Tino Balio, *The American Film Industry* (Madison, WI: University of Wisconsin Press, 1976); Robert C. Allen, "Motion Picture Exhibition in Manhattan, 1906–12: Beyond the Nickelodeon," *Cinema Journal* 18:2 (Spring 1979): 2–15; Douglas Gomery, "Movie Audiences, Urban Geography and the History of the American Flm," *The Velvet Light Trap* 19 (Spring 1982): 23–29; and the more recent forum on the subject, edited by Ben Singer in *Cinema Journal* 34:3 (Spring 1995): 5–35 and 35:3 (Spring 1996): 72–128.

16 Steven Ross, *Working Class Hollywood* (Princeton, NJ: Princeton University Press, 1998).

17 E.g. "Movies on Liners to Aid the Alien" *New York Times*, 8 November 1926, 19; Paul Boyer, *Urban Masses and Moral Order, 1820–1920* (Boston, MA: Harvard University Press, 1978); Dominick Cavallo, *Muscles and Morals: Organized Playgrounds and Urban Reform, 1880–1920* (Philadelphia, PA: University of Pennsylvania Press, 1981); Steven Hardy, *How Boston Played* (Boston, MA: Northeastern University Press, 1982).

18 E.g Maurice Henle, "A Non-partisan Political Medium," *Wireless Age* (December 1922): 27–29; "The Dawn of Radio in Politics," Special issue on politics and radio *Wireless Age*, October 1924.

19 Robert McChesney, *Telecommunicatons, Mass Media and Democracy: The Battle for the Control of US Broadcasting, 1928–35* (New York: Oxford University Press 1993); Louise Benjamin, *Freedom of the Air and the Public Interest: First Amendment Rights in Broadcasting to 1935* (Carbondale, IL: Southern Illinois University Press, 2001); F. Leslie Smith, Milan D. Meeske and John W. Wright, *Electronic Media and Government: The Regulation of Wireless and Wired Mass Communication in the United States* (London: Longman, 1994), 256.

20 This was made explicit in the 1946 Blue Book, an FCC guide to stations that specified what programming the FCC would consider serving the public interest. Programming qualifying as public service devoted discussion to public issues. See Smith *et al.*, *Electronic Media and Government*, 252. A second means of meeting the criterion was negatively, through self-censorship of programming that would be damaging or offensive to the public.

21 Harrison Summers, *A Thirty Year History of Radio Programs, 1926–1956* (Arno Press, 1971).

22 George Denny, "Bring Back the Town Meeting," speech at Harvard University July 26, 1937, NYPL Town Hall Collection; *Good Evening Neighbors* (Town Hall, 1950), 23; George Denny, "Radio Builds America," *Journal of Educational Sociology* 14:6 (February 1941): 373. Schudson, *The Good Citizen*, 222, briefly discusses *American Town Meeting of the Air* as well.

23 New York Public Library, Manuscript Division, Town Hall Collection, box 29.

24 Smith *et al.*, *Electronic Media and Government*, 256, 260.

25 Joan Shelly Rubin, *The Making of Middle Brow Culture* (Chapel Hill, NC: University of North Carolina Press, 1992).

26 George Denny, "Radio Builds Democracy," *Journal of Educational Sociology* 14:6 (February 1941): 375–76

27 Elaine Tyler May, *Homeward Bound* (New York: Basic Book, 1988); Kenneth Jackson, *Crabgrass Frontier: The Suburbanization of the United States* (Oxford; Oxford University Press, 1985).

28 Thomas Coffin, "Television Effects on Leisure Time Activities," *Journal of Applied Psychology* 32 (1948): 550–58; Charles Alldredge, "Television: Its Effect on Family Habits in Washington DC" (Alldredge Public Relations, 1950); Raymond Stewart,

"The Social Impact of Television on Atlanta Households" PhD Emory University, 1952; Douglas Gomery, *Shared Pleasures: A History of Movie Presentation in the United States* (Madison, WI: University of Wisconsin Press, 1992), 83–88, and Richard Butsch, *The Making of American Audiences* (Cambridge: Cambridge University Press, 2000), 247–49 on television and movie admissions.

29 Wiliam Kornhauser, *Politics of Mass Society* (Free Press, 1959); Paul Lazarsfeld, Bernard Berelson and Hazel Gaudet, *People's Choice: How the Voter Makes Up His Mind in a Presidential Campaign* (New York: Columbia University Press, 1944).

30 John Keats, *Crack in the Picture Window* (Boston, MA: Houghton Mifflin, 1956); Vance Packard, *The Status Seekers* (New York: David McKay Co., 1959); Sloan Wilson, *The Man in the Gray Flannel Suit* (New York: Simon and Schuster, 1955), Clare Barnes, *White Collar Zoo* (Garden City, NY: Doubleday, 1949) and *White Collar Zoo Revisited* (Garden City, NY: Doubleday, 1961). Also see C. Wright Mills, *White Collar: The American Middle Classes* (Oxford: Oxford University Press, 1951); William H. Whyte, *The Organization Man* (New York: Simon and Schuster, 1956); David Reisman, *The Lonely Crowd: A Study of the Changing American Character* (New Haven, CT: Yale University Press, 1953).

31 Vance Packard, *The Hidden Persuaders* (New York: David McKay Co., 1957).

Chapter 6

Seeking the historical audience

Interdisciplinary lessons in the recovery of media practices

S. Elizabeth Bird

In the last 15 years or so, scholarship on media audiences has moved away from studies of direct engagement with texts towards a consideration of the multiple articulations with media in everyday life. As I have suggested, "We cannot really isolate the role of media in culture, because the media are firmly anchored into the web of culture, although articulated by individuals in different ways".[1] Studies of reception of texts and genres are still important; as Curran writes, we should resist the tendency to paint the changes in audience studies as some kind of grand narrative in which each new approach is "better" than the previous one.[2]

However, this more holistic, culturally-based work has opened up some new ways to conceptualize the role of media in everyday life, with scholars approaching questions from different directions – for example, taking the family as a starting point, or "backing into" media through creative experimentation,[3] rather than asking direct questions about specific media response. In part, these new approaches are a result of the (re)discovery of practice as a guiding concept to theorize the media audience in the twenty-first century, which is seen as a way to tease out the very diffuse role of media in what are often described as "media-saturated" cultures. A practice-based study focuses on moments of articulation between individuals and media, while also exploring how these moments are indicative of larger structures and cultural processes. Thus it moves away from both earlier "effects" traditions and "second-wave" approaches to audience reception of media texts.[4] The relevant questions about media are no longer "what do media do to people and cultures?" or even "what do people do in response to media?" As Couldry suggests,

> If recent media research has foregrounded "media culture", practice theory translates this into two concrete and related questions: what types of things do people do in relation to media? And what types of things do people say in relation to media?[5]

To this I would add, "how are media incorporated into everyday communicative and cultural practices?" which I think is a slightly different, if related issue.

The study of media practices maintains the focus on local, grounded activities, rather than theoretical (and possibly speculative) analyses of "culture," but it does not disdain the use of texts in conjunction with direct study of practice.

This ethnographically-informed approach seems appropriate for exploring the mediated world in which many of us now live – but how might we translate this into the historical context, when we cannot observe such practices directly? Audience scholarship made significant advances when it moved toward an appreciation of the "active audience," building on the seminal "encoding/decoding" model of Stuart Hall, which opened the door to a flood of studies on specific audience responses to particular texts.[6] However, once the importance of the active audience had been established, as well as the concomitant distrust of the ability to construct audience meanings from the text alone, it became more problematic to draw inferences about direct "audience response" in the past (as Douglas points out in this volume).

I suggest here that contemporary practice-based approaches mesh effectively with a major recent growth in cultural history, even if this has not been fully recognized in communication and media history. These complementary approaches have proved very effective in reaching a more nuanced understanding of the role of media in everyday life, not only in the present, but also in the past. Furthermore, they start to paint a picture of everyday media practices as having continuity over time, rather than implying that the past is indeed "another country" altogether.

The interest in practice-based approaches in media studies has developed at the same time as they have experienced a resurgence in anthropology, partly in response to the need to move away from narrow, place-bound "fields" in order to understand culture more completely.[7] As early as 1984, anthropologist Sherry Ortner argued that a practice approach to cultural analysis is able to unite Geertzian-inspired symbolic analysis with the social drama approach of the British Manchester school, often associated with Turner and his approach to ritual practices.[8] Thus to truly understand culture we need both textual analysis and ethnography, ideally working together. When it comes to exploring the role of media in culture, such an approach would not only address specific media texts and audience response, but also texts about texts, texts about audiences, and so on, creating a rich, multi-sited and multi-dimensional reading.[9]

This kind of ethnographic rethinking does tend to assume that the ethnographer is working in the present – ethnography with living people may not be enough to achieve the full picture, but neither is textual analysis. Where does that leave history? Can we ever hope to understand the past with the same kind of multi-dimensional, ethnographic richness we hope for in the present? Geertz suggested that we can.[10] He anticipated the "crisis of representation" that caused turmoil in anthropology in the mid-1980s (associated most strongly with Clifford and Marcus), suggesting that even in the present it is unrealistic to claim that we can accurately and unproblematically describe another culture through ethnography.[11] However, he argued that this should not prevent us from trying – and he suggested that exploring culture in another place presents the same problems as exploring it in another time:

> the truth of the doctrine of cultural (or historical – it is the same thing) relativism is that we can never apprehend another people's or another period's imagination neatly, as though it were our own. The falsity of it is that we can therefore never genuinely apprehend it at all.[12]

Thus he advises we should try to read past cultures in multiple, interpretative ways, just as we might today. When it comes to media, a practice-based approach takes us beyond the text and the moment of reception, and searches for connections across multiple practices and discourses. In studying the past, this presents complicated challenges, that take us away from the specific texts in which we might be interested, but there is work in several disciplines that demonstrates the value of this, as I shall show.

In some contexts, of course, we can employ such approaches as oral history and life history, directly engaging with people's memories, as Jensen recommends.[13] Although not without limitations, such methods are commonplace in anthropology[14]; almost by definition, such approaches produce a much broader and culturally embedded understanding of media than some narrowly-focused "response" studies. The work of Moores on recollections of early radio in Britain is a well-known example of such an approach, in which he suggests that the introduction of radio led to the construction of a "family audience," which had not really existed previously.[15] In a similar study of early television in Britain, O'Sullivan found oral histories to be rich sources from which to gain "greater critical insight into the shifting historical and contemporary significance of television … in the transformation of post-war British culture".[16]

But of course the memories of the living only take us back so far, and past that point, we must look elsewhere for evidence. As Douglas suggests, in studying the past, we should not be afraid to try to capture audience experience from text, but the more we can also recover and understand the larger cultural context, the more likely our interpretations are to hold true. With this in mind, I would like to draw attention to existing work across disciplines, most notably cultural history and literary studies, that foregrounds a broad, cultural approach to recovering a sense of everyday life in the past. I am not presenting original, first-hand research here, but rather suggesting how we might broaden the purview of media and communication history away from text and toward context, in order to enrich our understanding of past audience practices.

From spectator to everyday media practice: Lessons from cultural history

Much of the kind of rich, contextual history we have of past audience practices comes from studies of actual audiences at performances, such as Butsch's definitive study of Jacksonian era theater audiences.[17] By casting his net as widely as possible over primary accounts of audience activities, as well as multiple social and cultural histories, Butsch was able to paint a rich, multi-dimensional picture of the class-based practices that provided the context for the rise of the working class "Bowery B'hoys" audience, as well as the elite theater audiences. His goal was less to recreate the audience experience, and more to understand the way the various audiences came to be defined in the culture at large. As he points out, this is most feasible when the various "audiences" are visible, defined, and describable. In fact Livingstone argues that there was a radical shift in audience activity from the eighteenth to the nineteenth centuries: "Consider the shift from the physically contiguous mass spectatorship of the eighteenth century theatre or show to the spatially separated virtual mass of press and broadcasting audiences in the nineteenth and twentieth century." She continues, "the invisibility, or privatization, of what audience members are thinking, or learning, or feeling, is a new (twentieth/twenty-first century) problem."[18]

However, I believe the historical changes outlined by Livingstone are not as straightforward as she suggests. Rather, the "dispersed audience" (and thus the audience that is difficult to pin down for study) is most certainly not only a modern phenomenon. Consider, for example, the audience for news. James Carey, in a now-famous essay on journalism history, made a plea for a cultural history of journalism, drawing on anthropological perspectives. He invokes Geertz in asking, "how did it feel to live and act in a particular period of human history? However, Carey gave scant attention to the question of the audience for journalism, calling rather for what amounts to a historical ethnography of news reporting. From that, the response of the audience could be implied: "From the standpoint of the audience the techniques of journalism determine what the audience can think..."[19] It is still debatable how much the cultural turn in history has penetrated journalism history, which has largely remained focused on institutional histories, "grand narratives" of press progress, or biographical accounts of "great journalists."[20]

In part, the challenge to recovering the historical audience for news is the same as that faced by contemporary researchers. Understanding how people receive news in their daily lives is a nightmare even today, because of the diffuse nature of news – what is it; how does it move from text to audience; what do people do with it? News takes on meaning in context, as people listen, talk, pass on, and process the stories. As I have argued elsewhere, "the story" of a news event develops through interpersonal communication, sometimes filtered through opinion leaders. In today's complex news environment, the ability to discuss and analyze the news has spread across cyberspace.[21] Capturing the daily experience of news reception is a huge challenge. And how much more of a challenge it becomes when we are trying to recapture history.

However, there is some interesting and fruitful work that might help us progress in that direction, both starting from texts and starting from contexts.

As Zelizer comments, journalism history has tended to be very insular, and has not been interested in exploring the insights of historians, literary critics, or scholars from other disciplines.[22] It has been widely assumed that the audience is largely unrecoverable, except through texts. Some, however, have begun to look to work in cultural history, and the field of literary studies is also potentially fertile, as I shall show. For example, Darnton convincingly finds the dispersed, active, news audience as a vibrant reality in the eighteenth century, the very period when we think of audiences as static groups sitting in theaters. He poses the question: "How did you find out what the news was in Paris around 1750? Not, I submit, by reading a newspaper, because papers with news in them – news as we understand it today, about public affairs and prominent persons – did not exist." Rather, he suggests, we look for contemporary accounts of what people actually did in order to stay informed.

> You went to the tree of Cracow. It was a large, leafy chestnut tree, which stood at the heart of Paris in the gardens of the Palais-Royal ... Like a mighty magnet, the tree attracted *nouvellistes de bouche*, or newsmongers, who spread information about current events by word of mouth. They claimed to know, from private sources (a letter, an indiscreet servant, a remark overheard in an antechamber of Versailles), what was really happening in the corridors of power and the people in power took them seriously, because the government worried about what Parisians were saying.[23]

In addition to the documented activities at the tree, there were organized networks of people who were printing, copying, and reading aloud the news of the day, showing "that news (nouvelles) circulated through several media and by different modes – oral, manuscript, and print,"[24] although all outside the law. Using a rich selection of sources, Darnton suggests that eighteenth-century France was not the kind of simple, media-free culture that contrasts neatly with our contemporary "media-saturated" experience. Rather,

> It was merely different. It had a dense communication network made up of media and genres that have been ... so thoroughly forgotten that even their names are unknown today and cannot be translated into English equivalents ... there were so many modes of communication, and they intersected and overlapped so intensively that we can hardly picture their operation.[25]

Darnton stresses that he is not describing "messages transmitted down a line of diffusion to passive recipients but rather a process of assimilating and reworking information in groups – that is, the creation of collective consciousness or public opinion".[26]

Darnton's picture of news circulation is strikingly similar to ethnographically inspired glimpses of news reception today. Gray, for example, discusses the way online "fans" of news debate, discuss, speculate, insult, and generally enjoy their involvement with the news of the day, making the Tree of Crakow and the internet seem not quite so far apart as we might assume.[27] Peterson also argues that an understanding of news reception (in this case in India) can only be reached through rich, ethnographic study of the way news is embedded in cultural practices, drawing attention to

> the wide range of possible discoveries ethnography of news consumption may produce once we abandon the nearly ubiquitous *a priori* assumption that news consumption is primarily about the transmission of content, and that contexts of consumption merely affect the nature of reading and interpretation. Instead … contexts of consumption constitute social fields in which people engage in narrative and performatory constructions of themselves, reinforce social relations with other actors, negotiate status, engage in economic transactions, and imagine themselves and others as members of broader imagined communities.[28]

This description of the contemporary everyday news environment feels closer to Darnton's characterization of the eighteenth century than to social scientific accounts of "news responses".

Darnton acknowledges that he has no way of knowing for sure exactly how people read the quickly produced "news books" he also discusses as part of the news process. However,

> I don't think it extravagant to insist on a quality of reading in general: it is an activity that involves making sense of signs by fitting them in frames … The general readers in eighteenth-century France made sense of politics by incorporating news into the narrative frames provided by the literature of libel. And they were reinforced in their interpretations by the messages they received from all the other mediagossip, poems, songs, prints, jokes, and all the rest.[29]

Darnton has, of course, built a career on the exhaustive study of everyday life in eighteenth-century France, with some digressions towards other societies in the same period. Through that thorough knowledge, he is able to tease out the multiple references to media-related practices, and weave them into a coherent story about how news operates in a specific time and place. The richness of his data, along with his historical skill, allows that story to be very compelling. Most scholars working in media history are not specialist historians of this kind. However, what Darnton's work suggests, in terms of understanding the dispersed audience in history, is that we do indeed need to turn to the large and growing body of historical scholarship on social and cultural history, rather than media texts alone. This is a painstaking process, because so little historical work directly addresses media usage as a central theme. Rather, we have to "back into" the question of the media's role by starting with other practices. In the case of the eighteenth century, this could be learning about activities in coffee-houses, salons, or market-places, as we come across accounts of, for example, the way broadsheet ballads and scandal sheets were passed around in public places, or read to the illiterate. We are looking, therefore, for social practices *around* media. And in fact, this kind of approach is in many ways similar to that espoused by media scholars of practice today.[30]

A similarly rich analysis is provided by Horner and Brewin, who also approach the question of news and political engagement through discussion of a series of texts and practices that mesh to once again offer an alternative to the concept of the static audience. Their historical period is the early-to-mid nineteenth century, during the Jacksonian era and a few decades beyond. They focus on "Salt River Tickets," which were quickly-produced and very ephemeral cards intended to "tease and mock the supporters of losing candidates in the days following local, state, and national elections." As they suggest, such ephemera provide an "entry point" into unraveling what they describe as the "carnivalesque political culture of the past." As they put it, at this time period

> newspapers and other forms of print borrowed from the festivals and celebrations that were such a prominent feature of civic life ... Political broadsides mixed genres and media forms, drawing on popular visual traditions, literate culture, and public performance and burlesque. Political rituals and printed materials mutually reinforced one another.[31]

More directly than Darnton, Horner and Brewin draw comparisons between the twenty-first century media scene, with its perhaps equally chaotic landscape of free-for-all political debate across the real and virtual worlds. Weblogs and political ephemera alike are "produced by individuals or small groups outside established media and political institutions. They encourage interaction between the text's producer and audience. They often use satire or parody to achieve their points, and they operate within a strongly partisan universe".[32]

However, perhaps the most direct exploration of historical news audiences is found in the career of David Paul Nord. Nord has long taken issue with Carey's focus on cultural history of news production; as he writes, "For me, ordinary people reading and using journalism, not just the content of journalism itself, was the locus of cultural history".[33] In a series of works, Nord recreates the world in which news audiences lived, by using a variety of sources, such as unpublished and published letters to the editor. He explores the strategies that readers used to make sense of what they read, and argues that newspaper readers show a range of individual and very personal responses, that are nevertheless located within recognizable structures of cultural and political power.

This kind of deeply textured analysis starts to paint a rather different picture from the broad strokes of media history we often see. When we approach moments of communication from the perspective of surrounding context and practice, activities around news, for example, do not look so strikingly different over long periods of history. At the same time, as Darnton warned earlier, we must be cautious about drawing too-easy analogies between familiar practices and past practices that seem similar but whose contexts might be very different: "nothing is easier than to slip into the comfortable assumption that Europeans thought and felt two centuries ago just as we do today – allowing for the wigs and wooden shoes".[34] Horner and Brewin offer similar cautions, discussing, for example, the very different way in which racism was inscribed in the period under study. We should not minimize the significant social and technological changes that can transform the very nature of audience activity, as Butsch shows in his thorough analysis of the arrival or radio, especially in rural areas. Thus my intent here is not to deny changes in the audience, but to suggest that our conceptions of the audience are also shaped by the methodologies that have been used to study them. As historians such as Darnton (who acknowledges a major debt to Geertz) develop more effective ways to delve into the complex cultural contexts of the past, we may find more, and more varied audience activity than we expected.

Literary scholars recover the historical audience

The history of news and journalism is only one strand in a larger history of mediated practices. And, as Zelizer points out, it is a rather isolated strand.[35] The work of scholars like Nord and Darnton suggests that in reality, we will better understand the audience for news if we see news reception as embedded in other forms of audience activity, rather than as something distinct and separate. I shall return to this point, but now move away from journalism to point in the direction of a significant body of work deriving from literary studies, in which scholars have investigated the reception of media, especially books. I argue that communication and media history can also profitably look here for an understanding of past audience practices. Communication and literary studies have not always meshed well, with various sub-disciplinary themes in communication tending to focus on either journalism or popular culture (or occasionally the intersections between them), while literature scholars have focused more on "high" culture. Literary scholarship has certainly discovered "the audience," but until recently most reader-response criticism has applied such concepts as "implied readers," "informed readers," or other categories of hypothetical reader. It is this kind of response work that communication-based audience scholars often disdain, because of its entirely text-based universe.

However, as Rose argues, "the history of the common reader, at least after 1800, is recoverable," although it requires "the cooperative efforts of an organized body of scholars".[36] Communication and media historians should have a place among that body. Rose takes as his starting point the work of Charles Dickens, who we might describe as a populist author who rose to the status of literary giant, and Dickens is a useful entry point from which to attempt to recover the reading practices of his time period. Rose takes the most direct route to the reader; he shows, for example, that there are British surveys of readers that go back as far as the 1830s, including surveys of readership among working class audiences. He reports, for example, on an 1888 survey of school children aged 11 to 19, in which Dickens was reported as the favorite author by both boys and girls. Unexpected themes from the surveys included that adventure writers (such as Jules Verne), usually assumed to appeal to boys, were also very popular among girls. The surveys also included qualitative comments from respondents, some of which Rose quotes; for example, he cites one young woman's long essay, which included the comment,

> A great many girls never read so-called "girls" books at all; they prefer those presumably written for boys. Girls as a rule don't care for Sunday-school twaddle; they like a good stirring story, with a plot and some incident and adventures – not a collection of texts and sermons.[37]

Edward Salmon, who reported the survey results, concluded that "many girls' books sold well only because they were given as presents by adults"[38] – an interesting and very modern conclusion that would not be recoverable through analysis of either texts or sales figures.

Rose goes on to point out that while literary critics have often assumed the complete unavailability of first hand sources on reading practices, especially among non-elite groups, such sources can be found. He cites the work of Vincent, in which the author "was able to assemble 142 memoirs by early-nineteenth-century British workers and showed that they could be used to reconstruct a detailed history of reading response".[39] From these and multiple other sources, Rose shows how autobiographical accounts spoke clearly of the way Dickens' novels addressed their personal experiences.

Rose adamantly denies any value in textual study as a way to recover reading practices. He argues, for example, that

> If you want to know how Dickens shaped attitudes toward women in the minds of his readers, you are not going to find the answer in *The Pickwick Papers*, or anything else Dickens wrote ... To put it bluntly, a large body of recent literary criticism, based as it is on the receptive fallacy, should be scrapped.[40]

However, other literary scholars, more aligned perhaps with Douglas's cautious approach to texts, suggest that there is still value in doing careful textual analysis, showing how different elements articulate with other cultural realities. Curtis, for example, explores the connection of advertising images in Dickens' published works, pointing us to the important role of the visual in the reader's experience. Dickens' serialized works were bound in distinctive green covers bearing detailed pictorial representations that referenced both the novel and the advertiser. For instance, Dakin Tea company framed its cover advertisement for *Bleak House* in the form of a letter to Dickens, noting "that the reader will profit from reading both the serial and the ad".[41] Curtis notes that there was a continual flow between ads and texts,

> For example, Rowland's Kalydor complexion cream, advertised extensively in *Martin Chuzzlewit* and *Nicholas Nickleby*, appears ... in *Nicholas Nickleby* when an old man proclaims that the miniature portrait painter Miss La Creevy is more beautiful than "Mrs. Rowland who every morning bathes in Kalydor".[42]

Curtis' analysis does not amount to a reader-response study; however, it suggests ways in which we might look at the interaction between books, advertising, printed texts and visuals, in combination with historical contextual information, to help us recreate the contemporary meaning of a mediated phenomenon such as Charles Dickens. This point is further emphasized by Altick, who explores the significance for readers of the celebrated illustrations by "Phiz," which were disliked by some critics, because they allowed readers to be "lazy" by saving them the mental work of imagining the characters.[43]

Without using any direct audience responses, Vlock also argues for the validity of recovering the audience experience through both text and through a careful exploration of contexts. In this case, her central point, the meaning of Dickens, can only be fully understood within a much broader context than the novels themselves, primarily as part of a vibrant theatrical and performative culture, coupled with a strong printing industry and a vital street-culture. As she points out, Dickens' novels were constantly being adapted for the theater, with multiple versions playing at any one time, and this too assured that any given Dickens text would be reinterpreted constantly for audiences. Vlock's conceptualization of the audience contrasts with "the privatized subjectivity that has been so frequently invoked by cultural theorists," and which she believe is inadequate to capture the nineteenth-century imagination. Although not using the word, her argument echoes the work of many contemporary audience scholars, who insist on the "intertextuality" of mediated experience, in which any encounter with a particular text constantly overlaps with other discourses.

> The Victorian reading subject ... performed his or her reading in a highly public "space," drawing upon a set of consensual popular assumptions,

cultural stereotypes regularly published on the stage and generally accepted as representative of Victorian social reality ... We cannot, perhaps, enter fully into that experience, but we can examine for ourselves the multiple "texts" – novels, plays, voices and gestures, reviews – that resounded in the Victorian reader's head, and hence imagine how Victorians read.[44]

Altick echoes Vlock's discussions of intertextuality, with particular reference to the specific conditions that Dickens' (and others') novels were published – the serial form. It has been widely accepted for a long time that in his earlier novels Dickens changed the course of the narrative in direct response to audience feedback[45]; as Altick points out, Dickens received enormous amounts of "fan mail," most of which unfortunately he destroyed. The first time he composed an entire novel (*Dombey and Son*) before serialization, he speculated to correspondents about whether the audience would be traumatized by the death of a central character. Once again, the value for audience study here is not direct access to reader experience, but rather the creation of a more complex picture of an active, demanding audience, who interacted directly with the author, and may have helped shape the text itself – prefiguring, perhaps, the activist fan of the internet age.[46] Indeed, Hayward, in an exhaustive study of audiences of serialized fiction, from Dickens to TV soap operas, points to the active and communal role of the audience in both shaping the text and reconfiguring it through personal interaction.[47]

Perhaps the most striking points emerging from literary scholars' more recent recovery of the audience (outside the text itself) is that, first, there are sources available that reach into the lived experience of the reader; and second, that reading in the past was not necessarily an internalized, unrecoverable transaction between text and individual reader, but also had important social dimensions. Both are important insights for media historians. On the first point, Rose, comments that "Twenty years ago the historiography of reading scarcely existed".[48] Today, he points to a virtual revolution in the field, drawing on the influential work of cultural historians such as Darnton, but also on a broad range of other historical studies of everyday life and media interaction. As well as the reader surveys addressed above, he offers a list of sources (and works drawn from them) that can be grist to the scholar's mill, including police records, probate and booksellers' records, minutes from reading groups and literary societies, memoirs and diaries, commonplace books, records of educational institutions, library registers, letters to the editors, and more. He marshals an impressive bibliography of recent work that reaches rich and subtle understandings of reading practice, and concludes: "There is an important scholarly lesson here: the next time a fellow historian tells you 'The sources simply don't exist,' ask: 'How hard have you looked?'".[49]

On the second point, as Rose demonstrates, many authors have pointed to the interactive and social dimensions of reading. Price for example, argues that

"Part of the problem is that literary critics tend to act as if reading were the only legitimate use of books".[50] She cites Davis's work on the book as a valuable item in social exchange and currency, as well as Long's work on "textual interpretation as collective action" which links social activities around the book from the nineteenth century to contemporary times. For example, "Empirical studies of mid-twentieth-century American adults have shown that reading correlates with social involvement: readers need others to set an example, to provide a sounding board for reactions to texts, to recommend and criticize and exchange books".[51]

Stevenson shows that this association of reading and social involvement is not a new phenomenon. Discussing Victorian US society, she focuses attention on the large literature of what she calls "reading advice," which helped middle-class readers negotiate the large array of possible reading materials, and how to use them in everyday life: "Besides contributing to personal growth, books also had a social meaning … people had to be aware of the authors and books alluded to in polite conversation. In most families, reading provided some of the substance of everyday conversation." Advice literature would help families decide what books were important, and how they might put together a collection that fit their circumstances and budgets. And clearly, at least in the more leisured middle classes, organized social activities developed around reading, at times almost approaching the level of "fan clubs".[52]

Recovering the historical "fan audience"

As we have seen, some culturally-oriented literary and historical work is now hinting at the value of thinking about "fan-like" activity in the past. The study of "fan" activities has enjoyed a boom in contemporary audience studies, for a number of reasons. Contemporary fans are engaged in a huge variety of active, media-related practices that connect them, media texts, and multiple other texts together in an articulation that is anything but static and linear. Inspired by the early work of *Star Trek* researchers Jenkins and Bacon-Smith, a series of scholars have explored the world of complex fan practices, in which fans not only watch and talk, but also create fan fiction, video mash-ups, conference events and so on.[53] For the most part, there has been little attention given to fan activities in the past, again for understandable reasons. First, perhaps, it is only recently that scholars have acknowledged that one can conceive of "fans" of media other than television and movies. Second (at least until the 1990s, when scholars discovered the rich range of practices that surround actual viewership), fan activity has long been perceived as an individual psychological response, which certainly cannot be recovered historically. Now that the focus has tended to move away from psychology toward media-related practices, we are beginning to see work on historical fan audiences. This work, like contemporary fan studies, is often effective in illuminating audience practices more generally.

We can certainly look for hints of this in the work on popular novelists and poets, such as the scholarship on Dickens described above, through which it is clear that audiences did have a very active role in determining the direction of storylines and theater adaptations. Like today, not all readers would have written fan letters or picketed theaters (or their contemporary equivalents), but those who did would have had a particularly intense "audience response." But when we do learn about it, we can get a sense again of mediated activities that go far beyond the individual. Fisher, discusses the energetic, informed and very active theater audiences of eighteenth-century England, who essentially played the role now filled by critics in determining whether productions succeeded or failed.[54] Some tantalizing early work exists that suggests the possible rich troves of fan mail that may directly have influenced writers and the directions in which they went, such as a brief nod to an archive of fan mail for the novels of nineteenth-century British Prime Minister Benjamin Disraeli.[55] However, perhaps the most developed argument for the fan as a historical reality is that of Cavicchi, whose best known previous work focused on present-day fans. In his latest work, Cavicchi uses the diaries of young female opera fans, such as 24-year-old Lucy Lowell, who wrote seven volumes of diary entries in the 1880s.

> She attended performances by almost every touring opera and symphonic star that passed through Boston, every rehearsal and concert to the new Boston Symphony Orchestra, and many local festivals, band concerts, and musical theatre productions. … she wrote page after page of description about her experiences of hearing music.[56]

Cavicchi, like Rose, Darnton, and Butsch in other contexts, studied diaries, scrapbooks, and letters of the period. Like them, he makes the important point that "many of the materials have not been studied as evidence of musical life".[57] In other words, we cannot only expect to find evidence of media-related practices in sources that directly relate to those media, but must approach these practices by finding moments in which they articulate with more general accounts of social and cultural life. He goes on to discuss the career of stars like opera singer Jenny Lind, who inspired passionate responses in fans, who not only wrote about their personal attachment to her, but also to the other like-minded people who came to the theater to share the experience. Thus fan practices, past and present, represent a fruitful way to examine the intersection of media events and everyday life, showing in particular how individuals actively *choose* to articulate with media in a wide range of often unpredictable ways. This helps us move from a perception of "the media" as a monolithic, even sinister force, to an appreciation of individual choices and agency.

Cavicchi is careful not to make simple-minded analogies between the past and the present: "I don't wish to discount the significant transformations wrought by the mass media in the twentieth century".[58] However, he argues convincingly that a recovery and re-evaluation of past activities, by making the most effective use of extensive and under-utilized primary sources, can help us understand both changes and continuities in audience practices. Nineteenth-century music lovers, he writes, "were among the first to assume the role of the audience-consumer and to create the strategies many use today for understanding the world of stars, merchandizing, and spectacle".[59]

Conclusion: Audience practices and media history

As Zelizer argues, consideration of history has been problematic in communication studies. "For instance, in the United States, a preference for social science research in many communications schools drew queries about the reliability of the historical methods studies."[60] Journalism history, media history, and communications history tended to be separate enterprises, with different methodologies and objects of study, and little connection among them. With a few notable exceptions, none of these fields drew extensively on broader movements in cultural history or historically based literary studies, and interest in audiences was minimal. I believe that the rise in more practice-oriented contemporary audience research can help change that. Central to such scholarship is the dissolution of the kind of generic boundaries that have often marked "active audience" studies. We, "the audience," are not fixed groups paying attention to "the news," or "soap opera," or whatever, but individuals moving among media and articulating with them in a large variety of ways. Certainly, we may pay attention to specific genres in different ways, but basically we live as "audiences" all the time, developing our views of the world from across the mediated (and non-mediated) spectrum. This view of the audience has necessarily started to break down the disciplinary boundaries that kept some scholars studying television, others studying news, or movies, or advertising, and so on.

Sometimes, we might not even study a genre directly at all. For instance, I have suggested that one way to approach practice would be to explore what I call "mediated rituals".[61] We might start, for instance, with weddings, one of the central social and individual rituals in almost all cultures. We could use direct ethnographic methods, but would also include analysis of the voluminous texts of the "wedding industry;" representations of weddings in television, movies, and the news; internet discourse; analysis of wedding photographic practices; and so on. The goal would be to reach an understanding of the extent to which the contemporary wedding is a "mediated practice" for those who participate. We are no longer studying "news audiences," or "new media audiences," or any such fragment of the media universe, but rather cultural practices and how media intersect with them. I suggest that this approach could also work in a historical setting. Diaries and letters might substitute for ethnographic interviews, and analysis could be done of such texts as catalogs, magazines, newspapers, and so on.

My point here is not to advocate for a specific study, but rather to suggest that the move to a more diffuse notion of "the audience" may help create a more realistic picture of mediated practices in the past as well as the present. As Nord writes, the most pressing need for historical audience study is not more theorizing of the audience. Rather, we need more "empirical research, research that links different levels of analysis, research that links actual readers not only to texts but to social contexts in which the readers lived and the texts were read."[62] Nineteenth-century theater-goers, for example, were not just theater audiences, but also consumers of news, popular and serious literature, music, and multiple forms of ephemera, all of which are relevant to a full picture of the everyday life of the audience. All studies must have a starting point, of course; the authors discussed in this chapter have begun with the book, the theater, the news, and so on. But the most successful have moved from that genre to explore the connections between it and the culture in which it was embedded, between them weaving a rich cultural tapestry that points the way to a more nuanced and complete understanding of the media audience in history.

Notes

1 S. Elizabeth Bird, "Mediated Practices and the Interpretation of Culture," in J. Postill and B. Braeuchler, eds, *Theorising Media and Practice* (Oxford: Berghahn, forthcoming); S. Elizabeth Bird, *The Audience in Everyday Life: Living in a Media World* (New York: Routledge, 2003), 3.

2 James Curran, "The 'New Revisionism' in Mass Communication Research: A Reappraisal," *European Journal of Communication* 5, no. 2 (1990): 135–64.

3 See, for instance, Stewart Hoover, Lynn S. Clark. and D. F. Alters, *Media, Home and Family* (New York: Routledge, 2003); D. Gauntlett, *Creative Explorations: New Approaches to Identities and Audiences* (London: Routledge, 2007).

4 Perti Alasuutari, "Three Phases of Reception Studies," in Perti Alasuutari, ed., *Rethinking the Media Audience* (London: Sage, 1999), 1–21.

5 Nick Couldry, "Theorising Media as Practice," *Social Semiotics* 14, no. 2 (2004): 124.

6 For excellent overviews, see Perti Alasuutari "Three Phases of Reception Studies," and N. Abercrombie and B. Longhurst, *Audiences: A Sociological Theory of Performance and Imagination* (London: Sage, 1998).

7 See, for example, A. Gupta and J. Ferguson, eds, *Anthropological Locations: Boundaries and Grounds of a Field Science* (Berkeley, CA: University of California Press, 1997); Arjun Appadurai, *Modernity at Large: Cultural Dimensions of Globalization* (Minneapolis, MN: University of Minnesota Press, 1996).

8 Sherry B. Ortner, "Theory in Anthropology Since the Sixties," *Comparative Studies in Society and History* 26, no. 1 (1984): 126–66; Victor Turner, *The Ritual Process* (Chicago, IL: Aldine, 1969).

9 George E. Marcus, *Ethnography Through Thick and Thin* (Princeton, NJ: Princeton University Press, 1998).

10 Clifford Geertz, *Local Knowledge: Further Essays in Interpretive Anthropology* (New York: Basic Books, 1983); Clifford Geertz, *The Interpretation of Cultures* (New York: Basic Books, 1973).

11 James Clifford and George E. Marcus, eds, *Writing Culture: The Poetics and Politics of Ethnography* (Berkeley, CA: University of California Press, 1986).

12 Geertz, *Local Knowledge*, 44.

13 Klaus Bruhn Jensen, "The Past in the Future: Problems and Potentials of Historical Reception Studies," *Journal of Communication* 43, no. 4 (1993): 20–28.

14 M. Angrosino, *Doing Cultural Anthropology: Projects for Ethnographic Data Collection* (New York: Waveland, 2006).

15 S. Moores, "The Box on the Dresser: Memories of Early Radio and Everyday Life," *Media, Culture and Society* 10 (1998): 23–40.

16 T. O'Sullivan, "Television Memories and Cultures of Viewing, 1950–65," in John Corner, ed., *Popular Television in Britain: Studies in Cultural History* (London: BFI, 1991), 159–81.

17 Richard Butsch, *The Making of American Audiences from Stage to Television, 1750–1990* (New York: Cambridge University Press, 2000).

18 Sonia Livingstone, "The Changing Nature of Audiences: From the Mass Audience to the Interactive Media User" (London: LSE Research Online, 2003), 4–5, 24. Available at http://eprints.lse.ac.uk/archive/00000417

19 James W. Carey, "The Practice of Journalism History," *Journalism History* 1, no. 1, (1974): 3–5, 27.

20 Barbie Zelizer, *Taking Journalism Seriously: News and the Academy* (New York: Sage, 2004).

21 Bird, *The Audience in Everyday Life*.

22 Zelizer, *Taking Journalism Seriously*.

23 Robert Darnton, "An Early Information Society: News and the Media in Eighteenth-century Paris," *The American Historical Review* 105, no. 1 (2000): 2.

24 Darnton, "An Early Information Society," 4.

25 Darnton, "An Early Information Society," 7.

26 Darnton, "An Early Information Society," 26.

27 Jonathan Gray, "The News: You gotta Love It," in C. Sandvoss, J. Gray and C.L. Harrington, eds, *Fandom: Identities and Communities in a Mediated World* (New York: New York University Press, 2007), 75–87.

28 M.A. Peterson, "Getting the News in New Delhi: Newspaper Literacies in an Indian Mediascape," in S. Elizabeth Bird, ed., *The Anthropology of News of Journalism: A Global Perspective* (Bloomington, IN: Indiana University Press, forthcoming).

29 Darnton, "An Early Information Society," 34.

30 Couldry, "Theorising Media as Practice".

31 Jennifer R. Horner and Mark Brewin, "The Salt River Ticket, Democratic Discourse, and Nineteenth Century American Politics," *Critical Studies in Media Communication* 24, no. 1 (2007): 1, 5.

32 Horner and Brewin, "The Salt River Ticket, Democratic Discourse, and Nineteenth Century American Politics," 15.

33 David P. Nord, "James Carey and Journalism History: A Remembrance," *Journalism History* 32, no. 3 (2006): 122–27; David P. Nord, *Communities of Journalism: A History of American Newspapers and Their Readers.* (Urbana and Chicago, IL: University of Illinois Press, 2001), 125.

34 Robert Darnton, *The Great Cat Massacre and other Episodes in French Cultural History* (New York: Basic Books, 1984), 4.

35 Zelizer, *Taking Journalism Seriously*, 4.

36 Jonathan Rose, "How Historians Study Reader Response: Or, What did Jo Think of *Bleak House?*" in J.O. Jordan and R.L. Patten, eds, *Literature in the Marketplace: Nineteenth Century British Publishing and Reading Practices* (Cambridge: Cambridge University Press, 1995), 195.

37 Rose, "How Historians Study Reader Response," 201.

38 Rose, "How Historians Study Reader Response," 201.

39 Rose, "How Historians Study Reader Response," 205; see D. Vincent, *Bread, Knowledge and Freedom: A Study of Nineteenth Century Working Class Autobiography* (London: Methuen, 1982).

40 Rose, "How Historians Study Reader Response," 209.
41 G. Curtis, "Dickens in the Visual Market," in J.O. Jordan and R.L. Patten, eds, *Literature in the Marketplace: Nineteenth Century British Publishing and Reading Practices* (Cambridge: Cambridge University Press, 1995), 213–49, 220.
42 Curtis, "Dickens in the Visual Market," 222.
43 R. D. Altick, "Varieties of Readers' Response: The Case of *Dombey and Son*," *The Yearbook of English Studies* 10 (1980): 70–94.
44 D. M. Vlock, "Dickens, Theatre, and the Making of a Victorian Reading Public," *Studies in the Novel* 29, no. 2 (1997): 164–93.
45 See, for instance, G. G. Grubb, "Dickens' Pattern of Weekly Serialization," *ELH* 9, no. 2 (1942): 141–56.
46 H. Jenkins, "Afterword: The future of Fandom," in Cornell Sandvoss, J. Gray and C.L. Harrington, eds, *Fandom: Identities and Communities in a Mediated World* (New York: New York University Press, 2007), 357–64.
47 J. Hayward, *Consuming Pleasures: Active Audiences and Serial Fictions from Dickens to Soap Opera* (Lexington, KY: The University Press of Kentucky, 1997).
48 Jonathan Rose, "The History of Education as the History of Reading," *History of Education* 36, no. 4 (2007): 595–605.
49 Rose, "The History of Education as the History of Reading," 597.
50 L. Price, "Reading: The State of the Discipline," *Book History* 7 (2004): 303–20. See also N. Davis, *The Gift in Sixteenth-Century France* (Madison, WI: University of Wisconsin Press, 2000); Elizabeth Long, "Textual Interpretation as Collective Action," in J. Boyarin, ed., *The Ethnography of Reading* (Berkeley, CA: University of California Press, 1992), 180–211.
51 Davis, *The Gift in Sixteenth-Century France*, 306.
52 L.L. Stevenson, "Prescription and Reality: Reading Advisers and Reading Practice, 1860–80," *Book Research Quarterly* 6, no. 4 (1990): 43–52.
53 Henry Jenkins, *Textual Poachers: Television Fans and Participatory Culture* (New York: Routledge, 1992); Camille Bacon-Smith, *Enterprising Women: Television Fandom and the Creation of Popular Myth* (Philadelphia, PA: University of Pennsylvania Press, 1992); C. Sandvoss, L. Harrington and J. Gray, eds, *Fandom: Identities and Communities in a Mediated World* (New York: New York University Press, 2007); M. Hills, *Fan Cultures* (London: Routledge, 2002).
54 J.W. Fisher, "Audience Participation in the Eighteenth Century Theatre," in S. Kattwinkel, ed., *Audience Participation: Essays on Inclusion in Performance* (Westport, CT: Praeger, 2003), 55–70.
55 B.R. Jerman, "Disraeli's Fan Mail: A Curiosity Item," *Nineteenth-Century Fiction* 9, no. 1 (1954): 61–71.
56 D. Cavicchi, "Loving Music: Listeners, Entertainments, and the Origins of Music Fandom in Nineteenth Century America," in C. Sandvoss, J. Gray and L. Harrington, eds, *Fandom: Identities and Communities in a Mediated World* (New York: New York University Press, 2007), 235–49; D. Cavicchi, *Tramps Like Us: Music and Meaning Among Springsteen Fans* (New York: Oxford University Press, 1998), 235.
57 Cavicchi, *Tramps Like Us*, 236.
58 Cavicchi, *Tramps Like Us*, 249.
59 Cavicchi, *Tramps Like Us*, 249.
60 Zelizer, *Taking Journalism Seriously*, 85.
61 See S. Elizabeth Bird, "Mediated Practices and the Interpretation of Culture," forthcoming.
62 Nord, *Communities of Journalism*, 270.

Part 3

Technology

Introduction

Technology, communication and history

Deborah Lubken

Communication scholars are reputed to be uncommonly susceptible to the forbidden charms of technological determinism. We are well-schooled in the dangers of thinking about media as natural objects with fixed edges, and we have been cautioned against pursuing the consequences of technologies without also inquiring into their genesis.[1] Yet the excitement of exploring a particular gadget or system lowers our guard, and, in the heat of the moment, active verbs consort with technologies to produce unqualified cause-and-effect statements. Such is our reputation. Although the bulk of this notoriety may be based more in caricature than a representative sampling of scholarship, examples that perpetuate the myth are not difficult to find.

Remedies to technological determinism, both prophylactic and treatment-oriented, may be found by looking to the practices of historians, beginning with the sideways reading advocated by John Durham Peters earlier in this volume – the habit of looking away from obvious topics and questions to "incidentals and contingencies."[2] Each of the authors in this section turns away from familiar lines of inquiry to pursue issues of communication technology and history from fresh perspectives.

Peter Stallybrass directs our gaze away from the "revolutionary" – and controversial – effects of the printing press to the materiality of the artifacts it was used to produce. The truly revolutionary consequences of the printing press, Stallybrass contends, are found not in books (which constituted a relatively small portion of early printed material) but in printed blank forms, which provide the material basis for compulsory literacy by inciting hand-written completion. By examining the circumstances of reception of first indulgences, then almanacs, and finally the US Constitution, Stallybrass dispels the commonly held assumption that print replaced manuscript, instead locating print within a system of communication. Indulgences, for example, were "sold by a revolutionary conjoining of speech (sermons), printing (blank indulgences), and writing (the completion of the blank forms in manuscript)."[3]

Anna McCarthy encourages us to scrutinize the assumption underlying public service media: that the audience's views toward citizenship can be influenced through media consumption. She then directs our attention away from opinions, attitudes, and beliefs – where media scholars are accustomed to looking for evidence of television's effects – to the discursive spaces generated by public television. Through an archival investigation, McCarthy assesses the production processes of post-World War II public service programs, concluding that public service television emerged as a space to accommodate complex elite conversations about governance: "They were not communicating with the audience, or at least not only with the audience. They were using the idea of the audience to communicate with each other."[4]

John Nerone, after endorsing a social constructionist approach that de-centers technology and conceptualizes media as institutions, looks to the interplay of workplace structures and various technologies within the mid-nineteenth- to early twentieth-century newsroom to arrive at more complicated versions of certain episodes in media history. The economy of words associated with news work did not come about, as is commonly held, from the invention of the telegraph, but from a confluence of workplace roles and expectations, space limitations, the influence of nineteenth-century oral culture in the US, and beliefs about the political role of the press, among other factors. Likewise, while the incorporation of photography into news work did encounter technological obstacles, the differing goals of photojournalism and news illustration, each of which emerged out of different roles within the newsroom, constituted a more significant barrier. Even the impact of major printing technologies, including first the steam and then electrical press, was mitigated by their introduction into larger work structures and cultural systems.

The essays in this section suggest that sideways reading can provide the perspective to resist the wiles of technological determinism. Causal relationships that seem obvious when viewed from the expected point of view may seem less seductive – certainly more complex – when seen from a different angle. In addition to exploring the incidentals and contingencies of their respective topics, Stallybrass, McCarthy and Nerone each attempt to situate communication technologies within larger systems: within social, political, and economic spheres; alongside other technologies in general, and, more specifically, in their articulation with other modes of communication.

Notes

1 For a discussion of the pitfalls of the "artifactual" approach to communication history, see the introduction of Carolyn Marvin's *When Old Technologies Were New* (Oxford: Oxford University Press, 1988): 3–8. See also Leo Marx and Merritt Roe Smith, "Introduction," in Merritt Roe Smith and Leo Marx, eds, *Does Technology Drive History? The Dilemma of Technological Determinism* (Cambridge, MA: MIT Press, 1994).
2 John Durham Peters, "History as a Communication Problem," this volume, 21.
3 Peter Stallybrass, "Printing and the Manuscript Revolution," this volume, 113.
4 Anna McCarthy, "Governing by Television," this volume, 132.

Chapter 7

Printing and the manuscript revolution

Peter Stallybrass

In 1980, Elizabeth Eisenstein published *The Printing Press as an Agent of Change: Communications and Cultural Transformations in Early-Modern Europe* in two volumes.[1] But despite the book's massive influence, its thesis has been continually challenged since then and it is widely thought by most scholars working in the field to have been finally discredited by Adrian Johns's *The Nature of the Book*.[2] Johns rejects just about every aspect of Eisenstein's thesis: printed books are, he argues, no more fixed, reliable or standardized than manuscripts. Moreover, they were often sold in small print runs for narrowly defined groups. And the conditions of the reception of printed books was highly variable, depending upon how, why, or whether they were read. I will argue that for all of the problems with Eisenstein's thesis, its main argument – the revolutionary effects of printing – is even stronger than she originally proposed and that the attempt by recent scholars to argue for the *persistence* or even the *coexistence* of manuscript and print is misconceived, depending upon an elision of printing with the printing of *books*. When the first British Census of Production was made in 1907, books constituted only 14 per cent of the total value of print production. Printers do not print books. They print sheets of paper. Printing, I will argue today, did indeed produce a revolutionary transformation in communications, but not primarily through books. Its most radical effect was its incitement to writing by hand.

Half an hour before landing in the United States, the flight attendants issue all passengers with printed customs declaration forms. This is followed by the usual scramble to find a working pen; to recall what the flight number is; to retrieve your passport so as to fill in its number and the place where issued; to recall whether or not you've been on or near a farm; to remember that you've forgotten to buy all those gifts for your friends that you now won't need to declare; and finally, anxious and exhausted, to put your seat in the upright position, make sure that your seat belt is securely fastened, and prepare for landing. Among the many things that a flight to the US may be, it is an exercise in compulsory literacy. The nation-state demands that one reads and writes or (today humiliatingly, unless one is very young or doesn't read or write English) find someone who will fill in the form in one's stead. The work of the nation-state is done through a printed form that elicits writing by hand.

We are heirs to the Catholic Church, which, in 1476, inscribed the manuscript names of Henry Langly and his wife on William Caxton's first dated work: the single sheet of an Indulgence, published by the Catholic Church in the shape of a blank form.[3] Printing and manuscript are compulsorily conjoined in the printed blank form – a form that only fulfills its function *as* a form when it has been completed by hand. And there are two things above all that you must be able to write: your name and the date. A third, more variable, element is place – country of origin, place of birth, home address. The revolution of printing-for-manuscript that provides the material basis for compulsory literacy has little to do with reading. It demands that we fill in name and date, whether or not we have actually read our passports, our tax returns, or the fine print on customs declaration forms. The printed forms that shape our daily lives do not require us to read; they demand that we participate in the revolutionary transformation of writing by hand. A perverse thought: some of the most fundamental technologies of communication that shape and control our lives are not primarily communicative at all.

Europeans first encountered printed blanks to be filled in with name, date, and place in the form of indulgences, published at the expense of the Catholic Church and printed in millions in the first century of printing. The first dated text that survives from Gutenberg's press is not a book but a printed indulgence. An indulgence was usually a single piece of paper, printed on one side only. Gutenberg stopped work on his great Bible to print 2,000 copies of an indulgence in 1454–55.[4] But Gutenberg's 2,000 indulgences were only a foretaste of what was to come. In Augsburg in 1480, Jodocus Pflanzmann printed 20,000 certificates of confession, four to a sheet, and Johan Bämler printed 12,000 indulgences. In 1499–1500, Johann Luschner printed 142,950 indulgences for the Benedictine Monastery at Montserrat.[5] As Clive Griffin has shown, so profitable was the printing of indulgences that printers competed fiercely for the patents to print them. Successful printers sometimes had to set up new printing houses to cope with the work. Varela, for instance, set up a second house in Toledo where he printed indulgences from 1509 to 1514.[6] But the staggering increase in indulgences required not only printers but also new kinds of scribes. These scribes no longer needed to know how to copy out the whole of a Latin bible. Like us, they needed to know how to fill in printed forms with name, date, and place.

The sale of indulgences typically depended upon a complex interaction of speech, manuscript, and print. This indulgence, issued by the Archbishop of Mainz and Magdeburg, has blank spaces for the name of the recipient, the month of the year and the day of the week.[7] It was issued for the use of John Tetzel, the immediate cause of the Reformation, since it was he who took over Luther's church, ejecting him from his own pulpit, so that he could sell his indulgences. It was in direct response to Tetzel's usurpation of his church that Luther wrote and published the 95 Theses – theses whose overwhelming subject is the sale of indulgences.[8] Just how they were sold is carefully depicted in a German Lutheran woodcut.[9] In the center of the cut, in front of an altar, is the indulgence cross that was set up with papal banners either side of it. On the right, a monk encourages two parishioners to put their money into the collection box directly below the cross. On the left, the indulgence preacher stands in the pulpit, holding up a manuscript papal bull with five seals, while he delivers the indulgence sermon. And in the right foreground, a clerk sits at a table, around which three men and a woman are gathered. With his right hand, the clerk hands out one of the printed and sealed indulgences, while, with his left hand, he either records the transaction in manuscript or fills out the blanks in the next indulgence. In front of him are other sealed indulgences, and wax seals.

The indulgences are advertised orally by a preacher; they are distributed as printed forms; they are filled in and recorded in manuscript by clerks. Indulgences were thus sold by a revolutionary conjoining of speech (sermons), printing (blank indulgences), and writing (the completion of the blank forms in manuscript). Printing also produced the mechanical means by which this woodcut image was itself reproduced. Finally, this woodcut depicting the sale of indulgences is itself part of a polemic against what I believe was the single most important form of printing in the first seventy years of printing: the printing of millions of blank indulgences that, while only a small portion of the total number of sheets being printed, had a disproportionate impact upon the whole of Europe, becoming a central means of raising money to wage war against the Ottoman Empire and to subsidize the papacy. Plenary indulgences, giving remission of all sins committed before the indulgence was granted, could only be conferred by the Pope. Partial indulgences, on the other hand, were administered by local officials and constituted a system of taxation for subsidizing hospitals, rebuilding churches, mending roads and harbors, and lining the pockets of pardoners and bishops. Indulgences were not, as is usually thought, some strange aberration; they were the successful means by which both the Church and local communities raised taxes.

They also provided the model for the first government tax forms. In 1512, parliament granted Henry VIII a subsidy for war against France. The subsidy was proclaimed both in folio booklets and in printed broadsides that were posted. But more important for its future implications was Cardinal Wolsey's order for the printing of blank forms to assist in the collection of the tax. These "bureaucratic forms," like indulgences, "provided blank spaces for the name of the buyer and date of purchase."[10] One of the three surviving forms is a blank that Richard Pynson printed in 1515

for thorderynge and assessynge of eruey [sic] p[er]sone dwellynge, aby-dynge, or hauynge theyr moost resorte to, or in the sayde Cytie of London chargeable and contributory to a subsydie graunted to our sayd soueraygne lorde, by auctoryte of his Parlyament last holden in Westm [inster].[11]

The tax form thus doubles as a state census, combining in a single piece of paper the founding bureaucratic forms of the modern nation-state.

But printed blank forms were only one way in which printing produced blank paper for completion by hand. Equally significant was the transformation of the most popular of all small pamphlets: the almanac. At first, almanacs were entirely printed, although one often finds blank margins and end-leaves used for practicing writing, making contracts, or writing down recipes. But in 1568, Joachim Hughbrigh printed an almanac for merchants, mariners, students and "trauellers both by sea and lande." And Hughbrigh's almanac is composed not only of printed pages but also of blank pages – or rather of pages on which only the days of the month have been printed in the left margin. In other words, these "blank" pages are not added by the binder but are a constituent part of the printing process. From small beginnings, these "blanks," as they came to be called, transformed both almanac-production and the history of writing by hand.

We are fortunate, then, that the Stock Book for the Stationers' Company from 1663/4 to 1713/4 has survived, and with it evidence of the thousands of copies that were printed in London every year. Almanacs accounted for nearly 40 per cent of the Stock's total expenditure on paper, printing, and authorship from 1673 to 1682. If the sheer quantity of almanacs is astonishing, so also is the fact that almanacs *without* blank pages were outnumbered by almanacs *with* them. The distinction between these two kinds of almanacs was registered in their official names: "sorts" usually consisted of two printed sheets (32 octavo pages), "blanks" of two and a half sheets (40 octavo pages), the extra half sheet providing the blank pages for manuscript accounts and notes. In 1664, the Treasurer of the Stationers' Company recorded that he had received 167,550 blanks compared to 122,850 sorts; in 1665, 194,300 blanks compared to 126,900 sorts; and in 1666, 173,650 blanks compared to 116,850 sorts. Blanks also accounted for nearly all the newly authored almanacs produced during the reign of Charles II.[12] In other words, the most popular form of the most popular printed text in Restoration England was *an almanac printed for manuscript*. Whether or not the owner of a blank almanac wrote on the blank pages, the very existence of those pages presumed his or her literacy and desire to write. From the sixteenth to the nineteenth centuries, "blank" almanacs elicited and organized the keeping of daily manuscript notes. While all almanacs provided the ideological framework of daily events recorded on a yearly basis, blanks provided the material precondition for keeping a diary.

The assumption that printing means the printing of *books* has helped to reinforce the further false assumption that printing somehow displaces manuscript. In fact, "manuscript" is a concept that was produced by printing. In the OED, there is not a single use of the word prior to 1597. Yet, paradoxically, the novel concept of "manuscript" emerges as always-already nostalgic. "As we all know," manuscript precedes printing. Indeed, one definition of "manuscript" is "a book, document etc. *written before the general adoption of printing* in a country." In this last sense, manuscript is quite literally a thing of the past, which disappeared in Europe some time in the middle of the fifteenth century. Yet this concept of manuscript as a thing of the past emerged in English, according to the OED, in 1600, a hundred and fifty years *after* the invention of printing. In fact, every early example of the use of "manuscript" in the OED defines the word *in opposition to printing*: a manuscript, we are told, is "written by hand, *not printed*." It is "a written document that *has not been printed*," "an author's written (or typed) copy *as distinguished from the print of the same*," or "'writing' *as opposed to 'print.'*" What makes "manuscript" a novelty is that it can only exist *after printing*. Before printing, there was writing, no end of writing, but no manuscript and no manuscript*s*. The concept of a "manuscript" is a back formation that can be conceptualized for the first time when writing by hand no longer dominates the whole field.

What follows from the fact that manuscript comes after printing? First, printed forms like indulgences and checks literally precede the written additions of signatures, dates, and sums of money. Secondly, more and more writing is a direct response to the stimulus of print. We can consider the relationship between printing and the most famous manuscript in the history of the United States, the manuscript that, indeed, *founds* the United States: namely, the Constitution. Here, surely, we have left behind the dizzying Derridean world in which effects precede causes. Here, we have a manuscript that has generated millions of printed documents. A manuscript that contains what has become so central to the value of these unique works – the signature of the author. Or, in this case, author*s*, whose names we can read at the bottom of the fourth page. So crucial are the authenticating signatures that in the most popular facsimile of the manuscript, the four pages of the Constitution have been illegibly condensed onto a single small fake-parchment scroll, while the signatures are still large enough to read. Among the authors of the Constitution we can find our own founder here at Penn: Benjamin Franklin.

On the May 25, 1787, the Constitutional Convention met here in Philadelphia for the first time.[13] From then until September 17, with a two-week break in the late summer, the Convention met for five or six hours every day for six days of the week. How should we imagine the Convention proceeding? With endless debate, to be sure. But who recorded the debates? It was agreed at the beginning of the Convention that the debates should be conducted in secret, and in fact much of the evidence of the debates was deliberately destroyed. On the evening of September 17, immediately after the Convention had finally concluded its business, William Jackson wrote to George Washington that he would bring him the official Journals "after burning all the loose scraps of paper which belong to the Convention."

I do not know what Jackson considered "loose scraps," but it is possible that they included at least some of the printed drafts of the Constitution that *preceded* the "true, original" manuscript by six weeks. For on the 6th of August, when the Convention resumed work after its summer recess, the Committee of Detail presented each member of the Convention with a printed draft. John Dickinson's copy, dated by hand "7 August 1787," survives at the Library Company. It is a printed document that is immensely wasteful in its use of paper, with a huge margin on the left. The reason for the margin is immediately apparent from Dickinson's copy: this is a printed text that has been designed for additions by hand. If the Convention is getting closer to a final version of the Constitution, implicit in the printing and distribution of this very draft, the distance that still has to be traveled is materialized in the printed expectation of changes, additions, and deletions – changes that will require the blank space in which to write. And changes will be made, although John Dickinson is not here interested in correcting the opening, which begins:

> We the People of the States of New-Hampshire, Massachusetts, Rhode-Island and Providence Plantations, Connecticut, New-York, New-Jersey, Pennsylvania, Delaware, Maryland, Virginia, North-Carolina, South-Carolina, and Georgia

The "People" here remain the people of a federation of separate states, even if they may (or may not) agree that "the stile of this Government shall be, 'The United States.'" The wide margins of the printed draft, however, call out for further considerations and emendations. When copies of a new draft of the constitution were distributed to the Convention on the 12th of September, the layout was significantly different. The size of the left-hand margin in the new draft is still apparent by comparison to the right margin. There's still space for additions both in the margin and in the blank spaces within the text block. But the margin has been radically reduced in comparison with the earlier draft. Delegates are still encouraged to make additions – but not on the same scale as a month before. Because the different states that authorized the Constitution on August 7 have been displaced by a new sovereign power: "We, the People of the United States." How precarious that entity seems in its infant state. And there remains much that cannot be printed because it is unknown. Here "manuscript" is anything but nostalgic. In the draft, printing preserves what has already been discussed, whereas manuscript is the technology of an uncertain and unknown future. This is materialized in the sheer range of blank spaces in these printed drafts.

In fact, the draft Constitutions of August 6 and September 12 contain three of the kinds of blank spaces, to be completed by manuscript:

1) Margins designed for writing by hand
2) Blank windows to be completed when something in the future is known (here, the number of States that will be necessary to ratify the Constitution.

Notice also the need for manuscript corrections to the printed text: the numbers of the sections have been changed because of the earlier addition of a new manuscript section). In fact, the numbers of the sections are often deliberately left blank so as to avoid having to make such corrections. And some of the blanks remain blank to this day: "I, BLANK, do solemnly swear" – the hope that someone better may turn up one day, who might even uphold the Constitution.

3) Blank space: the blank paper provided by the unprinted page at the end of the September 12 draft, in which John Dickinson has written: a manuscript blank form!

Only on September 17, the day on which the Constitution was ratified amd six weeks after the first printed drafts, was the Constitution written down as a "manuscript" in what would become the most nostalgic and sentimental of senses. This manuscript of the Constitution was written by Jacob Shallus, assistant clerk of the Pennsylvania Assembly, and it is not an original manuscript at all. It is a copy of a printed draft of September 12 that contained manuscript corrections. The printed Constitutions both materially and temporally preceded the manuscript Constitution. To rethink manuscript as a means of communication that is subsequent to printing, we need to rethink the revolutionary implications of printing as an incitement to writing by hand.

Notes

1 Elizabeth L. Eisenstein, *The Printing Press as an Agent of Change: Communications and Cultural Transformations in Early-Modern Europe*, two vols. in one (Cambridge: Cambridge University Press, 1980).

2 Adrian Johns, *The Nature of the Book: Print and Knowledge in the Making* (Chicago, IL: University of Chicago Press, 1998).

3 George D. Painter, *William Caxton: A Biography* (New York: G. P. Putnam, 1977), 83–84. That this is the first *dated* work does not mean that it is necessarily early. See Lotte Hellinga, *Caxton in Focus* (London: The British Library, 1982), 81. However, given the staggering rate of loss of both copies and whole editions of indulgences, earlier editions of Caxton indulgences are more likely than earlier editions of pamphlets or books.

4 Albert Kapr, *Johann Gutenberg: The Man and his Invention*, trans. Douglas Martin (Aldershot: Scolar Press, 1996), 189–90; and John Man, *Gutenberg: How One Man Remade the World of Words* (New York: John Wiley and Sons, 2002), 154–55. See also Eisenstein, *Printing Press*, 375, Keith Maslen, "Jobbing Printing and the Bibliographer: New Evidence from the Bowyer Ledgers," in his *An Early London Printing House at Work: Studies in the Bowyer Ledgers* (New York: Bibliographical Society of America, 1993), 139–52, esp. 140.

5 See John L. Flood, "'Volentes Sibi Comparare Infrascriptos Libros Impressos … ': Printed Books as a Commercial Commodity in the Fifteenth-Century," in Kristian Jensen, ed., *Incunabula and their Readers: Printing, Selling and Using Books in the Fifteenth Century* (London: The British Library, 2003), 139–51.

6 Clive Griffin, *The Crombergers of Seville: The History of a Printing and Merchant Dynasty* (Oxford: Clarendon Press, 1988), 52.

7 Indulgence issued by Albrecht von Brandenburg, Archbishop of Mainz and Magedeburg, Houghton Library *54-303-304F.
8 John L. Flood, "The Book in Reformation Germany," in Jean-François Gilmont, ed., *The Reformation and the Book* (Aldershot: Ashgate, 1998), trans. Karin Maag, 21–103, esp. 26–27.
9 See Martin Brecht, *Martin Luther: His Road to Reformation 1483–1521.* (Philadelphia, PA: Fortress Press, 1985), 181.
10 Pamela Neville-Sington, "Press, Politics and Religion," in Lotte Hellinga and J. B. Trapp, eds, *The Cambridge History of the Book in Britain*, vol. 3, 1400–1557, (Cambridge: Cambridge University Press, 1999), 576–607, 583. See also Arthur J. Slavin, "The Tudor Revolution and the Devil's Art: Bishop Bonner's Printed Forms," in Delloyd. J. Guth and John W. McKenna, eds, *Tudor Rule and Revolution* (Cambridge: Cambridge University Press, 1982), 3–23; and "The Gutenberg Galaxy and the Tudor Revolution," in Gerald P. Tyson and Sylvia S. Wagonheim, eds, *Print and Culture in the Renaissance: Essays on the Advent of Printing in Europe* (Newark, DE: University of Delaware Press, 1986), 90–109.
11 STC 7767. The 1513–15 subsidy forms, based upon indulgences, provided in turn the models for the blank taxation forms issued by Bishops Longland, Bonner, and Jugge after 1534 (STC 9175b.5, 9175b.10, 9175b.15, 9175b.20, 9175b.25, 9175b.30, 16794). See Neville-Sington, "Press, Politics and Religion," 591.
12 The information in this paragraph is taken from Cyprian Blagden, "The Distribution of Almanacks in the Second Half of the Seventeenth Century," *Studies in Bibliography* 11 (1958): 107–19. See especially 110, 113–15 and Table 1.
13 Information on the Constitutional Assembly is drawn from Merrill Jensen, ed., *The Documentary History of the Ratification of the Constitution*, vol. 1, "Constitutional Documents and Records, 1776–87" (Madison, WI: State Historical Society of Wisconsin, 1976).

Chapter 8

Governing by television

Anna McCarthy

Public service media form a complex nexus of policy, practice, and debate, one in which ideas about the uses of media technology meet ideas about governance. Historically, the term *public service* has been used to describe the goals that shape how media technologies and institutions are regulated, and to characterize forms of media programming. In each case, the assumption is that a particular technological arrangement, or aesthetic and rhetorical voice, will somehow contribute to the collective welfare of a state and its people. In this chapter, I am concerned with the methodological and political consequences, for progressive or leftist media historians, of this close association between public service broadcasting and conceptions of governance. How we understand this relationship influences our interpretations of the role of media technology in cultural history, encouraging certain conclusions while potentially, at least in some cases, foreclosing upon the possibility of others. These consequences extend beyond the question of whether we construct "accurate" accounts of a certain medium's history. Debates about how the airwaves are governed are also debates about how the people who tune into to those airwaves are governed, or rather, in the language of liberal democracy, how they are helped or hindered in their ongoing aims of governing themselves.[1] It follows, then, that at any given moment, assertions of what broadcast regulation should be, or what public service media should look like, are windows onto political history more generally, indices of someone's sense of the sociopolitical problems blocking the process of democratic governance at that time.

It also follows that media historians must be careful to avoid imposing their own standards when measuring the levels of democratization achieved by particular media processes in the past. This is not because presentism is always bad, or because historical relativism is always good. It is because to do so is to *replicate*, rather than scrutinize, the basic axiom on which causal claims about public service media and democratic life rest, namely, that you can change people's orientation towards citizenship by changing how they consume media, or by changing the media they consume. The point is that concepts of citizenship change, and so do ideas about what public service media can and should do. Determining the material arrangements, structures of ownership, and forms of expression which ensure that broadcasting provides a public service is a social process that shifts over time, although it always involves making a claim about what democracy *is*. It also always involves defining its deficiencies at any particular moment, and forming a picture of how it might be vulnerable to anti-democratic forces. The particular form of broadcast regulation or programming that one defines as a public service, from this perspective, is best understood as an expression of a particular sense of what needs to be done to preserve democratic processes, or even, in some cases, correct the flaws that make their current operations less than perfect. The historian's task is to unravel the interests and conflicts that underlie these historical definitions of mediated democracy, that motivate particular descriptions of its failings, and which make any particular technological fix seem natural or inevitable; it is not to offer a Whiggish or prelapsarian account of democratic progress from the perspective of the present day.

In going about this task, it is helpful to think about the uses of public service media to diagnose and treat problems in democracy as expressions of a persistent technocratic fantasy in US political culture: the fantasy of governing by television. Like all fantasies, this one proceeds from particular historical and material circumstances. Laurie Ouellette, whose work on the US Public Television network is an exemplary case study of this fantasy, notes that political contests of the late 1960s led elite social managers to see TV "as a device capable of solving problems, resolving conflicts, and reconstructing TV viewers as citizens instead of consumers of washing machines and potato chips."[2] Indeed, although the idea of governing through TV might conjure up Orwellian imagery – the minds of the people entirely controlled by government screens! – Ouellette's work shows us that this fantasy is less totalitarian dystopia than democratic utopia, fusing McLuhan and Jefferson in an unquestioned equation of technological diffusion and civic participation. This equation is troubling from the perspective of the progressive historian of technology and media committed to methods of historical materialism. This is because it assumes that "democracy" is a pre-given, self-evident, and historically transcendent category, an ideal that can be achieved by "actually existing" social relations insofar as they approach it asymptotically, their proximity enhanced by the development of technological and regulatory instruments.

Such models do not allow for the possibility that definitions of democracy always emerge from historically specific organizations of power, authority, and political economy. As Michael Warner notes in a critique of techno-determinist approaches to the history of print, "enlightenment and democratization, instead of being seen as politically contested aspects of social organization, now appear as the exfoliation of material technology."[3] This is the kind of thinking that leads people to debate the question of whether, say, something like youtube.com helps or hinders the process of democratic participation, as if the answer is a clear "yes" or "no." Such debates only make sense if we assume that "democracy" has some kind of fixed ontological integrity external to the contexts in which it is invoked, and to which these contexts must be made to conform. They also require that we ignore the possibility that what people actually mean when they say *democratic participation* might change over time, in relationship to political, economic, cultural, and technological, shifts.[4]

The following assessment of the issues at stake in the historical analysis of public service television proposes an alternative approach to the liberal appeal to self-evident and transcendental conceptions of democratic governance. It draws on some examples from the immediate postwar period, when "educational" films aimed at securing particular governance objectives frequently appeared on people's television screens. After examining how this historical moment might shed light on the conceptual stakes involved in how historians define "public service," we move to the question of how to analyze the films themselves as historical documents. It is important to identify the assumptions about media effects often brought to bear upon them, I argue, and to evaluate the possibility that print and manuscript archival materials might provide crucial material for understanding the broader political import of these films.

This last point is important because it brings up the technological conditions that enable the writing of history at any given moment. This essay is a product of the digital age given that the visual material to which it refers – the ephemeral films that populated the airwaves in the early years of American commercial television – have become increasingly available in recent years thanks to digital infrastructures such as the Internet.[5] This ease of access comes with an obligation, however. Because we encounter these films under circumstances so alien to those of their initial circulation, we must work that much harder to understand their original modes of production and reception. We must also work hard to see beyond their formal and rhetorical styles. The camp didacticism and technical crudeness styles of films with titles like *The Story of Chemicals* and *Communism—and You* makes them highly amenable for "repurposing" as stock footage, so we are likely to encounter them now in an entirely new context, where their kitschy "Fiftiesness" is a shorthand tool for communicating the otherness of the past. In these decontextualized forms, these films often elicit hilarity among contemporary viewers, who don't know what to make of them and who can't imagine that anyone took them seriously. I will address this question of technology and access at the end of this essay, as it relates to the more general concern of this volume, namely, how thinking about communications history shapes inquiry about technology and vice versa.

Despite (or perhaps because of) their style, these media artifacts represent exciting possibilities for historians of television, allowing us to look beyond the well-preserved and often commercially available entertainment products of TV's "Golden Age," towards those works on the margins – industrial films, religious programs, and propaganda films of all sorts – with which local television stations filled the broadcast day in the medium's early years. These transient filmed programs and public relations advertisements are not generally included in television's entertainment canons. As a category, they are distinct from other TV forms of the period in that their primary goal was promotional and pedagogical, against the combination of product sales and entertainment that defined mainstream programming. Not all of them were officially designated as "public service" programming, in that the cost of the airtime in which they appeared was not donated by the station or network. Many were privately sponsored educational and cultural programs that fell into the once-prevalent but now largely defunct category of sponsored broadcast known as *institutionals*. These seemingly noncommercial programs would offer viewers plays, historical biographies, news material or documentaries interspersed with "messages" explaining pro-corporate positions on such issues as monopoly and regulation to a mass audience. Other noncommercial television films, however, did air for free. Produced by nonprofits – business organizations, labor unions, religious denominations, and other state, civic, and nongovernmental groups – they sought to foster particular opinions and attitudes in the general population. These programs were often syndicated without charge to local TV stations for use as educational material airing in their federally mandated public service hours. It was a chance at free programming that many station managers gladly accepted.

Whether airing in paid or free time, these programs spoke in the language of liberal pluralism that suffused postwar public rhetoric, their shared goal the moral, political, or economic education of the TV audience.[6] They sought to *govern*, but not by dominance or force. Rather, they addressed viewers as individuals – "ethically incomplete" ones, to borrow Toby Miller's phrase – in need of guidance and enlightenment.[7] However, it is important to note that acknowledging these programs' aspirations of governance does not necessarily mean that we must affirm their efficacy in shaping ideas and conduct within the general population. It is distinctly more likely, for reasons outlined below, that the cultural power and longitudinal significance of these broadcasts does not reside in their direct effects in the sphere or reception – their claimed impact on opinions and attitudes. As I will argue, it is primarily through archival investigation of the conflicting processes of their *production* that the broader significance of these films becomes clear. Specifically, this methodology leads us towards a more comprehensive understanding of how educational and public service broadcasting were constituted as a sphere of elite problem solving within the postwar political arena, an area of submerged social conflict that framed commercial TV's sociopolitical possibilities in enduring ways.

This approach to public service broadcasting diverges in key terms from existing critiques and histories, specifically those that detail the increasingly vexed efforts of progressives and educators to retain public ownership of the airwaves and secure a space for noncommercial programming and alternative voices over the twentieth century.[8] This is not to deny the importance of these struggles over ownership and accountability. American commercial broadcasting was defined from the first, as Tom Streeter has compellingly demonstrated, by corporate liberal ideologies of private stewardship of public resources and it has kept up with the changing political rationalities of advanced liberalism over the course of its history.[9] Indeed, the demise of public service broadcasting mandates exemplifies the neoliberalization of broadcast policy that crystallized in Reagan era deregulation.

But if, as Liz Jacka concludes disparagingly, existing histories render "democracy as defeat" in the media realm, it is in no small part because some of them tend to define public service in terms that conform to those of welfarist liberal broadcast policy and its technological administration.[10] Under this definition, public service programming in commercial TV is programming that serves the community and which should (as it was until 1960 in the United States) be protected from the pressures of the market in the form of fees for broadcast or competition for airtime. Public service emerges from such models as an imperiled and disappearing resource that must be defended from its corporate violators and, by extension, from the taint of popular culture.[11] As neoliberal "de"regulation (more aptly, "re"regulation) continues apace, progressive historians are left bemoaning the fact that public service broadcasting, which was problematically defined and inadequately administered from the first, is on the verge of disappearing.

There is nevertheless much to be gained from these approaches, and I do not dismiss them. They are crucial for activist work in numerous spheres, from policy to pedagogy. But I think this focus has prevented us from seeing – and really taking on – the fact that the concept of public service is far more expansive, and appropriable, than the strict policy definition of the category as unpaid programming. In practice, alongside programs that conform to this definition, American television has always included a penumbral category of programs that were partially or fully sponsored by commercial interests, or else which indirectly promoted particular corporations and their products, but which nevertheless articulated their missions in terms of public service. The National Association of Manufacturers, for example, presented its filmed documentary series *Industry on Parade* as public service (as opposed to commercial) programming even though it focused on particular consumer products; moreover, in attempting to illustrate the manufacturing sector's contributions to the nation's economic and cultural wealth and turn public opinion against organized labor, its status as a public service might seem highly questionable. Similarly, private companies interested in the creation of a public relations message and the discrediting of New Deal regulatory frameworks routinely presented their messages as noncommercial, educational messages. Although they aired in paid commercial time, these programs, like DuPont's historical biography series *Cavalcade of America*, worked to create the impression that their sponsor was committed to the public interest. Moreover, even as public service programming has historically served as a venue for progressive political causes such as civil rights, it has also provided a forum for groups speaking against leftist and social justice causes, including segregationists and white supremacists.[12] Politically, fiscally, and aesthetically, in short, the practical appearance of public service concepts in commercial broadcasting is a profoundly *impure* phenomenon, extending far beyond the definitions created by the state.[13]

Given this situation, I propose a historical approach that sees public service in American commercial television not as a fixed ideal but rather as a flexible discursive relationship between audiences, sponsors and broadcasters. Moreover, I suggest that we see this relationship in political, rather than administrative or normative terms. In other words, it is a relationship defined by the question of how television might best be used as a benevolent tool of liberal governance, teaching the responsibilities of citizenship to a mass audience – a pedagogical opportunity that many political groups and constituencies sought for themselves in the postwar period. Such an approach would not limit its sources to programs defined as public service within the narrow confines of FCC policy as it happened to have been defined at the moment (although this does not mean it should exclude such programs). Nor would it expend a great deal of intellectual energy exposing the falsity of such programs' claims to serve the public. Rather, it would focus on *all* broadcast material that presented itself, for whatever reasons, via an often strategic disidentification with commerce and the market, and which spoke in a civic voice even if it expressed no discernable democratic commitment. The communality uniting the range of institutional relations and aesthetic forms, including commercially sponsored ones, that fall into this discursive approach to the category of public service is thus performative rather than economic or ethical, and it is based in their manifest articulation, at once moral, epistemological, and generic or aesthetic, of a conception of sponsorship and programming that goes beyond "mere" entertainment and for that matter the single-minded pursuit of profit in order to pursue loftier goals.[14]

This more flexible understanding of the public service obligation of broadcasting reflects the degree to which, as Lynn Spigel, citing Tom Streeter, has pointed out,[15] public service is a concept always intertwined with public relations (and, one might add, the management of public opinion) in television history. What remains to be explored are the implications of this conjuncture for actual projects of governance through media as they were conceived and attempted over the course of US history. In the case of the postwar period, defining public service as an occupiable discourse rather than a protected policy territory opens it up for investigation as a cultural realm in which the broad-ranging problems of particular political rationalities, by which I mean the many variants of liberalism active in this period of US history, could be debated and played out. At this particular moment, New Deal political culture, with its popular front sensibilities, its invocation of "the people," and its broad-ranging debates over political economy was giving way to a politics of interest groups, in which a healthy demos was defined in terms of "balance" and "reason" and in which the basic unit of democracy was no longer the people but rather the individual.[16]

Broadcasting's public service ideal in this context is marked by the quandaries of interest group realpolitik. The strongest position in a polity defined by interest groups is, after all, the position that seems to *transcend* interest, or alternately, subsume all interests in the assertion of some kind of universal good. Identification with this space of reasonable, seemingly neutral enunciation was a matter of intense struggle for any number of groups – organized labor, civil rights activists, liberal internationalist policymakers, and of course the corporate sector – that were constituted as interests in postwar political culture. Public service television sponsorship was a realm of speech in which the restricted nature of discourse, defined by the norms and rationalities of education, identified it with values of reason and disinterest. It represented the possibility of speaking from a position above material and personal interests, from the authoritative position of the universal liberal subject capable of knowledge and action on behalf of others. To speak to the television audience from within the voice of public service was to link sponsorship to citizenship.

In practice, the process of annexing this prized discursive position was very complicated, a complexity reflected in the research methods a discursive approach requires. Divergent interests and aesthetics of governance through media came together in the production of particular programs so that the final product onscreen, although it might seem on the surface to be a coherent expression of a singular impulse to govern through media, is itself the end product of numerous mediations and compromises. Tracing this process of mediation is a genealogical operation in the Foucauldian sense, as it involves the incorporation of alterity and disjuncture to produce what might be called a history of the present. This requires a suspension of conventional modes of political–historical critique. Instead of asking of any particular telefilm "does it or does it not serve a public service, as I define it" the historian should be asking "how well does it manage to align itself with a public service position, and what organizational, institutional, and cultural processes got it there? To what extent is its status as a public service under contestation, and by whom? On what terms and to what ends?"

Archival research is, I think, indispensable for anyone about to embark upon a genealogical account of public service broadcasting. Primary documents provide material for tracing the mediation of interests in the production process, and in that respect they illustrate the extent to which public service telefilms were not only communication from "elites" to "the masses," they were also complicated forms of communication *among* elites. Many audiences were imagined and addressed in the organizational process of propaganda production, audiences that might have included other members of the establishment (both "allies" and "opponents"); broadcasters who needed to be persuaded to air the programs; federal policymakers and policy enforcers; members of corporations and business groups who might be impressed by the fact of television sponsorship as much as by the content; and state functionaries outside the broadcast policy arena.[17]

We can see this process working itself out in the production of public service programs about civil rights, a TV sponsorship activity that grew steadily throughout the 1950s and 1960s. On the most manifest level, such programs were an attempt to govern conduct and ideas by talking to the mass audience as a collectivity composed of "black" and "white" citizens. Less obviously, but more crucially for understanding public service television as an arena of rule, they was also as an opportunity for white people in power to talk to each other about how to negotiate the enfranchisement demands of Black US citizens. The films and broadcasts that resulted reflected the input of any number of intermediary audiences, each with their own agendas and investments in particular modes of representation, including those cultural workers who produced these programs for sponsors and broadcasters who authorized their airing.

Examples drawn from the archival records of public service programs about civil rights will serve to illustrate this last point. The first comes from the files of a liberal philanthropic organization called the Fund for the Republic, which deposited its papers in the Public Policy archives at Princeton University. If the negotiations of representation and viewership that surrounded public service programming allow us to see its inscribed viewer-citizen as the product of multiple intersecting governance ideals, and thus understand how some representational strategies endured while others did not, what we see in the case of the Fund for the Republic is the inflexibility of well-intentioned liberal elites in their support for civil liberties and civil rights. The program in question was the first television project developed by Fund officers, who pitched it to NBC in 1954. A filmed pilot for a series focused on incidents of prejudice in American life, the program presented acted sketches illustrating common situations in which prejudice might occur. It interspersed these sketches with "humorous" commentary by cartoonist Al Capp, whose task was to point out the absurdity and illogic of discrimination to the viewer. The Fund screened the program for NBC president Sylvester "Pat" Weaver with high hopes. But Weaver's response was less than positive. Summarizing the meeting in a memorandum to Fund officer W.H. Ferry, a staff member reported that he reacted with utter distaste, questioning both the humor and the direct treatment of racism. As the memo further noted, Weaver explained that the program went against NBC's policy for racial representation, described as combating discrimination by using "Negro actors wherever they should be used without any emphasis on the actual fact of their use".[18] Needless to say, the show was not picked up by the network.

Moments such as this offer important insight into archival methods as a tool for understanding the significance of public service television, and they give form to the latter's historical status as a venue for struggles over television as a resource for governing. Most obviously, as this example illustrates, archival records allow us to examine failed efforts in this arena. Moreover, they illustrate the very different degrees of comfort with popular culture as a whole that elites in the realm of sponsorship brought to public service television. Weaver's concern with the advisability of adopting such a didactic voice reflected both his, professional sense of the audience and its receptivity and the narrownesss of network policy on matters of race. If the Fund saw viewers as open vessels for ideology, Weaver saw the audience as recalcitrant and ultimately resistant to lectures from above. Such archivally documented interactions between producers and sponsors in public service television also allow us to see how different conceptions of television's effects entered into the adjudication of appropriate forms of civic pedagogy. Weaver's response is instructive in highlighting both the manifest differences and the underlying similarities between the liberal sensibilities of representational policy at the networks and the assumptions of the Fund's officers. Both groups believed that setting examples was a crucial mechanism for civic pedagogy in TV, but their sense of the effects of these examples were wildly different. In Weaver's view, social change was best effected through the unremarkable representation of black people. The unstated, and pathologizing, assumption in his policy was that such treatment would normalize them in the white mind. Fund officers, on the other hand, sought to set examples in the realm of behavior, seeking to normalize liberal *attitudes*, rather than particular populations, in the minds of the average white viewer.

Obviously, to make such claims involves using archival documents not simply as evidence of what people said, or wrote. It also involves some kind of exegesis, in which one looks beyond facts for a sense of the underlying assumptions on which particular ideas about representation and persuasion rest. In the case of the Fund for the Republic, archival documents reveal a somewhat top-down and unsophisticated model of the relationship between television viewing and civic action effects, one that its officers refused to relinquish despite consistent challenges from industry professionals. As the example above illustrates, Fund officers assumed a television viewer for whom the divestment of prejudice was a matter of rational choice, a calculation based on the identification of self interest which ultimately, somehow, contributes to the social good.[19] Television's task was to motivate that choice by illustrating its benefits as a social good.

This image of the individual liberal subject capable of disinterested reflection on action was in keeping with the Fund's goal of reactivating the principles on which the American Republic was founded. Indeed, one might say that when Fund officers saw problems in their projects, their judgments turned on whether the program appeared to activate this sense of enlightenment in themselves. Although they were highly scornful of popular culture, Fund officers relied on popular cultural figures like Capp to appeal to viewers. Yet at the same time, they could only conceive of the television viewer as a rational being capable of becoming fully aware of the social costs of prejudice. Unable to resolve these contradictory understandings of medium and viewer, the Fund failed to get most of its projects on the air.

In contrast to this view of television as an instruction manual for rational civic activity based on negative examples, the television activities of the corporate-dominated Advertising Council suggest a very different understanding of the viewer – no doubt a reflection of the Council's staff and membership, all advertising professionals. Advertising Council civil rights spots tended to address the viewer as a member of a locality, rooted in daily interactions. After the 1965 passage of the landmark Voting Rights act the Council launched a campaign to promote "better race relations." The civic model on which this campaigns rested, like campaigns on other matters such as mental health awareness, economic security, and public safety, was the ideal of community self-management. Like many Advertising Council solutions, the solutions offered in its civil rights spots were implicitly opposed to government regulation.[20] Indeed, despite the legislative context surrounding its launch, the campaign did not take voting or government as its model of civic participation. Rather, it focused on the importance such voluntaristic community structures as "bi-racial committees." As the Council's chairman told the Association of National Advertisers, the Council drew its mandate from conversations with Black Americans about their relationship to Whites:

> The predominant attitude of Negroes, we were told, is one of frustration arising from the feeling that no-one wants to do things *with* Negroes, although many whites want to do things *for* Negroes. Yet experience has already shown that if Negroes and Whites will only sit down together and discuss their community's racial problems, they can usually be alleviated or solved.[21]

The campaign thus began on a basis not dissimilar to that of the Fund for the Republic, in that it sought to reform civic behavior through television. Yet its tone was very different. The Fund staged examples of everyday interactions and asked viewers to judge those interactions, and themselves. The Council's spots adopted an interpersonal focus, offering concrete solutions within a civic framework outside the traditional mechanisms of the state, and appealed to the viewer as a participant in everyday racial interactions rather than a judge of them.

This seeming sensitivity to context extended into the process of refining the representational strategies of these programs. In 1965, the Council showed a print of one advertisement to the representatives from labor, civil rights, and philanthropy whom it invited to serve on its Public Policy Advisory Committee, the body that approved "controversial" campaigns before they aired. The minutes of the meetings record dialogs addressing the problems of identification and inclusion involved in representing interracial exchange. Labor leader Joseph Beirne noted that the film would annoy black viewers because "the camera did not focus on the Negro when he was speaking." Beirne's critique suggests that the film *illustrated*, rather than addressed, the charge that white people's ideas of racial reform were based in a certain sense of distance between the races. The remark helped pinpoint the need for reediting, but it also became an occasion for the sharing of white resentment. Helen Hall, a prominent social worker, supported Beirne's observation by noting, in what reads today as an aggrieved tone, that this detail was important because

> it was not possible these days to have a Negro group visit any establishment without having them count the number of Negroes on the staff, and look to see whether they were being treated with the same degree of courtesy and importance as the whites.[22]

The committee meeting here serves as a venue for white complaint and also, the begrudging accommodation of Black critique in the formation of a public service address.

For leftist critics and historians, what is important (and depressing) about these dialogs on visibility, community, and respect among the Advertising Council's advisory officers, especially when compared with the failures of the more socially liberal Fund for the Republic, is the degree to which the process of devising their public service programs reflect the articulation of civil rights with the broader neoliberal program of the organization. The Advertising Council's pro-business, anti-regulation agenda took shape not via the crudely propagandistic forms preferred by DuPont and other institutional advertisers, but rather through rhetorics of personal responsibility.[23] Whereas progressive voices like the Fund for the Republic failed to gain access to television as a medium of governance in part because of their preaching tones and ill-formed models of viewership, the corporate activists of the Advertising Council, for whom civil rights was merely a pretext for advancing claims of corporate citizenship, were able to successfully occupy the enunciative position of fair-minded, neutrality that public service broadcasting promised. Access to the paper trail that led to this occupation is, in a sense, a window onto the relative disorganization of the center-liberal establishment when it came to media strategies, and the far more sophisticated techniques of those sectors ultimately interesting in rolling back the social democratic gains of the New Deal.

In both cases, however, the archival record allows us to see the processes of negotiation and conflict that go into the production of a public service voice in television. And moreover, in terms of the sociopolitical issues at stake, it reveals a heretofore unanalyzed aspect of television's role in racial conflicts in the postwar period. Reading through the papers of such groups as the Advertising Council and the Fund for the Republic, despite their distinct ideological orientations, it becomes clear that public service television was an important vehicle for white elite conversations about Black claims for racial justice, and that it played this role not as a medium of mass communication per se, but rather as an institution in which powerful members of the so-called establishment could network with each other. This effect of public service TV, its emergence as a space for a dialog about governance among elites, is just as important historically as whatever its effects upon viewers might have been.

Does this mean that reception is unimportant? Or might this discursive, genealogical approach shape research in the sphere of reception? Even if one believes, as I do, in the profound unknowability of actual viewers, that does not remove the need to account for those moments when audiences *did* make themselves known. After all, producers were highly concerned with achieving particular effects in viewers' behavior and patterns of thought, and they sought numerous ways of interacting with audiences with these effects in mind. Can we incorporate an understanding of "actual audiences" in narrating the history of public service television as a form of governing?

The answer, once more, lies in the archive, in the files labeled "audience research." The officers of the Fund for the Republic had little inclination to test the efficacy of their pedagogical media strategies through audience research, preferring to rely on the authoritative insights of their leader, Robert Maynard Hutchins. But corporate sponsors spent a great deal of time analyzing their viewers' responses. The papers of the DuPont corporation, for example, provide a useful example of the kinds of challenges audiences posed for the process of governing, and suggest that a range of interpretive options are possible for historians interested in the institutional relations of market research. This is because researchers often found, to their likely annoyance, that viewers did not exactly conform to the naïve cognitive templates their studies established. Quite the opposite: many fully understood DuPont's pro-free enterprise advertising to be propaganda. Some of them expressed this awareness with cynicism. In one study, a respondent labeled "M11" told researchers interested in his reaction to a commercial, "They said that they work with small industry which is a lot of malarkey. Du Pont is interested in Du Pont".[24] Others, however, approached the process of audience research as a form of consultation, in which their job was to give feedback to the company on its techniques of persuasion.

In this particular study, interviewers sought to gauge whether viewers "got" the basic messages implied in institutional commercials aimed at boosting DuPont's corporate image. But instead of indicating merely that they were or were not aware of the message, respondent feedback suggests that audience members saw themselves as experts helping the company improve its commercial techniques:

I think it would inspire women to buy something like that (M14)
The commercial was too broad or too institutional. It didn't mean anything to me (M35)
I thought the commercials were not clear-cut Sunday commercials. (M48)

They mentioned their slogan, "better things for better living through chemistry." Anything makes a strong case for your company when they can connect it with your welfare. Their slogan does this. (M44)

the commercial was alright, but they could have done better (M53)

I think people are more prone to look at models modeling things than they are at chemicals. (F70)

I thought the commercial was for an immature mind. It's not really life. It's just what they think people want us to see. (F52)

These assessments, coded in the research firm's report with a number and the letters M and F indicating the respondent's sex, addressed the commercials' conformity to conventions of public service ("educational" and "Sunday" being signifiers of the public service voice) as well as their effectiveness as persuasive texts.

I hasten to note that the existence of such knowing audiences does not mean that scholars should adopt some simplistic interpretation of the "resisting audience" paradigm as the only alternative to the propaganda model, recapitulating the hegemonic/subversive binarisms that people use to caricature cultural studies. A preferable option is to understand the audience researcher interaction as itself a moment of media governance. From this perspective, viewers may have understood these texts to be instrumentalist and propagandistic, but they could have interpreted the invitation to participate in audience research as an invitation to voice their sense of the acceptable limits within which the corporation might seek to exert rule. Experientially, the audience research process registers as a form of civic empowerment, allowing viewers to assert their freedom in statements about how far the sponsor, the state, or big business can go. In itself, then, as a form of social exchange, audience research might constitute a form of governing – establishing norms and restrictions on conduct and speech, naming and balancing interests – on the microlevel on which audiences encounter media representatives.

This alternative possibility is important, as it suggests another way that particular ways of reading in archival research can enhance our understanding of how power is exerted in media. This is a form of interpretation that is informed by Foucault's notion of *governmentality* and which looks at media institutions, technologies and programs as pathways through which advanced liberalism's political rationalities take form, at the moments when "the popular and the civic brush up against each other".[25] Moving analysis away from the state, the concept of governmentality focuses attention instead on the promulgation of myriad dispersed techniques of self-regulation aimed ultimately at the "conduct of conduct".[26] Archival research forestalls any easy collapse of governmentality and old-school Althusserian ideology, as it makes it impossible to see the elite fantasy of governing by television as a watertight and seamlessly implemented technocratic program. As the example of DuPont's expert, active audience illustrates, investigations of the archives of public service media production can move analyses of political culture and governance beyond what O'Malley *et al.* trenchantly criticize as the governmentality literature's tendency to create "ritualized and repetitive accounts of 'governing' in increasingly diverse contexts" (p. 514). This is because they provide us not with fully formed projects of rule but rather with access to the internal forms of conflict, compromise, and contradiction that shaped particular efforts to align persuasive techniques with the liberal-pedagogical public service ideal. The result is a very concrete view of media production as a key site in "the ongoing work of elaborating and negotiating political rationalities".[27]

From this perspective, we can see the work of propaganda films and public service programs in political culture more clearly. Their readily apparent *inability* to rule hegemonically, through mind control, is what enables their proliferation and deployment. Moreover, their transparent limits as instruments of governance allows for the restaging and replication of debates among sponsors, producers, and broadcasters about how to rule through broadcast words, sounds, and images, bringing together powerful constituencies in what was then called the Establishment in negotiations that could only solidify the authority of the governing classes. In their shared encounters with popular media the elites who sponsored public service television affirmed the moral mandate to rule, distilled the epistemological certainties about the viewing population through which this rule might be known and measured, and consolidated, if only through dissension, the language in which the populace might be addressed. The specific organization of broadcast technology in the postwar period aided these conversations in that the concept of the national television audience provided a convenient collective noun for talking about the nation as a population, one with discrete characteristics, reachable through certain aesthetic and rhetorical techniques, and knowable via statistics and other forms of empirical measurement. Elites, in short, were not communicating with the audience, or at least not only with the audience. They were also using the idea of the audience to communicate with each other.

The nature of the elite encounter with popular media via public service sponsorship was less conspiracy than problem solving, however. A full understanding of the influence of the public service voice in political culture must consider how conflicting or divergent understandings of the ways that TV viewing might lead to self-governance might have shaped this form of expression and defined its normative appearance. The archives can tell us how sponsors and producers negotiated the translation of *ideas* about audience and medium into concrete representations and modes of address oriented towards the reification of particular images of citizenship, and they can reveal the obstacles and pitfalls they saw hampering this process. In so doing, I think, we can identify tensions within and between particular projects of rule and their technologies of implementation, and understand how the local and diffuse contestations that shaped them might be amplified for future activist purposes. Digital technologies may make it easier to access the films, but perhaps the real narrative they tell lies in the communications issued on paper that preceded their release, and which remain largely inaccessible to researchers in cyberspace. Until the day that we can access all collections everywhere by entering a few keystrokes, communications history must still depend upon shoe leather and pencils if it is to get the full story.

Notes

1 In television studies, the most comprehensive account of the equation of public service television with popular government is Laurie Ouellette's *People Like You* (New York: Columbia University Press, 2002).

2 Ouellette, *People Like You*, 113.

3 Michael Warner, *The Letters of the Republic: Publication and the Public Sphere in Eighteenth Century America* (Cambridge, MA: Harvard University Press, 1992), 6.

4 A good example of this tendency is a study of the role of emotion in the public sphere, specifically in relation to the creation of "good" citizenship practices, carried out in the Netherlands after two prominent political murders: the assassination of xenophobic political candidate Pim Fortuyn and the slaying of filmmaker Theo Van Gogh, notorious for his use of derogatory language in criticisms of Islamic fundamentalism (M. Pantti and L. Van Zoonen, "Do Crying Citizens Make Good Citizens?" *Social Semiotics* 16, no. 2 (2006): 205–22). The authors conclude, having interviewed a number of distraught and angry Dutch citizens, that "emotions … did nothing to revive or promote citizenship, either in its political or its cultural dimensions." Citizenship, within their methodology, was a resolutely static phenomenon, easily identifiable, and effortlessly divided into "political" and "cultural" modes. What they failed to take into account is that this definition might be inadequate as a framework for categorizing the political affiliations and energies at stake in the conflict the study was trying to understand.

5 See, for example, the Prelinger archives at www.archive.org/movies/prelinger.php and the AV Geeks archive at www.archive.org/movies/collection.php?collection = avgeeks

6 Programs that aired in paid time were, for some sponsors, a place for the expression of more "controversial" views. As G.W. "Johnny" Johnstone of the National Association of Manufacturers explained to his colleagues in a memorandum (G.W. Johnstone, "NAM Radio-TV Credo," National Association of Manufacturers Collection, Hagley Business Museum and Library, Greenville, DE, 1956), "controversial subjects should be presented in the best showmanship fashion in sponsored (paid) time. Public service time should … be utilized for the single purpose of gaining good will."

However, even in paid television programming the expression of the pro-capitalist viewpoint almost always adopted a positive or prosocial tone in demonstrating the benefits of US corporate wealth for the citizenry and the nation. This was a distinct shift from the more distinctly illiberal tone of similar institutional advertising on radio in the pre-war years (W.L. Bird, *Better Living: Advertising, Media, and the New Vocabulary of Business Leadership, 1935–1955* [Evanston, IL: Northwestern University Press, 1999]).

7 Toby Miller, *The Well-Tempered Self: Cultural Citizenship and the Postmodern Subject* (Baltimore, MD: Johns Hopkins University Press, 1993).

8 Robert McChesney, *Telecommunications, Mass Media, and Democracy* (New York: Oxford University Press, 1993).

9 Tom Streeter, *Selling the Air: A Critique of the Policy of Commercial Broadcasting in the United States* (Chicago, IL: University of Chicago Press, 1996).

10 Elizabeth Jacka, "'Democracy as Defeat:' The Impotence of Arguments for Public Service Broadcasting," *Television & New Media* vol. 4 (2003): 177–91.

11 Ouellette, *People Like You.*

12 S. Classen, *Watching Jim Crow: The Struggles over Mississippi TV, 1955–1969* (Durham, NC: Duke University Press, 2004).

13 There are a number of excellent histories of these forms of sponsored film and television (E. Fones-Wolf, *Selling Free Enterprise The Business Assault on Labor and Liberalism, 1945–60* [Urbana, IL: University of Illinois Press, 1994]; R. Marchand, *Creating the Corporate Soul: The Rise of Public Relations and Corporate Imagery in American Big Business* [Berkeley, CA: University of California Press, 1998]; Bird, *Better Living*).

14 It is possible to think of public service as a voice among other voices in the polysemy of any particular television text – the prosocial codes woven into any program or genre. Thus, for example, when a character in a situation comedy learns the proverbial "valuable lesson" and understands why it is important to say no to drugs, we can see that moment as one in which the public service voice finds expression. John Hartley (*Uses of Television* [London: Routledge, 1999]) demonstrates that civic engagement is an omnipresent mode of TV viewing when he examines the new forms of citizenship that emerge with television.

15 Lynn Spigel, "The Making of a TV Literate Elite," in C. Geraghty and D. Lusted, eds, *The Television Studies Book* (London: Arnold, 1998).

16 I. Katznelson, "Was the Great Society a Lost Opportunity?," in S. Fraser and G. Gary Gerstle, eds, *The Rise and Fall of the New Deal Order, 1930–1980*. Princeton, NJ: Princeton University Press, 1989), 185–211; Warren Sussman, *Culture as History: The Transformation of American Society in the Twentieth Century* (New York: Random House, 1985).

17 My formulation of this understanding of the multiple audience for a particular programming form owes much to Heather Hendershot's discussion of the multiple audiences addressed by children's television (Heather Hendershot, *Saturday Morning Censors: Children's Television Regulation Before the V-Chip* [Durham, NC: Duke University Press, 1998]).

18 Edward Reed, E. Correspondence between Edward Reed and W.H. "Ping" Ferry (Box 108, Folder 5). Fund For the Republic Papers, Seeley Mudd Library, Princeton University, Princeton, NJ, 1954, January 9.

19 S.M. Amadae, *Rationalizing Capitalist Democracy: The Cold War Origins of Rational Choice Liberalism* (Chicago, IL: University of Chicago Press, 2003).

20 David L. Paletz, Roberta E. Pearson and Donald L. Willis, *Politics in Public Service Advertising on Television* (New York: Praeger, 1977).

21 E. W. Ebel, Presentation to the Association of National Advertisers. Historical File Folder 1230, document 113/2/207. Advertising Council Archives, University of Illinois Library, Urbana, IL, 1965, May 11.

22 Advertising Council, "Report of the Public Policy Committee Annual Meeting, November 10, 1965," Public Policy Committee Box, no folder number, document 13/2/209. Advertising Council Archives, University of Illinois Library, Urbana, IL, 1965.

23 Perhaps the most notorious example of this use of public service is the Keep America Beautiful Campaign, sponsored by bottling companies, which promoted community-based solutions to littering (as opposed to government-imposed bottle deposits) (Paletz *et al.*, *Politics in Public Service Advertising on Television*).

24 Gallup and Robinson, Inc., *Television Impact Report on Du Pont Show of the Month 'Crescendo.'* September 29, (Box 18, Folder 1) DuPont Collection, Hagley Business Museum and Library, Greenville, DE, 1957.

25 Toby Miller, *Technologies of Truth: Cultural Citizenship and Popular Media* (Minneapolis, MN: University of Minnesota Press, 1998), 4.

26 Michel Foucault, "On Governmentality," in J.D. Faubion, ed., *Power: Essential Works of Foucault, 1954–1984, Volume 3*, trans. R. Hurley (New York: The New Press, 2001).

27 P. O'Malley, L. Weir and C. Shearing, "Governmentality, Criticism, Politics," *Economy and Society* vol. 26 (1997): 501–51, esp. 514.

Chapter 9

Newswork, technology, and cultural form, 1837–1920

John Nerone

History, communication, and technology

The standard practices professional historians use to produce scholarly narratives have often run counter to the historical habits and uses of communication scholars. Professional history established itself as a discipline by separating itself from the many other ways intellectuals represented the human past. History, unlike philosophy or sociology or anthropology or economics, would construct idiographic accounts of the past, in which concrete human actors consciously made history, using philological analysis of archival documents. These accounts would differ from what Robert Nisbet called "natural histories," the large-scale accounts of law-like tendencies found in Rousseau, Voltaire, Comte, Hegel, Marx, and Weber.[1] Not that professional historians didn't hope for grand narrative. Rather, the discipline proclaimed the modernist faith that all their specific narratives would assemble themselves brick by brick into a great cathedral of knowledge. Historians have long since lost that faith.[2] But the practices of professional history have endured. Individual historians still craft narrative bricks out of archival sources, although they no longer expect them to make sense of each other, to yield up grand narrative. Instead, each individual work tries to make sense in itself by a bottomless contextualization; Hayden White sees historical work as dominated by the trope of irony.[3] Grand narratives are suggested, tentatively offered, argued about, but ultimately deferred, and professional historians have come to accept the fact that even their specific narratives will have a limited shelf-life.

Communication scholars, on the other hand, still want grand narrative in their histories. Innis and McLuhan, for instance, who represent a recurring persuasion in communication history, stand in a direct line of descent from Enlightenment "natural historians" like Rousseau and Voltaire;[4] Marxism is another recurring inspiration. To professional historians, the grand narratives of communication history look pre-professional, lost in a kind of religious fog. Even the more concrete histories of journalism and freedom of the press seem "spiritual" because they appeal to almost Hegelian notions of progress – toward freedom, or toward professional autonomy.

The divergence between historical work and communications scholarship is not as wide as it was a quarter of a century ago. Historians have lost some confidence in their toolkit, and are more open to the ways other humanists and social scientists represent the past. Ultimately, history is superbly inter-disciplinary, and the best historians have always been open to a full range of scholarship; now, it is expected that any historian approaching a specific topic, like communication technologies, will engage deeply with the work of other disciplines. And in the history of technology there is a borderland in which historians and communication scholars overlap.

There is still a divergence, however. The practices and inclinations of pro-fessional historians tend to lead them away from a focus on a particular sector, like communication, or from social forces that might be seen as reified, like technology, and toward an ever more diversified and overdetermining contextualization. Communication scholarship can still make historians grit their teeth and mutter "technological determinism."

The practices of professional historians tend to inflect histories of technol-ogy in three ways. They instill an allergy toward what is called "technological determinism." They prefer the notion of media-as-institutions to the notion of media-as-technologies. And they decenter specific media or technologies, even when those are the subjects of their narratives, by deploying the trope of social construction. I'll discuss each in order.

First, the allergy toward technological determinism. David Nye has asserted that among historians of technology, technological determinists are a virtually extinct species.[5] This is an observation that specialists often make with con-fidence, the same way that other specialists might say that, among scholars of racial identity, there are no racists. Technological determinism, so-called, is as obnoxious as racism. But of course one of the points of scholarship on racial identity is that, in some measure, everyone is a racist inasmuch as everyone approaches the world with a map of the races culturally implanted and operational. And one of the points of the history of technology is that tech-nologies HAVE a history. So it is somewhat disingenuous to say that there are no technological determinists. It would be more honest to say that there are no monocausal technological determinists.

This is a point that the late James Carey was fond of making. The tele-graph, for instance, had powerful effects, in his account, in many dimensions, and it would be hard to find any student of the history of the telegraph who would say otherwise. Why else would you study it? Carey's influential essay on the telegraph is illuminating in this sense.[6] One could say it is of two minds about the way the telegraph influenced history. Part of its influence came from its inherent characteristics or habilities as a technology: in its nature, it sepa-rated individual acts of communication from transportation. But the bigger part of its influence came from its integration into other systems, and espe-cially transportation systems.[7] Did standardized time zones and commodity futures trading owe more to the telegraph as a technology or to the railroad/

telegraph system? Similarly, the influence of the telegraph on news styles, which I'll discuss in some detail below, may have come from its technological characteristics, or may be attributable to its integration into a system of news transmission that involved a particular configuration of markets, media, and reporters.

Carey's work on the telegraph implicitly follows a more general tendency of communication scholars to use the word "media" in two senses at the same time. One usage refers to the technologies of communication. In this usage, a medium is an instrumentality, like television, paper, or the electric telegraph. This usage derives from prior usage in fields like physics or art, in which a medium is that through which something moves (e.g. light through water) or of which something is made (e.g. a portrait of oil on canvas). The second usage refers to the institutions of communication. In this usage, a medium is a specific business or organization or institution, like the *New York Times* or the Associated Press.

Historical work conceived in the classic sense – as the philological analysis of documentary records preserved in archives (which are in turn defined as the records collections of concrete organizations) – will tend to emphasize the second meaning of "media" as institutions or organizations. It is much easier to write a conventional history of the *New York Times* than it is to write one of, say, television. So the pragmatics of historical scholarship push toward a particular sense of what a history of communication might mean.

The history of technology will not likely be in the foreground of media history understood as the history of institutions or organizations. The history of "the press" is hardly dominated by the history of the printing press, for instance. Because no one talked about an institution called "the press" for several centuries after the western invention of printing, historians simply don't argue that the technology caused the appearance of the institution. In such scholarship (including my own), technology tends to work in the background. If the fore-ground is occupied by the public sphere, for instance, or by news culture – two now venerable approaches to the history of communication – various tech-nologies will repeatedly intrude on the narrative, but usually in a fashion that's mediated by many other considerations. At the points when scholars argue for a strong determining presence for specific technologies – for example, that steam-powered printing presses caused the appearance of mass circulation newspapers, or that the telegraph produced a more economic writing style – historical work tends to qualify the assertion, if not to squash it altogether.

And correctly so, I think. Accounts that foreground technologies will inevi-tably come under criticism from subsequent historical work. Elizabeth Eisenstein's history of the printing press, to take the most respected example in this genre, made the fairly assertive argument that printing led to the rise of the nation-state by helping to regularize vernacular languages and by helping to produce the sort of stereotyped characters, like monarchs or other political leaders – around which a national public sphere could crystallize.[8] A generation later, Benedict Anderson qualified this argument with an account that has a particular variant of print culture – print capitalism – anchor the rise of national consciousness. In his version, print culture comes unmoored from the printing press per se, and the argument for powerful technology effects recedes.[9] And a while after that Adrian Johns argued that the printing press did not come to do the things that Eisenstein attributed to it until legal, economic, and literary structures "coded" it in a particular way.[10] Eisenstein had argued that print produced a new kind of "fixity." Johns argued that the first century of printing destabilized texts by producing a flood of variants, forgeries, and piracies. The bloody history of the printed Bible is a good case in point. Printing allowed what had seemed to be a fixed, unitary, divine text to become a site of contention as different versions found their way into the same marketplaces and public arenas. So another technology meets its "social construction."

It is almost redundant now to say that the history of technology is a history of the social construction of technology. Any term so universally used will have to be capacious.[11] I have argued elsewhere that the social construction of technology embraces a spectrum of positions, depending on who or what does the constructing: cultural factors, policy, political economy.[12] Previous generations did not think to group such positions under a rubric like social construction, and instead considered their work to be fundamentally at odds with each other. In addition to being a perfectly sensible approach on both a theoretical and practical level, social construction has the added benefit of dampening the tensions between cultural and political economic approaches that preoccupied and distracted earlier generations of scholars.[13]

Social construction decenters technology from its own history. Even in works that focus on particular technologies, like Susan Douglas's histories of radio or Dan Czitrom's landmark *Media and the American Mind*,[14] the career of any particular medium becomes the story of the many different actors and factors (government, markets, audiences, and entrepreneurs) that constructed it. If the technology itself has some sort of historical agency, it is only after it has been constructed in a particular way as a sort of cultural form, as Raymond Williams notes in his analysis of television.[15] In Williams' argument, the general social tendency of "mobile privatization" is the ultimate constructing factor. In Paul Starr's magisterial history of the media, the ultimate construction is set by a "path of development" that emerged from early national policy debates and political maneuverings.[16]

Work as social construction

In what follows, I will preview ongoing research into the history of the different occupations in the news business in the years 1837–1920. In this work I explore the relationship between work routines and news culture. Dan Schiller, in his book *Theorizing Communication*, argues that work is the neglected vital center of the processes of communication.[17] This insight suggests a connection between two kinds of work, which can be crudely designated as making meaning and making media. Schiller's sense, which I share, that the work practices and routines by which media are produced have something to do with the meaning that people make of the media, invites a focus on the materialities of communication that is similar to but different from that encountered in the softer versions of the "media ecology" approach to communication. In this case, the work environment (the newsroom, the pressroom) is the key media ecology.

Obviously, technologies will frequently enter into this history. Some of them will be the technologies that communication historians like to discuss, like telegraphy and photography. Others will be more unusual, like the linotype and the typewriter. Each of these technologies was integrated into news workplaces that already had somewhat defined occupational structures and cultures. Each was also integrated into a broader social system of news.

These technologies are largely less interesting to communication scholars. The simple reason is that they are not sites at which messages are communicated to audiences or readers. Those technologies – radio, television, the internet – are far more compelling, especially if the really big question is how media technologies change culture. But the same factor makes the news technologies I will discuss more amenable to responsible historical inquiry.

These technologies are interesting also because they seem to form part of a cluster. Particular periods or sectors often produce clusters of technological innovations, similar or dissimilar technologies which might share a common technological or social genealogy. Sometimes a cluster will be inspired by a scientific breakthrough – e.g. the transistor. Sometimes a happenstance occurrence will produce a cluster: the Civil War produced innovations in both naval architecture and mortuary science; World War I produced both antibiotics and rapid developments in aviation and radio. Sometimes clusters appear because some sort of social system harmonizes two technologically separable domains. Transportation and communication, for instance, live apart technologically but entail each other socially, so that the telegraph and the railroad worked together – although the steam engine had nothing technologically to do with electricity – and the automobile and the radio worked together – although the internal combustion engine had nothing to do technologically with the vacuum tube. Clusters can also group around a particular social vector, as Raymond Williams notes in his discussion of mobile privatization;[18] a legion of scholars see a host of identification, accounting, mapping, and recording technologies clustering around the vector of surveillance.

Friedrich Kittler discusses many of these technologies in his important book, *Gramophone, Film, Typewriter*.[19] In his account, these technologies are part of a massive change in discourse networks. Kittler is a literary scholar and not a historian by training, and his explorations in the histories of these technologies is frankly reminiscent of McLuhan in its poignancy of insight as well as its reliance on artistic and literary sources as evidence. Although I am not convinced by his argument, I do share the notion that the various tools that inflected newswork are somewhat connected, perhaps most strongly by the vectors of industrial efficiency – the mechanization and routinization of work – and by automatic fidelity.

The telegraph and the form of the report

To begin, we might return to Carey's rendition of the argument that the telegraph introduced a terser and more neutral style of reportage.[20] When we look at this argument through the lens of workplaces – the newsroom, the composing room, and the pressroom – we find a rather more complicated history. Let's begin with the newsroom. First, when the telegraph was introduced, "newsrooms" were what people called the rooms in hotels, taverns, and other public places where people read newspapers. There was initially no dedicated space within newspaper offices where newswork was done. Instead, newspaper shops typically featured a variety of editorial desks. The telegraph news at first came into the same desk that so-called "exchange" newspapers came to, generally; the telegraph reports looked like and read like the digests of items that this editor culled from the latest mailbag, or like the digests of European news that came on the latest ship from Britain. All three of these digests would tend toward terseness. The European news, because it was cooperatively gathered then distributed to newspapers of every political persuasion, also tended toward neutrality; coming before the telegraph, such digests probably provided a template for the development of styles of telegraphic reportage.

Meanwhile, another desk handled local news. At the larger newspapers, by the 1830s, this desk was staffed by the city editor (in earlier manifestations, the night editor), who ran a crew of "reporters." Reporters got their name from the legal system, where a reporter was either a stenographer or a volume of recent court cases; in either case, the connotation of the term was one of faithful reproduction – what Michael Schudson terms "naive empiricism".[21] Reporters scavenged for news at customary places – police offices, hospitals, city hall, the markets, political meetings, cultural events. Their job was to produce a steady flow of news. The city desk's job was to provide a routine supply of the novel and deviant.[22]

Reporters were distinguished from correspondents. A correspondent was a letter-writer, usually situated in a distant and important location, like a political capital. Unlike the reporter, whose work and work routines inclined toward voicelessness, the correspondent was supposed to be the readers' eyes and ears at the centers of power, and was supposed to inflect one's intelligence with personal insight and colorful observation. Typically, correspondents had other day jobs. In the early Republic, it was not uncommon for a newspaper to use the local Congressman as its Washington correspondent, for instance. Thurlow Weed worked as a correspondent while also lobbying for pet projects and organizing first the Anti-Masonic and then the Whig party in upstate New York.[23]

Weed, of course, was also an editor and proprietor of several important partisan newspapers. The editor – and here I mean what would later be called the editorial page editor – performed yet another kind of newswork. In smaller newspapers, the same editor would compose original material and handle the so-called "scissors and paste" work, clipping items from other newspapers and drafting brief introductions to them. The editor was the most public and personal of the workers; his or her name was on the newspaper – correspondents usually wrote over a pseudonym or a set of initials – and readers knew exactly where to find them. Violence often accompanied an editor's work, so commonly that it became a kind of humorous association, like prison rape is today, though later generations would not find either practice especially amusing.

In the fluid world of the mid-nineteenth-century newswork, people moved between these positions. In any given person's career, and in any given establishment, the different tasks and desks outlined here might blur together, but the generations between the solidification of the system of partisan newspapering and the rise of the institutional press saw an increasing differentiation of roles and division of news labor along these lines – reporting vs. correspondence vs. editing-as-compiling vs. editing-as-opinion. What we call journalism came from the merging of the roles of correspondent and reporter and the building of a wall of separation between journalists and editors, a process that occurred gradually, beginning I think in the mid-1890s, but was consummated suddenly in the second decade of the twentieth century, when newspaper shops reorganized to process their content according to domain rather than according to stream of transmission.

The development of the economy of words we associate with the telegraph must be understood within this context. The impact of the telegraph was mediated by diverse workplace roles and expectations. Within these workplaces, there were other factors pushing toward terseness or resisting it.

Terseness was imposed on reporters by the city editor and his (almost always) staff of copy editors, who trimmed copy to the bone. Reporters themselves sought to expand their copy for the simple reason that they were paid by the line. Anyone who has read in the early years of the files of the trade newspaper "The Journalist" will recognize the dilemma of the "space writer".[24]

This economy of words was in turn imposed upon the city editor by the foreman of the composing room. Until around the 1870s, at all but the most prosperous metropolitan dailies, there remained a hard four-page limit to the length of a newspaper. Within that four-page limit, all sorts of expansions occurred – larger paper sizes, smaller type, more columns – so the sheer content of a newspaper increased, but still there was a scarcity of space, so that the various editors and other content producers competed for it. The arbiter of the competition was the foreman of the composing room, who negotiated back and forth with the copy desk to drive down the amount of content to what would fit.

The city editor and the foreman tended to deflate copy in the same way that telegraphic digests – as well as the other digests I've mentioned – did. The remarkable thing is that even so it took so long to achieve terseness. News discourse remained quite longwinded well beyond the point at which we'd expect economic and technological factors to have driven out the excess verbiage. Why?

A series of factors resisted a tighter economy of words. Some of these factors were aesthetic or cultural. Nineteenth-century US Americans had been schooled in a florid oral culture – one of the reasons for the enduring popularity of Shakespeare's plays among ordinary people of that era[25] – and had come to expect significant public communication to have significant size and complexity as well.

Even while the reporter's text was subject to ruthless compression, other content providers received more tolerant treatment. Editors and correspondents especially continued to expand and embellish. Their work, along with the clipped news from exchange papers, remained independent of the iron hand of the city editor. This matter tended to reside in the middle of the newspaper (pages 2–3 in a four-page paper; pages 4–5 in an eight-page paper), in a position of priority, with telegraphic news, local items, and business news following afterwards.

Accompanying the resistance of oral culture and the resistance of the editors and correspondents, was the resistance of the political. As the newspaper commercialized, politics was not exiled from the press, but was rather sandwiched between other kinds of content. The political matter still claimed to be the "sacred" element of journalism, while the other matter was profane, and as such could trump the short-term requirements of brevity and compression. By the same token, the sacred political work of the newspaper also retarded the rationalization of the economic structure of the news business. Newspapers were slow to become local monopolies and slow to form national chains – even today they are far less consolidated than other forms of media – because of the power of the belief in the political work of the press.

The ability of editors and correspondents and political culture to resist the supposed imperatives of the market and technologies might also explain an incongruity in the deployment of the telegraph within the news system. Why weren't there partisan wire services? In the age of postal dissemination, parties had established campaign newspapers that were intended to work as bulletin boards for local editors to crib from; the most famous of these is 1840's Whig *Log Cabin*, edited by Horace Greeley. It would stand to reason that, with the rise of telegraphic news transmission, the parties would post a national wire report that local editors could access. Why not? Perhaps the expense – telegraphic news wasn't subsidized the way that postal news was, with free postage for newspapers exchanged between editors.[26] Perhaps because of the relative imperishability of political discourse. Older means of transmission would suffice for the sorts of editorial matter that Greeley printed in the *Log Cabin*, for instance. But neither of these explanations really holds up. The expense of telegraphic news was likely no higher than the expense of printing campaign newspapers – which, being short-lived, would enjoy very little advertising support and which were priced below cost to circulate widely among voters. Besides, cost is a practical problem with a host of available practical solutions; because partisans were indeed suspicious of the political motivations of the wire services, they could have found a way to add their content to the telegraphic stream had they so desired. As for timeliness, subsequent eras have seen the power of the accelerated news cycle; canny as they were, mid-nineteenth-century politicoes could easily have imagined what a daily diet of national party news would look like and what purposes it would serve.

Probably the absence of national partisan wire services had to do more with the culture of newspaper politics than with the practicalities of telegraphic communication. The partisan newspaper system was supposed to be decentralized, and within it each editor was supposed to have autonomy and independence – autonomy over the selection of content for his or her newspaper, and an independent voice that could be heard within the national party newspaper network. A partisan wire service would have violated the norms of that culture, in the same way that "professional" bloggers violate the norms of the contemporary blogosphere.

The telegraph's impact on news diction was muted, limited, and mediated by many other factors. These factors all have something to do with the workplace environment, which was in tension with some of the possibilities of the technology, and which contributed to its construction. The same is true for other aspects of news style – the "form of the report," as James Carey called it.[27] One common example is the inverted pyramid style.

The inverted pyramid style, in which a story is told backward, as it were, by beginning with the point of the story and then moving to its origins and contexts, had come to characterize reporting by the beginning of the twentieth century. It is surprisingly hard to find much earlier,[28] although in a sense the tall stacks of headlines above the typical news digest serves sort of the same purpose, outlining the content of the column to follow. A standard explanation for the rise of the inverted pyramid style involves the impact of telegraphic transmission. Telegraphic transmission invites turning the story upside down, beginning with the biggest points, and then tapering off toward dispensable details; this would allow an editor at the telegraph desk of a newspaper to simply excise the bottom paragraphs to fit the story into the available space.

But this form appeared elsewhere before it arrived in news stories. David Mindich makes a good argument for War Secretary Edwin Stanton's civil war dispatches as the first examples of inverted pyramid style.[29] Whether any particular dispatch is the first is relatively unimportant. What is significant is that this style was being imported from a bureaucracy. The inverted pyramid style would have been very useful to the emerging public and private bureaucracies of the mid-nineteenth century, just as the bullet-point executive summary is favored by administrators today. Again, what is remarkable about its adoption in news culture is the slowness of it.

Ironically, one of the factors that seemed to have hastened the adoption of both terseness and the inverted pyramid was the breaking of the four-page limit. Newspapers expanded their size gradually, and as they did they became significantly more attentive to the style and appearance of news matter. The reasons for this shift are rooted in the sorts of economic factors that Richard Kaplan has identified as creating economies of scale in local newspapering in the last ten or fifteen years of the century – especially lower paper costs and expanded advertising revenue. Lower paper costs was a direct effect of new technologies – the wood pulp process. The expansion of advertising revenue is associated with two factors – the rise of the department store and the rise of national product advertising – that are more tangentially related to technologies but are more crucially part of a large-scale social transformation.[30]

Advertising was consistently the vanguard of design and style changes in the newspaper. Every innovation in newspaper design, including the headline, illustration, and white space, appeared first in advertising matter and then was copied by the more austere news columns. The spaciousness and elegance of the advertising matter was off limits to the news in the age of the four-page newspaper, though. This applies to textual strategies as well. In the four-page newspaper, news items were crammed in without much regard to style, inverted pyramid or otherwise. As newspapers expanded, significantly more attention was paid to these elements.

Take these arguments as preliminary, and suppose that I'm correct in arguing, pending further research, that the sources of these elements of news style came not from the telegraph but from the complicated interaction of many factors in work structure and culture. If that is the case, then why did everyone think it was the telegraph? There is no shortage of contemporary commentary that attributed historic shifts in the culture of journalism to the telegraph. Was everyone simply wrong?

There are certainly plenty of parallel examples from today's news culture that would suggest otherwise. To take a personal favorite, Kevin Barnhurst and Diana Mutz have convincingly shown that, contrary to the common sense of working journalists, news stories have been getting longer over the past century or so.[31] Journalists think otherwise because they know that their own stories keep getting cut, and they have a ready explanation for the source of this cutting: the corporate ownership of their newspaper or broadcast outlet. This economic pressure is real. But journalists have been more effective than they think in pushing a different agenda. Long-form journalism and its sense of embattlement spring from the professionalization of news occupations – always a halfway professionalization, because journalists will always lack the autonomy and independence of the classic professions.

It is not hard to come up with a parallel explanation for the impact of the telegraph on news styles. The telegraph and other tools are the most readily available protagonists in the larger and far more complex reshuffling and reconfiguration of newswork in this period. And their impact was undeniably real, though not apparently sufficient to produce the effects claimed. There is also something in the explanation by technology that suits the habits by which journalists tell the story of their craft. Pending further inquiry, one might suggest that journalists and other professionals have a tendency toward collective memory by technique. Talk to a journalist who has worked through the past three decades and you will get a pretty precise and somewhat nostalgic overview of the different typewriters, pcs, telephones, fax machines, cameras, notebooks and pencils that one has used. And again, talk about the challenges facing the craft and you will get another list of the incoming tools of the trade, as well as a commentary on the corporate structure of the news industry. Perhaps journalists talk about tools because, as proto-professionals, they tend to repress other workplace factors, which they share with other workers but not so much with other professions.

One further reason that the role of technologies is played up in these accounts is the habit of the media industries generally to see their sector as the site of permanent revolution. Often this awareness comes in the form of the narrative of impending disaster, as each new tool threatens to destroy the existing industry. For a business that specializes in novelty, the news industry has often been surprisingly hostile to new technology. The ready adoption of the telegraph – many years after its invention and successful demonstration, but still well before other industries[32] – is a relatively rare example of an early adoption of a new technology by the newspaper industry. Other technologies occasioned significant resistance – radio and other broadcast technologies and the computer especially. Pablo Boczkowski's study of specific projects in which newspapers have tried to exploit the possibilities of the internet documents this sort of resistance; again it is to a large extent premised on a defense of professional standards, a point I'll return to in the conclusion.[33]

Picture technologies

The same period is known for the introduction of many other technologies: picture technologies, including photography and halftone printing; printing technologies, including the linotype and the web press; and other communication technologies that were integrated into the newsroom, including the typewriter and the telephone. Each of them has been seen as having a transformative effect on social communication generally and news culture specifically. If we look at them through the lens of the workplace, however, we see that their impact was considerably more complicated.

Picture technologies followed much the same path of development as the telegraph. Photography struck popular consciousness at roughly the same time as the telegraph, and spread rapidly in the 1840s. Its impact on news culture was expected to be revolutionary. In fact, Morse happened to be in Paris in 1839, and arranged for a visit to Daguerre's studio; afterwards, Daguerre visited his studio and saw an exhibition of the electric telegraph. Morse wrote up these events in a letter for the newspapers – the equivalent of a press release, meant to be a mutual promotion of the two inventions.[34]

But the integration of photography into newsgathering and reporting moved crabwise for half a century and more. One version of this history has it that photography's adoption was hampered technologically. Simply put, a technological barrier existed in the printing of photographs on the same page with text. This account is sort of true. Early on techniques were developed for printing photographs alone – hence the popularity of *cartes de visite* even before the Civil War. It was difficult to do the same thing in a newspaper. Instead, to reproduce photographs, it was necessary to engrave them onto wood or some other medium. The illustrated news that resulted strikes present-day readers as stilted and immature – photojournalism waiting to be born.

But on closer inspection it is clear that that is not the story. The illustrated news aimed to do a different task than photojournalism.[35] The photos that a photojournalist publishes are meant to provide a trace of an event. The illustrated news was meant to provide virtual presence. The theory was that the visual memory provided by a good news illustration would be similar to or identical to the visual memory that one would have acquired by being present at an event. The illustrated news was also meant as a form of report. A good news illustration was the result of a complicated process of gathering visual elements through sketches and other methods of visual recording, including photography, and composing them into a master record. Some of the resulting illustrations were complex works of visual reporting, compressing time and space and offering commentary and contextualization.[36]

This explains why it took a quarter of a century after the successful demonstration of the halftone process for news illustration to shift from engravings to photographs. The photographs were, in a word, simply not as lucid as the engravings.

In the illustrated press that was so popular in the years between the Civil War and the turn of the century, we see a complex construction of a social reality. Sketch artists were reporters in one sense and correspondents in another. They spent much of their time in the faithful reproduction of visual details, sketching this or that visual element to use in future compositions. But in constructing a picture of a scene, the sketch artist would use the same freedom to comment as a correspondent, without feeling compelled to depict something as it actually happened. Many of the larger images that appeared in the leading national illustrated journals, like *Harper's Weekly* or *Leslie's*, were team products, pieced together by a lead artist from elements contributed by sketch artists, then broken down and engraved by a team of specialist engravers.

The illustrated news anticipated in some key ways the later development of professional journalism. In illustrated news, a claim to fidelity based on both detailed sketches and photographic documentation supported an interpretation that required the intervention of an author. Like verbal journalism, pictorial journalism wrestled with the justification of its interpretive element. It produced an ideology in which the interpretation of the artist was explained in terms of the irreducible psychological processes of personal memory. The artist produced a representation on paper that could substitute for the mental image that an individual witness would have retained from one's lived experience. The illustrated news was ahead of its time in acknowledging the necessarily subjective element of objective journalism.

Photojournalists, by contrast, emerged first as reporters. As journalists, they were occupationally retrograde, practitioners of the naive empiricism of the reporter-as-stenographer. Photography became a journalism only after the period of this discussion.

It was only after the camera had been redesigned to allow it to achieve some of the lucidity of the artist's hand that it became a believable substitute. But even then the tasks of illustration changed. The news photograph became truly significant only in the 1920s, when the speed graphic camera allowed reporters to shoot on-the-spot action shots. This new camera was a tool that could be integrated into the work of the reporter in a new fashion. Its influence was mediated by work routines, too.

Through the 1920s, news photos were rarely live and candid. The impact of the new cameras was relatively diffuse in the established press. Photography's impact was more strikingly felt in the new tabloid press, the wild frontier of journalism.

It is a recurring pattern in the history of news for things to get out of hand in every generation. In the early 1870s, and again in the 1890s, new cheap newspapers appeared, challenging established news habits. In these and other cases, the unsettlement was attributed to technological change – steam presses, stereotyping, cheaper paper, wire service syndication. A moral panic ensued. The responses came in the form of calls for codes of ethics, in strengthened state press associations, and in journalism training programs in the new state universities. Joseph Pulitzer, whose "new journalism" had helped produce the moral panic of the 1890s, responded by seeking to endow a college of journalism at Columbia University.[37] In the first decade of the twentieth century, several such departments or schools of journalism were established.

The tabloid press, with its exploitation of the new photographic technology, helped touch off another moral crisis. In this case, the crisis was compounded by the demoralizing experience with media performance during World War I; the generalized anxiety over motion pictures, youth, and immigration; and the industrial and phenomenological shocks produced by the expansion of broadcasting, which invaded the news market and colonized the middle-class home rapidly in the same decade.

The present-day ideological apparatus of journalism was formulated in response to that crisis. It is tempting to see it coming straight out of the new machines. It is an old habit to see objectivity, for instance, emerging from the telegraph and its need to sell news to a variety of consumers, or from broadcasting's regulatory requirements, or from the eye of the camera. But if we turn our attention to the mediation of work routines and the division of labor, the process looks different, and it would seem that different outcomes might have resulted.

Technology and the mechanical department

Perhaps the largest technological shifts came from the introduction of new printing technologies. The period featured the introduction of steam and then electric-powered presses, shifting from flat beds to cylinders, culminating in the web perfecting press. It also saw the adoption of typesetting machines, culminating in the linotype. More peripherally, it saw a shift to electric lighting, a rather significant improvement in a workplace with so little fresh air and so much flammable material.[38]

The impact of new printing technologies was obviously felt in the mechanical departments of newspapers, but it is not clear what effect they may have had on content or its meanings. Within the mechanical department, a division of labor had been achieved between compositors, or typesetters, and pressmen. In the years following the Civil War typographical unions came to represent typesetters, and pressmen formed their own locals. These occupations were differently skilled. Typesetting work required complex literary skills and considerable dexterity, whereas presswork was more mechanical and physically demanding. In part, this divide invited a gendered distinction, as Ava Baron has shown.[39] Typesetters from the 1830s on had to struggle to keep their craft "manly," as large employers were inclined to hire part-timers and women and children to do some tasks.[40]

The typographical unions were quite solid, however, and a robust craft culture retarded "rationalization" and dampened emerging conflicts between workers and managers. One example was the way recurring disputes over the distribution of "phat" and "lean" matter within the print shop were handled. In any particular shop, but especially newspaper shops, there were especially desirable typesetting jobs that involved "phat," or emphatic, type, like headlines and display ads. By the scale of prices that most shops adhered to, typesetters were paid by the "em." When figuring the pay for display type, though, the "em" used was the body face, which might be 9-point or 8-point. Someone typesetting a headline might be paid as if he or she had set the same space in 8-point type. Now within a shop, all the typesetters would be paid by the "em" except the foreman, who would be paid a weekly salary. So it was always tempting for the owner to keep the phat for the foreman, rather than putting it "on the hook," that is in the usual assignment rack, from which typesetters would take jobs in turn. Work disputes often involved getting managers to guarantee that the phat would be put on the hook.[41]

Disputes like these tended to be worked out because foremen and proprietors at many shops remained culturally connected with the workers in the chapel. Nevertheless, there were repeated attempts to break the local unions in the years between the Civil War and World War I, with the conflict sometimes, but rarely, achieving levels of spectacular violence, the most famous being the bombing of the *Los Angeles Times* in 1910.[42]

Mechanization offered one way to supersede organized labor. Proprietors patronized inventors who experimented with ways to automate aspects of the production process, and the resulting machines ate away at the edges of the organized workplace.

The most dramatic mechanical invention in the period was the linotype. Much of the craft culture of the typographical unions had been built up around the notion of "working at the case," setting cold type into sticks and forms. Through the second half of the nineteenth century, a series of inventions patterned after the typewriter moved to replace this process. The most effective was Otto Merganthaler's device. In 1886, the *New York Tribune* became the first newspaper to use one. Other newspapers followed suit in a pattern that accelerated rapidly during the depression that began in 1893, with proprietors sensing an urgent need to cut costs.

In theory, the linotype could have demolished the typographical unions and transformed the lines of autonomy and authority in the print workplace. It did not. The ITU managed to avoid the most dire consequences, even while it accepted the linotype as the standard equipment in print workplaces.

The ITU was fortunate in that the introduction of the linotype coincided with massive growth in print production and consumption.[43] The combination of cheap paper; plentiful advertising from new sources (department stores, national consumer products); cost-saving industry practices (syndication, patent insides/outsides); and the rise of a new mass audience allowed for a tremendous expansion in the publishing industry, so that, even during the depression of the 1890s, proprietors could introduce new machines while continuing to employ large numbers of typesetters and pay them well. The unions did not do more to resist the technology because industry conditions allowed them to adapt to it without suffering. They did adopt some standards that limited the impact of the machines. So, for instance, they successfully placed members as operators of the new machines, and managed to keep typesetting shops closed. They also were able to insist that shops re-set rather than share matter like department store ads, making work for additional typesetters.

This domestication of the new technology depended on an effectively organized shop. The ITU and its member locals showed remarkable skill in managing to maintain local solidarity in the face of a fluid work force of migrating typesetters following seasonal work, and national solidarity in the face of broad regional differences in markets and cultures.

The ITU's effectiveness in resisting de-skilling is in vivid contrast with its ineffectiveness in spreading its organization into newsrooms. Reporters and copy editors faced many of the same workplace challenges as typesetters, and were a disgruntled bunch, overworked and underpaid, and terminally grumpy at the way occupational gratification was held hostage by the newsroom management. They also saw their work altered by new machines, especially the typewriter and the telephone.

The impact of the typewriter on newswork is yet to be understood. One certainly notices the changes in newsroom appearance. Photographs from the period show reporters – mostly men – seated at long benches, facing their typewriters.[44] These workplaces look very similar to garment shops in the same period, except that in those places it is women facing sewing machines. The typewriters seem to bind the reporters in place. They also seem to distort the work of reporters, though it is hard to specify how.

The sewing machine and the typewriter are technologically and socio-logically very similar. Both mechanize a particular activity which had pre-viously been rather personal and very time- and attention-consuming. Both also encourage the formation of small workplaces with workers numbering between a handful and a few dozen. The typewriter's chief effect was on the smooth running of offices. Anyone who has done research in the papers of an organization or firm in this period will recall the sense of deep change at the point when the records shift from handwriting to typewriting. Typewriting became a skill of its own; some reporters mastered it, but most accommodated to it less skillfully or perhaps more expressively. The reporter who was a vir-tuoso at two-fingered typing became a commonplace in newspaper lore, sug-gesting a manly two-fisted approach to the machine. The most accomplished "typewriters," as typewriter operators were called, were women, and the sophisticated use of the machines, like the sophisticated use of shorthand, came to be considered a feminine skill.[45] Ted Curtis Smythe points out that typewriting certainly improved communication between the newsroom and typesetters, who had previously been slowed down by the need to decipher handwriting.[46]

The telephone, like the typewriter, had been demonstrated at the 1876 Centennial Exhibition in Philadelphia, and was introduced into newspaper shops in the 1880s and 1890s. It also became a fixture in the iconography of journalism, with the reporter roaming around the city and phoning in raw material to "rewrite men" stationed in the newsroom at their typewriters.

It would be silly to suppose that these new newsroom technologies con-stituted the same kind of threat to occupational control and safety as the linotype, even though they came out of the same technological moment. Still, newsroom workers did not enjoy happy labor conditions. Why did they resist collective organization? Probably because they did not wish to think of themselves as workers.[47] Journalism wished to be a profession. And, for quite different reasons, proprietors also wanted journalism to professionalize.

The politics of professionalization

I have already argued that modern journalism developed on the material basis of a merging of the differing occupations of reporter and correspondent, and their separation from editorship. This realignment came in part in dialog with changes in technology, though these were never a determining factor. It also came accompanied by significant tensions between newsworkers and their employers.

The flip side to this occupational history is a political history that occurred outside newspaper workplaces. Throughout the industrialization of the newspaper, a concerned public viewed with alarm the growing power and apparent corruption of the press. This same public knew from this same press of the immense power and apparent corruption of the oil industry and the meatpacking industry and mining and organized labor. It invited legislative action to rein in the excesses of the press and its infrastructure. Congressional investigations into the telegraph monopoly were as frequent as investigations into the railroads. Perhaps the most interesting accomplishment of this broad public concern was the passage of the 1912 Truth in Publishing Act.[48]

Newspaper publishers of every stripe – partisan, commercial, honest or less honest – resisted restrictive regulation. When regulation came to railroads or meatpacking, it benefitted those industries by making it easier to refuse kickbacks to clients and easier to export to other countries. Honest practitioners would no longer be punished for their honesty. So those forms of regulation had crucial support from within their industries. This has rarely been the case with the news industry. Newspaper publishers supported the suppression of radicalism, which we might take to be a restrictive form of government regulation of expression, and sometimes have been as supportive as the general public of libel laws, but for the most part they have resisted any attempt to regulate their business environment or news practices. They have accepted some indirect forms of subsidy and special treatment, notably in the form of reduced postage and the easing of antitrust restrictions (in 1970's Newspaper Preservation Act), but beyond that have not welcomed government intervention.

So progressive-era regulatory movements caused significant concern among newspaper publishers, for good reasons and bad ones. The bad ones involved the fear that government intervention would hurt profitability. The good ones involved the recognition that the public had grounds for its disgruntlement. Press performance had not met reasonable expectations.[49]

The professionalization project emerged as a reasonable negotiated settlement to two battles at once. In newsrooms, professionalization mollified newsworkers by promising them increased autonomy while discouraging them from thinking of themselves as wage workers like the typographers and pressmen. In the larger arena, professionalization mollified the public by offering assurances that the press would rigorously separate its own business interests from its news content. And of course an entire apparatus was created in the early decades of the twentieth century to codify this deal. I've already mentioned the schools of journalism and the codes of ethics.

This national political history explains, I think, the development of a differently inflected culture of news in the United States than elsewhere in the industrializing world. The US has a form of news specific to it and recognized as such which it has been consciously exporting since at least World War II. The so-called Americanization of media in Europe, Asia, and South America is beyond the scope of this paper; I would only point out that no one would think Americanization remarkable if it came automatically from the tools of the trade.

Conclusion

One finds technologies everywhere involved in the history of newswork. Perhaps they made this history, but not in conditions of their own choosing. The impact of specific technologies was mediated by many other factors.

Does this more nuanced account change the meaning of the story, or does it merely retard it a bit? One could argue that the final outcome of this long and involved history was a news culture that was just as the machines would have had it; other factors simply slowed it down. The easiest case for this argument would be in picture technologies, where a photorealism did eventually emerge. But even there, the key factor is not the internal construction of any particular photo, which may be photorealistic, but the arrangement of those traces within an overall structure of newswork, alongside the professionalizing verbal journalism and the continuing editorial function. Besides, the realism of photorealism is hardly uncontested.

Technology is, or should be, decentered in the account of the development of modern newswork. If historical practice tends by default to consign technology to context, I think that is properly so. An account centered on technology deforms the history, essentializes the technology, distorts agency, and misconstrues not just the openness of the past but the possibilities of the present.

But I am not wholly satisfied that news culture needs be understood entirely or primarily as work. Making media is not the same as making culture, or making meaning. In the period I've been discussing, a line was drawn between mechanical work and newswork. The struggles of typographers and pressmen to retain control in their workplaces may have had something to do with the profitability of newspapers as businesses, and may even have had something to do with the appearance of newspapers, but I have found very few instances in which these mechanical workers intervened in shaping the content of newspapers.

I am not comfortable generalizing that point, however. The digitization of newspaper production has eroded the lines that had been drawn between journalism and mechanical work, as well as between content and design, even as corporate imperatives have eroded the division of newswork into beats. Meanwhile, the internet and the blogosphere have challenged the canons of objectivity and the construction of a journalistic subject position. Historians should stick to the past and not predict the future, of course, so I will remain agnostic as to whether all this turbulence and dynamism will result in the reinvention of journalism. Perhaps a new journalism has already been heralded by Matt Drudge and Rush Limbaugh, and will feature a personalization and re-partisanization of the news media. Or perhaps the next new journalism will be a reactionary move intended to save us from that world.

Notes

1 Robert Nisbet, *Social Change and History: Aspects of the Western Theory of Development* (New York: Oxford University Press, 1969).
2 Peter Novick, *That Noble Dream: The "Objectivity Question" and the American Historical Profession* (New York: Cambridge University Press, 1988).
3 Hayden V. White, *Metahistory: The Historical Imagination in Nineteenth-century Europe* (Baltimore, MD: Johns Hopkins University Press, 1973); Hayden V. White, *The Content of the Form: Narrative Discourse and Historical Representation* (Baltimore, MD: Johns Hopkins University Press, 1987).
4 Paul Heyer, *Communications and History: Theories of Media, Knowledge, and Civilization* (New York: Greenwood Press, 1988).
5 David E. Nye, "Technology and the Production of Difference," *American Quarterly* 58, no. 3 (2006): 597.
6 James W. Carey, "Technology and Ideology: The Case of the Telegraph," in James W. Carey, *Communication as Culture: Essays on Media and Society* (Boston, MA: Unwin Hyman, 1983, 1989), 201–30.
7 Jeremy Packer, "Rethinking Dependency: New Relations of Transportation and Communication," in Jeremy Packer and Craig Robertson, eds, *Thinking with James Carey: Essays on Communications, Transportation, History* (New York: Peter Lang, 2006), 79–100; Jonathan Sterne, "Transportation and Communication: Together as You've Always Wanted Them," in Jeremy Packer and Craig Robertson, eds, *Thinking with James Carey: Essays on Communications, Transportation, History* (New York: Peter Lang, 2006), 117–36; John Durham Peters, "Technology and Ideology: The Case of the Telegraph Revisited," in Jeremy Packer and Craig Robertson, eds, *Thinking with James Carey: Essays on Communications, Transportation, History* (New York: Peter Lang, 2006), 137–56.
8 Elizabeth Eisenstein, *The Printing Press as an Agent of Change: Communications and Cultural Transformations in Early Modern Europe* (Cambridge: Cambridge University Press, 1979).
9 Benedict Anderson, *Imagined Communities: Reflections on the Origin and Spread of Nationalism*. Rev. edn (London and New York: Verso, 1991).
10 Adrian Johns, *The Nature of the Book: Print and Knowledge in the Making* (Chicago, IL: University of Chicago Press, 1998).
11 Ian Hacking, *The Social Construction of What?* (Cambridge, MA: Harvard University Press, 1999).
12 John Nerone, "The Future of Communication History," *Critical Studies in Media Communication* 23, no. 3 (2006): 254–62; Carolyn Marvin, *When Old Technologies Were New: Thinking About Electric Communication in the Late Nineteenth*

Century (New York: Oxford University Press, 1988); Jonathan Sterne, *The Audible Past: Cultural Origins of Sound Reproduction* (Durham, NC: Duke University Press, 2003); Richard R. John, *Spreading the News: The American Postal System from Franklin to Morse* (Cambridge, MA: Harvard University Press, 1995); Paul Starr, *The Creation of the Media: Political Origins of Modern Communications* (New York: Basic Books, 2004); Robert W. McChesney, *Telecommunications, Mass Media, and Democracy: The Battle for the Control of U.S. Broadcasting, 1928–35* (New York: Oxford University Press, 1993).

13 James W. Carey and Larry Grossberg, "From New England to Illinois: The Invention of (American) Cultural Studies," in Jeremy Packer and Craig Robertson, eds, *Thinking with James Carey: Essays on Communications, Transportation, History* (New York: Peter Lang, 2006), 11–28.

14 Susan J. Douglas, *Inventing American Broadcasting, 1899–1922* (Baltimore, MD: Johns Hopkins University Press, 1987); Susan J. Douglas, *Listening In: Radio and the American Imagination, from Amos 'n' Andy and Edward R. Murrow to Wolfman Jack and Howard Stern* (New York: Times Books, 1999); Daniel J. Czitrom, *Media and the American Mind: From Morse to McLuhan* (Chapel Hill, NC: University of North Carolina Press, 1982).

15 Raymond Williams, *Television: Technology and Cultural Form* (London: Fontana, 1974).

16 Starr, *The Creation of the Media.*

17 Dan Schiller, *Theorizing Communication: A History* (New York: Oxford University Press, 1996).

18 Williams, *Television: Technology and Cultural Form.*

19 Friedrich A. Kittler, *Gramophone, Film, Typewriter.* Translated, with an introduction, by Geoffrey Winthrop-Young and Michael Wutz (Stanford, CA: Stanford University Press, 1999).

20 Carey, "Technology and Ideology," 11–28; Donald L. Shaw, "News Bias and the Telegraph: A Study of Historical Change," *Journalism Quarterly* 44, no. 1 (1967): 3–12, 31.

21 Michael Schudson, *Discovering the News: A Social History of American Newspapers* (New York: Basic Books, 1978).

22 Christopher P. Wilson, *The Labor of Words: Literary Professionalism in the Progressive Era* (Athens, GA: University of Georgia Press, 1985).

23 Thurlow Weed, *Life of Thurlow Weed Including his Autobiography and a Memoir* (New York: Houghton Mifflin, 1883); Glyndon G. Van Deusen, *Thurlow Weed: Wizard of the Lobby* (Boston, MA: Little, Brown, 1947).

24 William S. Solomon, "The Site of Newsroom Labor: The Division of Editorial Practice," in Bonnie Brennen and Hanno Hardt, eds, *Newsworkers: Toward a History of the Rank and File* (Minneapolis, MN: University of Minnesota Press, 1995); Ted Curtis Smythe, "The Reporter, 1880–1900: Working Conditions and Their Influence on the News," *Journalism History* 7 (1980): 1–10.

25 Lawrence W. Levine, *Highbrow/Lowbrow: The Emergence of Cultural Hierarchy in America* (Cambridge, MA: Harvard University Press, 1988), ch. 1.

26 Richard R. John, *Spreading the News*; Richard B. Kielbowicz, *News in the Mail: The Press, Post Office, and Public Information, 1700–1860s* (New York: Greenwood Press, 1989).

27 James W. Carey, "The Problem of Journalism History," *Journalism History* 1, no. 1 (1974): 3–5, 27.

28 Horst Pöttker, "News and its Communicative Quality: The Inverted Pyramid – When and Why did it Appear?" *Journalism Studies* 4, no. 4 (2003): 501–11; David T.Z. Mindich, *Just the Facts: How "Objectivity" Came to Define American Journalism* (New York: NYU Press, 1998).

29 Mindich, *Just the Facts*.

30 Richard M. Ohmann, *Selling Culture: Magazines, Markets, and Class at the Turn of the Century* (New York: Verso, 1996).

31 Kevin G. Barnhurst and Diana Mutz, "American Journalism and the Decline in Event-centered Reporting," *Journal of Communication* 47, no. 4 (1997): 27–53.

32 Menahem Blondheim, *News Over the Wires: The Telegraph and the Flow of Public Information in America, 1844–97* (Cambridge, MA: Harvard University Press, 1994); Menahem Blondheim, "The Click: Telegraphic Technology, Journalism, and the Transformation of the New York Associated Press," *American Journalism* 17, no. 4 (2000): 27–51.

33 Pablo Boczkowski, *Digitizing the News: Innovation in Online Newspapers* (Cambridge, MA: MIT Press, 2004).

34 "The Daguerreutipe," *The Farmers' Cabinet*, 26 April 1839, 37:35, 2

35 Joshua Brown, *Beyond the Lines: Pictorial Reporting, Everyday Life, and the Crisis of Gilded Age America* (Berkeley, CA: University of California Press, 2002); Kevin, G. Barnhurst and John Nerone, *The Form of News: A History* (New York: Guilford, 2001).

36 See, for example, the famous illustration of Garfield's assassination (Frank Leslie's *Illustrated Newspaper*, 16 July 1881, 332–3).

37 Joseph Pulitzer, "The College of Journalism," *North American Review* 178, no. 570 (1904): 641–80.

38 Ted Curtis Smythe, *The Gilded Age Press, 1865–1900* (New York: Greenwood Press, 2003).

39 Ava Baron, "An 'Other' Side of Gender Antagonism at Work: Man, Boys, and the Remasculinization of Printers' Work, 1830–1920," in Ava Baron, ed., *Work Engendered: Toward a New History of American Labor* (Ithaca, NY: Cornell University Press, 1991).

40 William S. Pretzer, "The British, Duff Green, the Rats, and the Devil: Custom, Capitalism, and Conflict in the Washington Printing Trade, 1834–36," *Labor History* 27 (1986): 5–30.

41 See, for example, Galveston (Texas) Typographical Union Records, 1860–1932. Office of the Secretary Treasurer, Minutes of Monthly Meetings, 1875–1889. Center for American History, University of Texas at Austin, Austin TX.

42 John Nerone, *Violence Against the Press: Policing the Public Sphere in US History* (New York: Oxford University Press, 1994).

43 Charles Johannigsmaier, *Fiction and the American Literary Marketplace, 1860–1900: The Role of Newspaper Syndicates* (New York: Cambridge University Press, 1997); Harry Kelber and Carl Schlesingerm, *Union Printers and Controlled Automation* (New York: Free Press, 1967).

44 Hanno Hardt and Bonnie Brennen, "Newswork, History, and Photographic Evidence: A Visual Analysis of a 1930s Newsroom," in Bonnie Brennen and Hanno Hardt, *Picturing the Past: Media, History, and Photography* (Urbana, IL: University of Illinois Press, 1999), 11–35.

45 Sharon Hartman Strom, *Beyond the Typewriter: Gender, Class, and the Origins of Modern American Office Work, 1900–1930* (Urbana, IL: University of Illinois Press, 1992).

46 Curtis Smythe, *The Gilded Age Press*, 128.

47 Daniel J. Leab, *A Union of Individuals; The Formation of the American Newspaper Guild, 1933–36* (New York: Columbia University Press, 1970).

48 Linda Lawson, *Truth in Publishing: Federal Regulation of the Press's Business Practices, 1880–1920* (Carbondale, IL: Southern Illinois University Press, 1993).

49 Hazel Dicken Garcia, *Journalistic Standards in Nineteenth-century America* (Madison, WI: University of Wisconsin Press, 1989); Marion Marzolf, *Civilizing Voices: American Press Criticism, 1880–1950* (New York: Longman, 1991).

Part 4

Journalism

Introduction

Journalism, communication and history

Nicole Maurantonio

In his canonical 1974 article, "The Problem of Journalism History," James W. Carey dubbed the study of journalism history "something of an embarrassment"[1] – an avenue of historical inquiry characterized by a seeming conceptual myopia. This lack of vision, Carey argued, relegated its practitioners to seeing journalism solely as the outgrowth of "those large impersonal faces buffeting the press: industrialization, urbanization, and mass democracy."[2] While undoubtedly these faces helped journalism historians understand the past, they provide, as Carey believed, only one narrative – and a tired one at that. This so-called "Whig history" became what journalism historians have since strived to define their work against, as David Paul Nord notes in his paper, "the history of journalism and the history of the book." While a collective dismissal of this Whig history has prevailed, as scholars have sought to reinvigorate a field once moving toward what Carey saw to be a dead end, journalism historians remain a fractured group, divided by varying ways of addressing the tensions that have characterized the field's own historical trajectory. Underlying these tensions are such questions as: What should constitute the locus of attention for journalism historians – the institution or the individual? Where should journalism historians turn for their theoretical frameworks – sociology or anthropology? How should texts themselves be positioned *vis-à-vis* their historical settings?

There are no "correct" answers to any of these questions, nor are the answers "either-or." Yet whether or not one agrees with Carey's 1974 call for studies of the cultural history of journalism,[3] journalism historians can agree on one thing – the assumption underpinning Carey's claims. Journalism must be foregrounded as the subject rather than the object of historical inquiry, not merely a source used by historians as evidence but an active agent. Journalism, according to Carey, is a "cultural act," "a state of consciousness, a way of apprehending, of experiencing the world,"[4] that requires sustained investigation. How to in fact negotiate journalism's place within culture and study it productively, without reverting to the pitfalls of journalism histories past, is a central theme uniting the papers of David Paul Nord, Michael Schudson and Robert McChesney. Approaching the study of journalism history from varying entry points, Nord, Schudson and McChesney highlight not only the internal fractures and points of departure within journalism history, but also what these avenues of inquiry can ultimately offer our understandings of the past, present and future.

Tracking the trajectories of the "new book history" and the "new journalism history," David Paul Nord grapples with the causes of their divergent paths. Arguing that "the new book history is largely a reaction against the decontextualized study of *texts*, while the new journalism history is a reaction against the decontextualized study of *institutions*,"[5] Nord compares surveys of media and book history by examining the themes and theoretical frameworks their respective practitioners choose to privilege. While these two branches share similar interests in texts – precisely how these texts are analyzed and positioned are issues that delineate them. While journalism historians, according to Nord, mine publications for content, fundamentally it is the publication itself that stands at the heart of the project. Historians of the book, in contrast, situate the text's content as the locus of inquiry. Similarly, as Nord points out, "the journalism historians pay more attention to professional practice and to the organizational side of media institutions, while the book historians focus more on forms and formats of printed material and the contexts of their use."[6] Despite their trajectories, the divergence of journalism history and the history of the book should not concern us, according to Nord. It should, however, force us to pause to consider the ways of answering questions that necessarily traverse the two modes of inquiry.

Michael Schudson similarly considers the issue of conceptual frameworks and categories in journalism history in his discussion of "Public spheres, imagined communities, and the underdeveloped historical understanding of journalism." Seizing the words of former American Historical Association (AHA) president and eighteenth-century French political, cultural, and intellectual historian, Robert Darnton, Schudson laments history departments' lack of attention to the field of communication history. While acknowledging Darnton's work in carving a space for communication on the historian's agenda, Schudson reflects upon Darnton's claims surrounding Jürgen Habermas's conceptualization of the "public sphere" and its subsequent reification. As Schudson writes, "Journalism is not something that floated platonically above the world and that each country copied down, shaping it to its own national grammar. It is something that – as we know it today – Americans had a major hand in inventing."[7] Acknowledging this, according to Schudson, means not only understanding news organizations as businesses or as arbiters of the oft-cited dream of objectivity. It means schools of communication and journalism must take the reins in efforts to reinforce journalism's place in the public sphere and in democracy.

In "How to think about journalism: Looking backward, going forward," Robert McChesney joins Schudson in reflecting upon the role of journalism in the public sphere. Considering the "crisis" of contemporary American journalism, McChesney argues that despite the "low grade"[8] earned by current news media – media which have unfortunately seen "the decline of investigative reporting, the degeneration of political reporting and international journalism, the absurd horserace coverage of campaigns, the collapse of local journalism, [and] the increased prevalence of celebrity and scandal"[9] – American journalism now stands at a crossroads. Yet productively "going forward" in ways that concurrently revitalize journalism and democracy in the United states more broadly requires an historical/political economy perspective, according to McChesney. However, understanding the structures and policies underpinning the contemporary "crisis" of American journalism, as McChesney argues is not the only advantage a political economy approach offers. It provides an interpretative frame encouraging dialogue between political and social movements, individuals and institutions seeking reform. As McChesney writes, "[I]t is only in the context of people coming together to struggle for social change that depolicization is vanquished and victory becomes plausible, even inevitable."[10] Historical context, for McChesney, thus provides the requisite backdrop against which the contemporary movement for media reform is set.

Nord, Schudson and McChesney provide us with lenses through which to read journalism histories past, reflect upon the current state of journalism research, and look toward a future of fresh research which would not only answer Carey's 1974 call but pose a different, albeit equally valuable, set of questions regarding journalism and its place within history. While these essays draw our attention to the areas in need of research, they should also excite us to the possibilities that await.

Notes

1 James W. Carey, "The Problem of Journalism History," *Journalism History* 1, no. 1 (Spring 1974): 3.
2 Carey, "The Problem of Journalism History," 4.
3 Carey, "The Problem of Journalism History," 4.
4 Carey, "The Problem of Journalism History," 5.
5 David P. Nord, "The History of Journalism and the History of the Book," this volume, 163.
6 Nord, "The History of Journalism and the History of the Book," 171.
7 Michael Schudson, "Public Spheres, Imagined Communities, and the Underdeveloped Historical Understanding of Journalism," this volume, 188.
8 Robert W. McChesney, "How to Think About Journalism: Looking Backward, Going Forward," this volume, 191.
9 McChesney, "How to Think About Journalism", 191.
10 McChesney, "How to Think About Journalism", 213.

Chapter 10

The history of journalism and the history of the book

David Paul Nord

I

It sounds simple enough: The history of journalism is part of the history of publishing, and the history of publishing is part of the history of journalism. They overlap. Journalism historians write about newspapers, magazines, and books, and so do historians of what is sometimes called "print culture" or the "history of the book." Each field might also seem to be encompassed by a broader category, such as the history of media or communication or information. Furthermore, journalism historians, publishing historians, and media historians increasingly see their fields as convergent, especially for the centuries before broadcast and film, when publication meant print. Each field consciously courts the other. Though they use the term "book," the practitioners of the "history of the book," for example, actually seek to study publishing and "print culture" in its broadest sense. They include in their field popular print media such as magazines and newspapers, tracts and broadsides, engravings and photo reproductions. Historians of journalism and mass media embrace those same popular printed materials. All of these historians take their subject to be mediated communication—that is, human communication in the age of mechanical reproduction, to borrow Stephen Greenblatt's phrase, which he borrowed from Walter Benjamin.[1] Scholars of journalism history, media history, and book history share much, including interests in language, information, technology, law, business organization, and popular culture. All are fascinated by (and sometimes worried about) the convergence of print and electronic media systems in our own digital age. All are self-consciously interdisciplinary and cheerfully ecumenical.

And yet, despite the will, the way to convergence in the fields of journalism history, media history, and book history has yet to be found, for even though they overlap on subject matter, they are theoretically and conceptually distinct. They are still largely nonintersecting academic fields. I believe these fields might be better understood—and perhaps improved—if we could see why they remain so different. In this essay, my method will be to examine several early, critical commentaries in the fields of journalism history and history of the book, and then to survey some recent scholarship in three specialized journals: *Book History, Journalism History,* and *American Journalism* (see Appendix). I believe that current book history and current journalism history (and media history more broadly) grew from critiques of older scholarly fields and from pleas in the 1970s for enriched historical and historiographical *contexts*. I will argue that the new book history is largely a reaction against the decontextualized study of *texts*, while the new journalism history is a reaction against the decontextualized study of *institutions*. As they have added historical breadth and context, the fields should be on the road to convergence. But they are not. Just as traces of earlier life forms persist in the DNA of living organisms, so the scholarly origins of these two species of history remain detectable at their core and guide their evolution still.

The gist of my argument can be illustrated in a comparison of two surveys published in 2005: *Comparative Media History* by Jane Chapman and *An Introduction to Book History* by David Finkelstein and Alistair McCleery.[2] In some ways these books are quite similar. Both are international in scope and sweep across centuries. Both are designed as textbooks and as guides to new scholarship and perspectives on the history of publishing. Both books seek to historicize print, to locate it in time and space, to set it into the contexts of culture. Both focus on technology and the material production and distribution of printed material. Both are concerned with the business of publishing and with politics, government, and law. Both assert the power of the press on audiences. But at every moment of harmony the two books remain just a bit out of sync. Chapman describes culture in terms of modernity, ideology, authority, democracy, capitalism, imperialism, globalization, and consumer society. Finkelstein and McCleery use some of those terms, but their notion of culture is more about regimes of knowledge associated with orality, literacy, and the changing uses of print. Technology for Chapman is mainly about the speed, capacity, and reach of distribution, while Finkelstein and McCleery are more interested in how technology shapes the form and therefore the use of printed material. The business side of publishing for Chapman is about publishers and media entrepreneurs; Finkelstein and McCleery pay more attention to other roles in the business, including author, translator, and artisan. In the realm of law, both books explore government censorship and regulation, but Finkelstein and McCleery are more concerned than Chapman with intellectual property and copyright. In Chapman's account, the press exercises power over audiences, but audiences are usually abstractions, off stage. Finkelstein and McCleery assign audience members a more active role in the transformation of print into meaning, into culture. And they give these people a more homely name: readers.

For Finkelstein and McCleery, the key theoretical perspective is the "sociology of texts," a term coined by Oxford University scholar Don McKenzie and adapted by historians such as Roger Chartier in France and Robert Darnton and David Hall in the United States.[3] McKenzie's crucial insight was, in the words of Chartier, simply this:

Against the abstraction of the text, it shows that the status and interpretation of a work depend on material considerations; against the "death
of the author," it stresses the author's role, at the side of the bookseller-
printer, in defining the form given to the work; against the absence of the
reader, it recalls that the meaning of a text is always produced in a historical setting and depends on the differing and plural readings that assign
meaning to it.[4]

McKenzie, Chartier, Darnton, and Hall do not appear in *Comparative Media
History* nor does the phrase "sociology of texts." For Chapman, the most
valuable theoretical perspective is political economy. The most useful social
theorists are those who study the sociology of institutions and ideology, such
as Benedict Anderson, Raymond Williams, Stuart Hall, and Anthony Giddens.
For Finkelstein and McCleery, the text is, in a sense, always the crucial
dependent variable, shaped and used in the contexts of culture. In a summary
statement at the end of Chapter 1, they write that the new "book historians
are increasingly framing their work in terms of 'mediation,' shifting the
emphasis from recovering exact meanings in text to understanding the place of
texts within contemporary society" (p. 27). For Chapman, "text" is not the
term of choice; she prefers "content," and content never seems quite so
important as the media organizations and operators who create it and wield it.
In a chapter on "Commercialism, Consumerism, and Technology," Chapman
writes, "The objective of this chapter is to explore how content creation and
technology were used to develop business" (p. 71). I can imagine a book historian writing that sentence in the opposite direction: "The objective is to
explore how business and technology were used to create content."

   Perhaps the most telling difference lies in the authors' use of the concept of
"media" itself. In their introduction, Finkelstein and McCleery write that
"book historians have increasingly taken to framing their work in terms of
'mediation,'" by which they mean the "mediation" of "texts" (pp. 25, 27).
Chapman would not dispute the importance of media. But in her introduction
she writes, not of the mediation of texts, but of the "mediazation of culture"
(p. 3). The roots of these differences reach back into the 1960s.

II

In every academic discipline, the 1960s and 1970s were hothouse years for criticism, and historical studies of printed media—newspapers, magazines, and
books—attracted their share.

   In journalism history and media history, a new generation of scholars,
working in research-oriented schools of journalism, criticized traditional histories of media for being too insular, too decontextualized, too uncritical, too
captive to the needs of professional training, and too enamored of the biographies of men and media organizations (usually famous newspapers).

Though he was not the first to raise criticisms of journalism history, James W. Carey assigned the problem a name that stuck: Whig history.[5] In Whig history—a term that Carey borrowed from nineteenth-century British historiography—the past is prologue to a glorious present. For Carey and his colleagues, traditional journalism history was servant to the profession of journalism. It provided the creation myth, the story of origins of contemporary businesses, institutions, and professional practices.

An early effort to escape Whig history and to chart a new course for journalism history was a slim, edited volume titled *Mass Media and the National Experience: Essays in Communications History*.[6] The authors, mostly new PhDs from state research universities, hoped to push journalism history into the mainstream of US history and historiography. "The essays that follow," Ronald Farrar wrote in the introduction, "reflect some of current scholarship's suggestions for rediscovering the common ground between the history of mass communications and the history of the country" (p. 3). Farrar and the other authors called for a history that moved beyond biography, both individual and organizational. Like sociologists, they used the term "institution" to mean something broader and more cultural than simply the media business. "A thoroughgoing inquiry into the institution and all its phases is imperative," Farrar wrote, "and the historical context must be far better described than it has been so far" (p. 13). Farrar's colleagues offered chapters on law, business, technology, and other aspects of media structure and practice.

This little volume was followed in the 1970s and 1980s by a stream of critical essays. Of the early critiques, perhaps the most ambitious was Garth Jowett's contribution to a special issue of *Journalism History* on "Seeking New Paths in Research."[7] Building on foundations laid by the economic historian Harold Innis and the media sociologist Melvin DeFleur, Jowett called for a new "history of communication," which he defined as "the examination of the development of man's ability to transmit thoughts, symbols and messages, both in the immediate spatial dimension and transtemporally" (p. 35). For Jowett, "the central problem confronted by communications historians is what takes place when a new medium of communication is introduced into a society" (p. 36). In other words, the subject was media as technology and as social institution—"modes of communication"—and their impact on social and cultural change. While few of the early critics were quite so abstract or expansive as Jowett, almost all pleaded for a broader reach for journalism history, a more sociological understanding of the institutions of media, and more historical and historiographical context.[8]

James Carey's own critique was different. In a now-famous essay in the inaugural issue of *Journalism History*, Carey repeated the familiar charge that "we have defined our craft too narrowly and too modestly".[9] But his plea was not for a sweeping historical sociology of media institutions and technologies but for a cultural history of the journalism itself—"the report," as he called it. Slightly out of step with the other new journalism historians, Carey actually paid attention to the content of media or at least to the concept of content. For Carey, journalism was a "symbolic form," a particular way that social experience was organized. "When we study the history of journalism we are principally studying a way in which men in the past have grasped reality," he wrote. "We are searching out the intersection of journalistic style and vocabulary, created systems of meaning, and standards of reality shared by writer and audience. We are trying to root out a portion of the history of consciousness" (p. 5).

Other commentators who responded to Carey's challenge tended to focus on what Carey himself had called the "methods, procedures, and canons" of professional journalism practice within the economy of mass production. In a set of three papers on "Operationalizing Carey" in a 1975 issue of *Journalism History*, each author proposed ways to use content analysis to uncover the professional or societal values embedded in the journalism of the past.[10] None of the critics who wrestled with Carey fully appreciated the radical epistemology of Carey's cultural approach to communications. "Journalism not only reveals the structure of feeling of previous eras," Carey declared, "it is the structure of feeling" (p. 5). The early Carey operationalizers—as I have called them—grasped the first clause of that sentence but were mystified by the second; and that mystification has largely persisted.[11]

Though the early critics of journalism history sometimes misunderstood or talked past one another, they did agree on several key points: Traditional journalism history was too narrowly focused on major individuals and institutions in the sense of media organizations; it was not properly contextualized in mainstream history and historiography; and it was too uncritical, too Whiggish, too closely linked to current media organizations and practices. The proper subject of journalism history should be *media institutions* in the broader sociological sense, including the methods and procedures of professional practice and the role of journalism (and media more generally) in the national experience. The apotheosis of the new institutional journalism/media history is Paul Starr's *Creation of the Media*.[12]

Like journalism history, the history of books has an ancient tradition of biographies of great publishers and antiquarian histories of famous publishing houses. But that traditional historiography was not the origin of the new book history, nor was it even the chief target of criticism in the 1960s and 1970s. The new "history of the book" grew from critiques mounted in four other disciplines: history of technology, analytical bibliography, literary criticism, and literacy studies. These streams of critique all found fault with a kind of ahistorical scientism that had arisen in these fields in the mid-twentieth century. Critics from these disciplines shared an abiding interest in written and printed texts. They now argued, in somewhat different ways, that texts could be understood only within the material and cultural contexts in which they were produced, distributed, and, perhaps most importantly, read.

By the 1960s the history of technology as it related to the history of books had dramatically split between narrow, descriptive studies of printing machinery and sweeping speculative pronouncements on media technology and society, the latter represented most vividly in the work of Harold Innis and Marshall McLuhan. Though French historians began the effort to set the study of printing technology more deeply into historical context, in America the work of Elizabeth Eisenstein was crucial.[13] Beginning in the 1960s, Eisenstein launched a historical test of McLuhan-style technological determinism. At the heart of her work lay an argument that the new technology of printing in the fifteenth and sixteenth centuries revolutionized how texts (scientific works, especially) were used. In an early report on her research, Eisenstein wrote in 1969:

> The advent of printing completely transformed the conditions under which texts were produced, distributed and consumed. It changed the way the contents of books were arranged, illustrated and presented. It arrested textual corruption, fixed texts more permanently, and enabled them to accumulate at an accelerated rate. It made possible new forms of cross-cultural interchange and systematic large-scale data collection. It extended the reach of authors through time and through space, introduced eponymous authorship and subverted traditional forms of collective authority (p. 24).

Subsequent historians of books and printing have discounted Eisenstein's most dramatic causal claims, arguing that printing technology was not an exogenous force but was influential only in cultural context. Book historians today stress the instability and mutability of even printed texts, which in turn suggests how historically contingent the technology of printing (perhaps all technology) has been.[14] Printing technology now seems to have had much less of a direct, independent effect on how texts were used by people in the past. Though Eisenstein paid much more attention to texts than did McLuhan or Innis, one of her chief critics, Adrian Johns, argues that she did not pay enough attention to actual books and the histories of their production, form, distribution, and use.[15] Journalism historians pay even less. Except for Barnhurst and Nerone's *The Form of News*, there is almost no exploration of the relationship between printing technology and how the texts of journalism were used. From time to time, journalism historians have paid some attention to the text-shaping power of another technology: the telegraph.[16]

The second stream of critique that helped to launch the new book history came in the field of analytical bibliography. In the mid-twentieth century, in an effort to inject scientific rigor into their field, some bibliographers had sought to limit bibliographical analysis strictly to measurable physical forms, not the elusive cultural meanings, of the objects they studied. This version of analytical bibliography, a strained variant of semiotic study, understood the physical features of a book to be "significant in the order and manner of their shapes but indifferent in symbolic meaning".[17] In order to sidestep the ambiguities, the messiness, of history, these scientific bibliographers declared "historical bibliography" (i.e. bibliography set into historical context) not bibliography at all. But a new generation of critics, coming of age in an era of cultural anthropology and social constructionism, rejected this rarefied analytical bibliography as ahistorical scientism. "Far from accepting that 'historical bibliography is not, properly speaking, bibliography at all,' it is tempting to claim, now, that all bibliography, properly speaking, is historical bibliography," declared Don F. McKenzie, in a now-famous series of lectures in 1985.[18] McKenzie argued that the *text*, not merely the object or the physical marks on paper or parchment, was the proper subject of bibliography—the text rooted in cultural context. "The principle I wish to suggest as basic is simply this," he said: "Bibliography is the discipline that studies texts as recorded forms, and the processes of their transmission, including their production and reception" (p. 4). Bibliography, then, should be understood as the "sociology of texts." According to McKenzie, "any history of the book which excluded study of the social, economic, and political motivations of publishing, the reasons why texts were written and read as they were, why they were rewritten and redesigned, or allowed to die, would degenerate into a feebly degressive book list and never rise to a readable history" (p. 5). For McKenzie and his colleagues, the history of the book was nothing less than the study of "the text in history" (p. 66).

Like the field of analytical bibliography, literary criticism also passed through an era of ahistorical scientism into a new era of historical contextualization, and in the process contributed another foundation stone to the new history of the book. Always fond of jargon and labels, literary critics gave names (often in capital letters) to these two eras: the New Criticism and the New Historicism. In the postwar era, some literary critics, allied with analytical bibliographers and editors of canonical literary editions, sought to objectify the texts they studied—that is, to limit literary analysis to the authenticated text alone, the words on the page, with no regard for the intent of the author, the physical form of the book, or the effect on the reader.[19] This was the New Criticism, a movement to transform the study of literature into an objective, empirical science. The New Historicism, which sought to root the text into historical context, emerged in the 1970s in reaction against the ahistorical formalism of the New Criticism.[20] Like critics in analytical bibliography, New Historicists such as Sacvan Bercovitch, Stephen Greenblatt, and Jerome McGann argued that literary texts did not exist as formal objects out of time and place but were necessarily constructed and understood in historical context. They insisted upon the "historicity of texts," a phrase used by Louis Montrose. "By the *historicity of texts*," he wrote, "I mean to suggest the cultural specificity, the social embedment, of all modes of writing—not only the texts that critics study but also the texts in which we study them".[21]

While many new historicist critics focused on the material forms of publication (books, magazines, etc.) one group of refugees from the New Criticism—reader-response critics—paid attention to how texts were used by readers.[22] One of the founders of reader-response criticism, Stanley Fish, argued that literature resides not in the text but in the reader—that is, a work of literature has meaning only in the reading of it. He wrote that "the objectivity of the text is an illusion, and moreover, a dangerous illusion, because it is so physically convincing".[23] For Fish and other reader-response critics, texts were "written" by their readers. These readings (writings?) were not random or idiosyncratic, however, because they were fashioned by interpretive strategies that were shared, more or less, by "interpretive communities." For Fish, "meanings are not extracted but made and made not by encoded forms but by interpretive strategies that call forms into being" (pp. 171–73). Such a model, as Fish understood from the beginning, is "radically historical" (p. 49).

The fourth stream of critique arose in another field concerned with reading and readers: literacy studies. By the 1960s the study of literacy, long the province of social-science research in education and international development, had been taken up by social historians. Proponents of the "new social history," these historians borrowed social science theory and methods to reconstruct patterns and trends of literacy in the past. In America, historians such as Kenneth Lockridge and Harvey Graff analyzed representative samples of historical documents (e.g. wills, deeds, and estate inventories) to estimate literacy rates and to correlate literacy with social variables such as religion and class.[24] By the 1970s, however, as the new social history was superseded by a new cultural history, some historians began to situate the act of reading more squarely into historical place and time. Dissatisfied with abstract generalizations about the incidence of literacy—that is, who could read and when—they asked what people read, why they read, how they read, how they learned to read, what their reading meant to them, and what role reading played in their lives.[25]

Three key figures in the transformation of the social history of literacy into a cultural history of reading were Robert Darnton and David Hall in the United States and Roger Chartier in France.[26] Like reader-response critics, they stressed the cultural embeddedness of reading. As Darnton succinctly put it, "reading has a history" (p. 187). That is, reading is a social practice that differs across time and place. "Both familiar and foreign, it is an activity that we share with our ancestors yet one that never can be the same as what they experienced" (p. 155). In his work on popular religion in early America, Hall found that the history of books and reading "forced a recognition of culture not as something uniform or imposed from above but ... fractured, local, and charged with oppositions" (p. 5). Both Darnton and Hall drew inspiration from Roger Chartier, who drew inspiration from Don McKenzie. Echoing McKenzie's mantra that "forms produce meaning," Chartier wrote in 1994 that readers and hearers, in point of fact, are never confronted with abstract or ideal texts detached from all materiality; they manipulate or perceive objects and forms whose structures and modalities govern their reading (or their hearing). ... We must keep in mind that reading is always a practice embodied in acts, spaces, and habits. (p. 3)

The history of books, therefore, must embrace the history of reading, and the history of reading must embrace the history of books, for "to read is always to read something" (p. 5).

For American scholars, it was Robert Darnton who wove these four strands of critique into a useful model for the study of the history of the book. In a 1982 essay titled "What is the History of Books?" Darnton surveyed the emerging field of book history and organized it into the shape of a "communications circuit," with key moments in the life of a book represented, from author to printer to bookseller to reader. He defined book history in a way that could have come out of the new journalism history: "the social and cultural history of communication by print." The purpose of book history, he said, "is to understand how ideas were transmitted through print and how exposure to the printed word affected the thought and behavior of mankind during the last five hundred years".[27] But in its attention to the "word," Darnton's formulation does not sound quite like journalism history. In his "communications circuit" model, Darnton was able to link themes and concepts from the histories of technology, bibliography, literature, and literacy because in each the *text* remained central. It is the text that shapes and is shaped, influences and is influenced. The communications circuit is the framework, the network; it is the text that moves within it.

III

Even a quick survey of a handful of recent articles suggests the patterns of similarity and difference that mark the fields of journalism history and the history of the book. I sampled ten articles in *Journalism History* (the Spring and Summer 2006 issues), eight in *American Journalism* (the Winter and Summer 2006 issues), and eleven in *Book History* (the 2006 annual issue). (See the Articles in the Appendix.) In some articles, the pre-1970s traditions live on. Three of the eighteen journalism history articles, for example, are narrowly framed biographies of individual journalists. None of the eleven book history articles are pure biographies, but most are very narrowly framed, and two deal with authors who were favorites of the old literary history: Mark Twain and Daniel Defoe. Perhaps the most striking similarity, though, is the tendency of scholars in both fields to focus on people and publications outside the older mainstream histories. The journalism historians write about topics ranging from obscure African-American weeklies to magazine articles on menopause. Indeed, ten of the eighteen articles are about women, African-Americans, or both. The book historians' topics range from a college yearbook to the politics of class and gender in Canadian pulp fiction. Clearly, both fields were influenced by the rise of social history in the 1970s and 1980s, with its attention to women, racial minorities, and other marginalized outsiders ignored by older historiography. Both fields now seem thoroughly embedded in the new cultural history, especially the history of popular culture.

But the differences are obvious and intriguing. Even when scholars deal with traditional canonical publications in their fields—the perennial subjects—they understand them in different ways. Famous mainstream publications dot the pages of *Journalism History* and *American Journalism*: *Life* magazine, *McClure's*, *Ladies' Home Journal*, the *New Yorker*, *Harper's Weekly*, the *Wall Street Journal*, the *Washington Post*, and Horace Greeley's *New York Tribune*. These publications are mined for content, but it is the magazine or newspaper itself that is the recognizable subject. In *Book History*, the canon under scrutiny is the content, the specific text. The articles on Defoe and Twain are not about Defoe and Twain but are about *Robinson Crusoe*, *Tom Sawyer*, and *Huckleberry Finn*. Specifically, they are about how those well-known texts were altered over time and how those alterations affected their use. The Defoe article describes how the original three volumes of Crusoe's adventures were variously abridged, combined, and repackaged in scores of editions across the centuries in ways that shaped how they were read. The Twain article is about *Tom Sawyer* and *Huckleberry Finn* in French translation and about how publishers packaged those translations for adult or youth audiences. In other words, the journalism historians tend to explore a variety of content within *canonical media*, while the book historians follow the *canonical text* as it travels across a variety of media platforms.

These patterns of difference in how scholars handle content and media appear throughout the sample of articles in *Journalism History*, *American Journalism*, and *Book History*. The journalism historians and the book historians both assume a connection between the printed word and the people who used it in particular historical contexts; this assumption is what makes them cultural history, rather than old-fashioned antiquarian publishing history. But in their handling of the printed word the journalism historians pay more attention to professional practice and to the organizational side of media institutions, while the book historians focus more on the forms and formats of printed material and the contexts of their use.

Of the eighteen articles in my sample from *American Journalism* and *Journalism History*, more than half deal in one way or another with the professional practice of journalists. The three pure biographies, for example, describe how individual journalists learned their trade and did their work. All four articles on African–American journalism focus on particular newspapers, ranging from local weeklies in Portland and Houston to the national *Chicago Defender* and the Garveyite organ, *Negro World*. In every case, the authors draw on the content of the newspapers to explore styles of professional

practice and the "booster" role of these forms of community-oriented journalism. Other articles deal with the development of particular genres of journalistic writing that still prevail today, including business reporting, popular
magazine "success stories," newspaper women's pages, and literary journalism.
In contrast, none of the eleven articles in *Book History* is directly about what I
would call professional practice, except for one article that is, interestingly,
about journalism. Other than the journalism article, the *Book History* article
that comes closest is perhaps the one on Canadian pulp fiction, which is a
study of publishers' business strategies as well as of genre. None of the articles
in *Book History* is about authorship as a professional practice or even
authorship in the traditional literary-history sense of creative genius. All of the
articles flow from a key insight of the new history of the book: that authors
may write texts, but they do not write books. The making of books is a collective
enterprise; it is the mediation of texts.

In seven of the eleven *Book History* articles, the mediation process involves
the physical form of publication: illustration, typography, binding, glossing,
abridgement, combination, arrangement, translation, and so on. Some of these
physical attributes of book construction fall under the rubric "paratext," an
important concept in the new book history. Sarah Covington's article,
"Paratextual Strategies in Thieleman van Braght's *Martyrs' Mirror*," is a good
example. *Martyrs' Mirror*, first published in 1660, is a Dutch compendium of
stories about the persecution of Anabaptists. The article follows *Martyrs'
Mirror* from its compilation from earlier collections of stories through its
transformation in later editions into a magnificent two-volume folio set, with
1,364 pages, 104 elaborate illustrations, several prefaces, indices, and countless
markers, subheadings, and marginal glosses. "With such abundance,"
Covington writes, "authorship itself receded, to be joined, or perhaps diluted,
by the contributions of the illustrator and later editors and publishers who
transformed the work into what was already a profoundly collective enterprise, and one that was as much materially assertive as it was spiritually so"
(p. 2). Several other articles describe the material forms of commercial books,
while two articles explore paratextual aspects of amateur publishing efforts.
Bernadette Lear writes about college yearbooks in the context of printing and
engraving technologies of the Gilded Age. Emily Oswald explores the publication of a small Christmas gift book by a photography club at a school for
black children in Virginia in 1899.

For book historians, the study of the physical forms of books (and other
publications) leads directly to the study of their *use*. Of the eleven *Book
History* articles, seven deal in one way or another with how books were used.
This is not to say that the authors provide much evidence of reading itself—
that is, evidence of readers making meaning. In fact, they don't. Only three of
the eleven articles include any direct evidence of reader response. But others
explore what might be called contexts of use. It is pretty clear, for example,
what role *Martyrs' Mirror* played in Anabaptist communities—and still plays.

Even today American Mennonites display some of the original copperplates in a traveling museum exhibit. The article on the selection, arrangement, and display of books in a royal library in the early eighteenth century is not about the actual reading of books but about the role of books in one reader's life. It is about the mind of a bibliophile who was a significant figure in the history of book collecting. The article by David Miall, one of the few literary scholars who does experimental studies of reading, is a plea for more attention to cognitive and evolutionary psychology in research on "real readers," including those readers who long ago passed into the realm of history. The journalism historians, in contrast, pay almost no attention to actual readers; most of the articles in *Journalism History* and *American Journalism* simply assume that media messages had an impact on audiences.

The different approaches of journalism historians and book historians may be seen vividly in a comparison of two articles that sit side-by-side in the 2006 volume of *Book History*. The articles are "Reporting for Duty: The Bohemian Brigade, the Civil War, and the Social Construction of the Reporter," by Andie Tucher, and "Anonymity, Authorship, and Recirculation: A Civil War Episode," by Ellen Gruber Garvey. The fact that Tucher's article appears in *Book History* suggests the desire of the editors to bring journalism history into the big tent of book history. But it's a different animal. Though Tucher and Garvey both write about newspapers during the American Civil War, their perspectives could scarcely be more different. Tucher is interested in the Civil War as a maelstrom in which newspaper reporters began to shape journalism into a profession. This "Bohemian brigade" wrote about the war, of course, but also about their own shared experiences and shared understanding of the reporter's role. "Journalists were, in other words, beginning to think of and present themselves as a class apart—as professionals," Tucher writes (p. 132). She brings the concept of "interpretive communities" into her analysis but cites Thomas Haskell, the historian of professionalization, rather than Stanley Fish, the reader-response critic (pp. 147 and 156). And readers do not appear in "Reporting for Duty." In contrast, Ellen Garvey is interested in the Civil War as a site for the study of how ordinary people used printed materials to cope with private grief. She traces the publication histories of two sentimental poems written in the voice of a dying soldier. These poems were reprinted in newspapers everywhere, North and South, in various altered forms, with anonymous or misattributed authorship. How these poems circulated and recirculated through the press, she writes, "tells much about how anonymity allowed publishers and readers to participate in, or even take over, some of the functions that authorship with a name attached to it occupies" (p. 160). In the second half of the article, Garvey describes how one grieving father used newspaper clippings of the poems in scrapbooks that he compiled in memory of his beloved son, Nat, killed in battle in 1863.

Though Garvey cites Michel Foucault in her discussion of authorship, her article is not especially theoretical. Nor is Tucher's. Tucher refers more often to historians of the professions than to sociologists of professionalization. Indeed, few of the authors of articles in my sample—both journalism history and book history—pay any attention to theory, whether sociological theory, media theory, or literary theory. These pieces are relentlessly empirical—properly so, in my opinion. On the rare occasions when they do venture into theory, they are, yet again, very different. In the *Journalism History* and *American Journalism* articles, the only thing that might be called theory is the concept of "framing," a favorite in media studies. On framing, two articles cite Gaye Tuchman; another cites Todd Gitlin. Two articles also cite works on research methodology, such as "discourse analysis." The *Book History* articles have an entirely different roster of theorists. If the authors need a sociologist, it's Pierre Bourdieu, not Todd Gitlin. Or they cite literary theorists: Foucault, Jerome McGann, Terry Eagleton, or Jonathan Culler. But most articles cite no theorists at all. Across both fields the authors mainly cite their own colleagues. The preferred journalism historians include James Carey, Michael Schudson, and old-timers such as Frank Luther Mott and John Tebbel. The book historians cite Meredith McGill, Lawrence Buell, Roger Chartier, Robert Darnton, Jonathan Rose, David Hall, *et al*. Save for Tucher's article, there are no overlaps in citations between the articles in *Journalism History* and *American Journalism* and the articles in *Book History*.

IV

So, what do these differences mean for the practice of history in these two fields? Does it matter that, despite their ecumenism, journalism history and book history still go their separate ways? Should we be concerned that the journalism professor Andie Tucher writes about newspapers and the Civil War in a way that is utterly different from the way the English professor Ellen Garvey writes about newspapers and the Civil War? My short answer is "no." Each of those articles is an excellent study in its own way; each contributes to the history of print culture in America. Still, something might be gained from a little more sharing or at least a little more recognition by each side of what the other guys are doing.

To summarize, what both fields have done well is contextualize and historicize the study of publishing and print. In that they are similar. The best literature of journalism history has long since moved beyond house histories of newspapers and biographies of famous editors and publishers. Journalism historians have followed the advice of that early volume of criticism, *Mass Media and the National Experience*. Especially in their attention to women and minorities, they have rediscovered the "common ground between the history of mass communications and the history of the country".[28] Book historians have also continued the drumbeat of historicism. Technology, bibliography, and literature no longer float free from history. Texts live in context. One of the most thoughtful practitioners of book history, Adrian Johns, put it well: "Books need to be seen as embedded in history through and through—not just in their creation and distribution but in their use".[29]

For book history, that final word in Johns' sentence is the key: "use." The new book history has taken seriously the advice of Roger Chartier, who has for more than twenty years been stressing the "close-knit relationship among three poles: the text itself, the object that conveys the text, and the act that grasps it".[30] The act that grasps the text, of course, is *reading*. And some of the most interesting work in book history has been in the history of readers and reading. From Carlo Ginzburg's) study of the mental world of a sixteenth-century Italian miller to Janice Radway's ethnography of late-twentieth-century American romance readers, the elusive reader has been a central figure in the history of the book.[31] For book historians, the author "recedes"—as Sarah Covington put it—and the reader comes to the fore. This is the signal contribution of the new history of the book.

In journalism history there was no need to banish the author because journalistic authorship has always receded from view. Only a few journalists, especially those who were also well-known literary writers, have ever been treated the way canonical authors were treated in traditional literary history. For the most part journalism historians have always viewed the production of texts as a collective, often anonymous, enterprise. That is why the medium—the business firm or organization—has usually been the recognizable subject. One of the projects of the new journalism history has been the recovery of the role of authorship in the form of professional practices, habits, and conventions. Andie Tucher's article in *Book History* is an example of the history of journalistic "authorship" understood as professional identity, community, and method. Several of the pieces in *American Journalism* and *Journalism History* take the same tack. In this effort, Tucher is consciously heeding the plea of James Carey for a cultural history of journalism.[32] In her article the culture in question is the culture of reporters. Hers is a cultural history of the institution of journalism—of "the report," as Carey put it (pp. 4–5). My sense is that when Carey called for a cultural history of journalism he did indeed have in mind communities of reporters and the kind of history that his protégé Andie Tucher is now doing. But Carey also hinted that what he called the "history of consciousness" in journalism must also involve its use by readers—though he did not specifically mention readers or the history of reader response.[33] Unlike historians of the book, historians of journalism have not moved very far into the history of readership. A few who have include Thomas Leonard, Ronald and Mary Zboray, David Henkin, and me.[34] For the most part, the signal contribution of the new journalism history has been, not the study of readers, but the study of the professional practice of journalists and the cultural institution of journalism.

If book history is strong on the form of printed texts and their use by readers and journalism history is strong on institutions and professional practice, what would a history look like that blended the two? It might look like the new library history that has been promoted for many years by Wayne Wiegand, Jonathan Rose, and others.[35] Library historiography has long been similar to the historiography of journalism. Scholars have focused mainly on the *institution*, the library, rather than on the texts contained in the library or the people who read them. Because library history, like journalism history, has been conducted mainly by professors in professional schools, they have always paid close attention to professional practice. Again like journalism history, library history in the 1970s became more critical, more contextualized, and more attuned to broader trends in social history.[36] But the subject remained the library and the librarian, not the books and the readers. This is changing, as library historians seek to ally their field more closely to the history of the book. As Wiegand put it in a plea to his colleagues, library scholars need "to concentrate much more attention on how people use (and have used) the texts libraries provide (and have provided) them." And they need "to understand historically not just the user in the library but also the library in the life of the user".[37]

Though Wiegand is still prodding his colleagues to do more reader-response research, in fact library historians have done a better job than journalism historians of integrating the history of their institution and their profession with the history of texts and their use by ordinary people. A now-classic American effort to construct a combined history of print-culture institutions, including libraries, with a history of readers and reading is William Gilmore's *Reading Becomes a Necessity of Life*.[38] A splendid recent example of what Wiegand has in mind is Christine Pawley's *Reading on the Middle Border* (2001), which explores the entire range of the "culture of print" in an Iowa town in the late nineteenth century.[39] Pawley's study is very institutional—there's the workplace, family, church, school, voluntary association, and library—but throughout the book, readers and reading hold center stage. Might such a book be written about the readers and the reading of journalism? Yes. In fact, Pawley provides more than just a suggestive template; she provides an actual example. Chapter 6 of *Reading on the Middle Border* is about yet another institution that was a key site of "interaction between print and daily life" in one small town: the newspaper. If a library historian can write a history of newspapers and their readers, journalism historians can do so as well.

Appendix

Articles

Journalism History, 32 (Spring 2006):

Sheila Webb, "The Tale of Advancement: *Life* Magazine's Construction of the Modern American Success Story."

Marilyn Greenwald, "'A Pen as Sharp as a stiletto' Cleveland Amory as Critic and Cctivist."

Gregory Borchard, "From Pink Lemonade to Salt River: Horace Greeley's Utopia and the Death of the Whig Party."

Brian Carroll, "Early Twentieth-century Heroes: Coverage of Negro League Baseball in the *Pittsburgh Courier* and the *Chicago Defender*."

Kimberly Wilmot, "The Penney-Missouri Awards: Honoring the Best in Women's News."

Journalism History, 32 (Summer 2006)

Andrew L. Yarrow, "The Big Postwar Story: Abundance and the Rise of Economic Journalism."

Harlen Makemson, "Beat the Press: How Leading Political Cartoonists Framed Protests at the 1968 Democratic Party Convention."

Jinx Coleman Broussard, "Exhortation to Action: The Writings of Amy Jacques Garvey, Journalist and Black Nationalist."

Martin Kuhn, "Drawing Civil War Soldiers: Volunteers and the Draft in *Harper's Weekly* and *Frank Leslie's Illustrated Newspaper*, 1861–64."

Julian Williams, "The Truth Shall Make you Free: The *Mississippi Free Press*, 1961–63."

American Journalism, 23 (Winter 2006)

Kimberley Mangun, "The (Oregon) *Advocate*: Boosting the Race and Portland, Too."

Ann Thorne, "Developing a Personal Style: Janet Flanner's Literary Journalism."

Marlene Cimons, "Menopause: Milestone or Misery? A Look at Media Messages to our Mothers and Grandmothers."

James Landers, "Island Empire: Discourse on U.S. Imperialism in *Century, Cosmopolitan, McClure's*—1893–1900."

American Journalism, 23 (Summer 2006)

Michael S. Sweeney, "Harvey O'Higgins and 'The Daily German Lie.'"

Laura Richardson Walton, "In Their Own Backyard: Local Press Coverage of the Chaney, Goodman, and Schwerner Murders."

Jane Marcellus, "These Working Wives: Representation of the 'Two-job' Woman Between the World Wars."

Mary M. Cronin, "C.F. Richardson and the Houston *Informer*'s Fight for Racial Equality in the 1920s."

Book History, 9 (2006)

Sarah Covington, "Paratextual Strategies in Thieleman van Braght's *Martyrs' Mirror*."

Emma Jay, "Queen Caroline's Library and its European Contexts."

Jeff Loveland, "Unifying Knowledge and Dividing Disciplines: The Development of Treatises in the *Encyclopaedia Britannica*."

Melissa Free, "Un-erasing *Crusoe: Farther Adventures* in the Nineteenth Century."

Andie Tucher, "Reporting for Duty: The Bohemian Brigade, the Civil War, and the Social Construction of the Reporter."

Ellen Gruber Garvey, "Anonymity, Authorship, and Recirculation: A Civil War Episode."

Bernadette A. Lear, "Book History in *Scarlet Letters*: The Beginning and Growth of a College Yearbook during the Gilded Age."

Emily Oswald, "Imagining Race: Illustrating the Poems of Paul Laurence Dunbar."

Ronald Jenn, "From American Frontier to European Borders: Publishing French Translations of Mark Twain's Novels *Tom Sawyer* and *Huckleberry Finn* (1884–1963)."

Michelle Denise Smith, "Soup Cans and Love Slaves: National Politics and Cultural Authority in the Editing and Authorship of Canadian Pulp Magazines."

David S. Miall, "Empirical Approaches to Studying Literary Readers: The State of the Discipline."

Notes

1 Stephen Greenblatt, "The Word of God in the Age of Mechanical Reproduction," in Stephen Greenblatt, *Renaissance Self-Fashioning: From More to Shakespeare* (Chicago, IL: University of Chicago Press, 1980), 74–114.

2 Jane Chapman, *Comparative Media History* (Cambridge: Polity Press, 2005); David Finkelstein and Alistair McCleery, *An Introduction to Book History* (New York: Routledge, 2005).

3 Don F. McKenzie, *Bibliography and the Sociology of Texts: The Panizzi Lectures: 1985* (London: British Library, 1986); Roger Chartier, *Forms and Meanings: Texts, Performances, and Audiences from Codex to Computer* (Philadelphia, PA: University of Pennsylvania Press, 1995); Roger Chartier, "Crossing Borders in Early Modern Europe: Sociology of Texts and Literature," *Book History* 8 (2005): 37–50; Robert Darnton, "What is the History of Books?" *Daedalus* 111 (1982): 65–83; Robert Darnton, "An Early Information Society: News and the Media in Eighteenth-century Paris," *American Historical Review* 105 (2000): 1–35; David D. Hall, *Worlds of Wonder, Days of Judgment: Popular Religious Belief in Early New England* (New York: Knopf, 1989).

4 Quoted in Finkelstein and McCleery, *Introduction to Book History*, 11.

5 James W. Carey, "The Problem of Journalism History," *Journalism History* 1 (1974): 3–5

6 Ronald T. Farrar and John D. Stevens, eds, *Mass Media and the National Experience: Essays in Communications History* (New York: Harper & Row, 1971).

7 Garth S. Jowett, "Toward a History of Communication," *Journalism History* 2 (1975): 34–37.

8 See Joseph McKerns, "The Limits of Progressive Journalism History," *Journalism History* 4 (1977): 88–92; John D. Stevens and Hazel Dicken-Garcia, *Communication History* (Beverly Hills, CA: Sage, 1980).

9 Carey, "The Problem of Journalism History."

10 John E. Erickson, "One Approach to the Cultural History of Reporting," *Journalism History* 2 (1975): 40–41, 43; Marion Marzolf, "Operationalizing Carey—An Approach to the Cultural History of Journalism," *Journalism History* 2 (1975): 42–43; Richard A. Schwarzlose, "First Things First: A Proposal," *Journalism History* 2 (1975): 38–39.

11 David Paul Nord, "James Carey and Journalism History: A Remembrance," *Journalism History* 32 (2006): 122–27; Barbie Zelizer, *Taking Journalism Seriously: News and the Academy* (Thousand Oaks, CA: Sage, 2004).

12 Paul Starr, *The Creation of the Media: Political Origins of Modern Mass Communications* (New York: Basic Books, 2004).
13 Lucien Febvre and Henri-Jean Martin, *L'Apparition du Livre* (Paris: Albin Michel, 1958. An English edition was published in 1976); Elizabeth L. Eisenstein, "The Advent of Printing and the Problem of the Renaissance," *Past and Present* 45 (1969): 19–89; Elizabeth L. Eisenstein, *The Printing Press as an Agent of Change: Communications and Cultural Transformation in Early-modern Europe*, 2 vols (Cambridge: Cambridge University Press, 1979).
14 Adrian Johns, *The Nature of the Book: Print and Knowledge in the Making* (Chicago, IL: University of Chicago Press, 1998); Daniel R. Headrick, *When Information Came of Age: Technologies of Knowledge in the Age of Reason and Revolution* (Oxford: Oxford University Press, 2000).
15 Adrian Johns, "How to Acknowledge a Revolution," *American Historical Review* 107 (2002): 106–25.
16 Kevin G. Barnhurst and John J. Nerone, *The Form of News: A History* (New York: Guilford Press, 2001); Donald L. Shaw, "Technology: Freedom for What?" in Farrar and Stevens, eds, *Mass Media and the National Experience* (New York: Harper & Row, 1971); Daniel J. Czitrom, *Media and the American Mind: From Morse to McLuhan* (Chapel Hill, NC: University of North Carolina Press, 1982); Menahem Blondheim, *News Over the Wires: The Telegraph and the Flow of Public Information in America, 1844–1897* (Cambridge, MA: Harvard University Press, 1994).
17 Fredson Bowers, *Bibliography and Textual Criticism* (Oxford: Clarendon Press, 1964).
18 McKenzie, *Bibliography and the Sociology of Texts*, 3.
19 William Wimsatt, Jr. and Monroe Beardsley, *The Verbal Icon: Studies in the Meaning of Poetry* (Lexington, KY: University of Kentucky Press, 1954).
20 Harold A. Veeser, ed., *The New Historicism* (New York: Routledge, 1989); Jeffrey N. Cox and Larry J. Reynolds, eds, *New Historical Literary Study: Essays on Reproducing Texts, Representing History* (Princeton, NJ: Princeton University Press, 1993).
21 Louis Montrose, "Professing the Renaissance: The Poetics and Politics of Culture," in Veeser, ed., *New Historicism*, 15–36.
22 Jane P. Tompkins, ed., *Reader-response Criticism: From Formalism to Post-structuralism* (Baltimore, MD: Johns Hopkins University Press, 1980).
23 Stanley Fish, *Is There a Text in This Class? The Authority of Interpretive Communities* (Cambridge, MA: Harvard University Press, 1980), 43.
24 Kenneth A. Lockridge, *Literacy in Colonial New England: An Enquiry into the Social Context of Literacy in the Early Modern West* (New York: W.W. Norton, 1974); Harvey J. Graff, *The Literacy Myth: Literacy and Social Structure in the Nineteenth-century City* (New York: Academic Press, 1979).
25 Hall, *Worlds of Wonder*; Richard D. Brown, *Knowledge Is Power: The Diffusion of Information in Early America, 1700–1865* (New York: Oxford University Press, 1989); Cathy N. Davidson, ed., *Reading in America: Literature and Social History* (Baltimore, MD: Johns Hopkins University Press, 1989); E. Jennifer Monaghan, *Learning to Read and Write in Colonial America* (Amherst, MA: University of Massachusetts Press, 2005).
26 Robert Darnton, *The Kiss of Lamourette: Reflections in Cultural History* (New York: W.W. Norton, 1990); David D. Hall, *Cultures of Print: Essays in the History of the Book* (Amherst, MA: University of Massachusetts Press, 1996); Roger Chartier, *The Order of Books: Readers, Authors, and Libraries in Europe Between the Fourteenth and Eighteenth Centuries* (Stanford, CA: Stanford University Press, 1994); Roger Chartier, "Texts, Printing, Readings," in Lynn Hunt, ed., *The New Cultural History* (Berkeley, CA: University of California Press, 1989), 154–75.

27 Darnton, "What Is the History of Books?," 65.
28 Farrar and Stevens, eds, *Mass Media and the National Experience*, 3.
29 Johns, "How to Acknowledge a Revolution," 116.
30 Chartier, "Texts, Printing, Readings," 161.
31 Carlo Ginzberg, *The Cheese and the Worms: The Cosmos of a Sixteenth-century Miller* (Baltimore, MD: Johns Hopkins University Press, 1980. First published in Italian in 1976); Janice Radway, *Reading the Romance: Women, Patriarchy, and Popular Literature* (Chapel Hill, NC: University of North Carolina Press, 1984).
32 Carey, "The Problem of Journalism History."
33 Nord, "James Carey and Journalism History;" David Paul Nord, "The Practice of Historical Research," in Guido H. Stempel III, David H. Weaver, and G. Cleveland Wilhoit, eds, *Mass Communication Research and Theory* (Boston, MA: Allyn & Bacon, 2003), 362–85.
34 Thomas C. Leonard, *News for All: America's Coming of Age with the Press* (New York: Oxford University Press, 1995); Ronald J. Zboray and Mary Saracino Zboray, *Everyday Ideas: Socio-literary Experience in Antebellum New England* (Knoxville, TN: University of Tennessee Press, 2006); Ronald J. Zboray and Mary Saracino Zboray, "Political News and Female readership in Antebellum Boston and its Region," *Journalism History* 22 (1996): 2–14; David Paul Nord, *Communities of Journalism: A History of American Newspapers and their Readers* (Urbana, IL: University of Illinois Press, 2001). David Henkin, *City Reading: Written Words and Public Spaces in Antebellum New York* (New York: Columbia University Press, 1998).
35 Wayne A. Wiegand, "To Reposition a Research Agenda: What American Studies Can Teach the LIS Community about the Library in the Life of the User," *Library Quarterly* 73 (2003): 369–82; Jonathan Rose, "Alternative Futures for Library History," *Libraries & Culture* 38 (2003): 50–60; Jon A. Aho and Donald G. Davis, Jr., "Advancing the Scholarship of Library History: The Role of the *Journal of Library History* and *Libraries & Culture*," *Libraries & Culture* 35 (2000): 173–91.
36 Michael H. Harris, "The Purpose of the American Public Library: A Revisionist Interpretation of History," *Library Journal* 98 (1973): 2509–14; Edward A. Goedeken, "Assessing What We Wrote: A Review of the *Libraries & Culture* Literature Reviews, 1967–2002," *Libraries & Culture* 40 (2005): 251–66.
37 Wayne A. Wiegand, "American Library History Literature, 1947–97: Theoretical Perspectives?" *Libraries & Culture* 35 (2000): 4–34.
38 William J. Gilmore, *Reading Becomes a Necessity of Life: Material and Cultural Life in Rural New England* (Knoxville, TN: University of Tennessee Press, 1989).
39 Christine Pawley, *Reading on the Middle Border: The Culture of Print in Late Nineteenth-century Osage, Iowa* (Amherst, MA: University of Massachusetts Press, 2001).

Chapter 11

Public spheres, imagined communities, and the underdeveloped historical understanding of journalism

Michael Schudson

From the viewpoint of most historians of the United States today, journalism is not a subject of great importance, nor has it ever been. There are few history departments in the country that offer a course on the history of journalism or, more broadly, media history. I suspect that there are no country-and-period-specific courses on the media in any PhD-granting history department in the United States the way there are specific courses on, say, "Colonial Economic History" or "Intellectual History in the Gilded Age" or "Twentieth Century US Diplomatic History." The media are sources for historians more than they are topics. The history of film is taught in film departments and the history of journalism in journalism schools and the history of books and libraries in library schools. Faculty in the history departments that have the greatest influence in defining what counts as a historical problem worth investigating rarely think of journalism as a topic fit for their graduate students or themselves.

Despite some notable individual achievements I will discuss, the result is a remarkable underdevelopment of studies in the history of journalism.

What's to be done? Not very much, at least not very much from outside prestigious PhD-granting history departments. Even to have a historian of the stature of Robert Darnton use his presidential address to the American Historical Association to announce the importance of "the problem of how societies made sense of events and transmitted information about them, something that might be called the history of communication" could not, by itself, transform the teaching of history in history departments, although the power of Darnton's work on eighteenth-century French political, cultural and intellectual history has certainly brought the topic of communication into much enlarged prominence in historical studies of pre-revolutionary France. But there has been no Darnton for American history, that is, no prestigious scholar inside a leading history department who has urged the formation of a new specialty in the discipline or exemplified it in his or her own work.

In his presidential address, published as an article in the American Historical Review, Darnton makes an off-hand remark about where his understanding of communication comes from. It is not from the theorists,

Benedict Anderson and Jurgen Habermas, who write about Europe in the period of Darnton's specialization. Instead, he attributes his understanding of the field to "conversations with Robert Merton and Elihu Katz" and, following Katz, finds inspiration in the work of Gabriel Tarde. For Darnton, as for Katz and Tarde, the process of communication

> always involved discussion and sociability, so it was not simply a matter of messages transmitted down a line of diffusion to passive recipients but rather a process of assimilating and reworking information in groups – that is, the creation of collective consciousness or public opinion.

But in identifying himself with this view of communication, he adds that this is in contrast to "the more voguish theories of Jurgen Habermas." Then, in a footnote, he writes that the notion of the public sphere is "valid enough as a conceptual tool" but that followers of Habermas "make the mistake of reifying it, so that it becomes an active agent in history, an actual force that produces actual effects – including, in some cases, the French Revolution."

When I read that, I took Darnton at his word; after all, we're all against reification! But an alert student of mine did not. She asked, doesn't Darnton himself, by the end of the article, suggest that the growing openness of literary and political communication in public places in the years before the French Revolution in fact helped bring on the Revolution? Darnton discusses at length the folk tales that were called *libelles* or *chroniques scandaleuses*. In these, "the court is always sinking deeper into depravity; the ministers are always deceiving the king; the king is always failing to fulfill his role as head of state" and so forth. The "meta-narrative that ran through the entire corpus" of these popular tales was that "politics was an endless series of variations on a single theme, decadence and despotism." The vast outpouring of these *libelles* "provided a frame for the public's perception of events during the crisis of 1787–88, which brought down the Old Regime".[1] For Darnton, "the general readers in eighteenth-century France made sense of politics by incorporating news into the narrative frames provided by the literature of libel".[2] Does this not make the claim, my student asked, that the public sphere is an actor in history?

Yes, exactly. How else to read Darnton's closing paragraph in which he affirms that the *libelles* "provided a frame for the public's perception of events during the crisis of 1787–88, which brought down the Old Regime"? How else to read the closing sentence that asserts, "the media knit themselves together in a communication system so powerful that it proved to be decisive in the collapse of the regime"?[3] There are subtleties here, to be sure. The *libelles* "framed" the public understanding; they did not storm the Bastille or pull triggers on muskets. But framing public understanding matters, and according to Darnton, matters fatefully. If popular media, oral and written, framed public understanding and public understanding influenced how individuals thought and acted, and if individuals acted on one another in ways that changed the course of history, then the popular media changed the course of history.

In a liberal democratic society – that is, a society with a representative government, the rule of law, and contested elections in which writers in the public press are free to criticize established power and to engage in discussion and debate on matters of public concern, journalism is often taken to be a primary institution in establishing or maintaining democracy. What matters above all else about journalism is its relationship to democracy. It is not the stock market quotations, the baseball scores, the advertisements, or even the human interest stories that in the end arouse passions and concerns about the fate of journalism. It is the role of journalism in making democratic self-government possible – or in failing to fulfill its potential to make democratic self-government possible.

And so the leading historical tales we tell about the news media concern the relationship of journalism and democracy. The most familiar of these tales is a "from slavery to freedom" story, a story of liberation, the progressive freeing of the search for truth from subservience to state power. Freed from state and party by the enterprise of advertising-supported business organizations, truth-tropic independent journalists are in inevitable tension with their profit-driven bosses, so eternal vigilance is as ever the price of liberty and truth. Drama remains in this tale, but it typically shows a general drift toward fearless truth-seeking.

A large amount of ink has been spilled by serious scholars to dispute this view of things. Many find it far too self-congratulatory and Whiggish, and point out that it ignores the ways that the marketplace exercises a censorship over free thought in many cases as forceful as that of the state. Although there are many critics of the triumphalist view, the most influential has been Habermas, who tells a tale as tragic as the Whiggish history is sunny and spirited. For Habermas, the media were indeed central to the emergence of a realm of critical and rational public discourse. But nearly as soon as this public sphere found its footing and helped to batter down the traditional world of monarchy and aristocracy, its liberatory potential was cut short by the invasive force of capital. The diversity and independence of a large variety of ideologically and politically driven publications was replaced by a commercially driven, lowest-common-denominator-seeking find-a-way-for-the-man-on-the-street-to-willingly-part-with-a-penny style of the news business. The news moguls were invariably supportive of capital, hostile to labor, and resistant to progressive political reform or change. A brief golden age was cut down in its youth, sacrificed on the altar of Mammon.

The general outline of this tale seems to me to be largely fantasy based on great exaggeration of the openness of public life in the late eighteenth century and inattention to the ways that the growth of parliamentary democracy and the expansion of the electorate in the nineteenth and early twentieth centuries expanded the range of public political expression, even in the commercial press Habermas found so stultifying.[4] The virtue of the Habermasian framework is not historical adequacy but normative reach. Habermas offers a model of public life in civil society that directs us far beyond "journalism" to the many vital institutions of public discourse and the public domain. He does not, in my judgment, go far enough. He does not recognize how much parliamentary institutions themselves become a domain of the public sphere, as much the critics of state power as the authors of it, the central stage – where there are opposition parties – of critical public discourse.

Still, Habermas and other critics of the commercialization of public life have seriously undervalued the progressive consequences of market forces. It is worth observing, as has Yuezhi Zhao, that "With the collapse of the Soviet model, this grand narrative of evolution from an authoritarian to a libertarian and finally to a social responsibility model of the press seems to have claimed world historical relevance."[5] Zhao herself is critical of this narrative in her fascinating study of the Chinese news media and she is critical of the advances of the market in China. Market reform in a formerly command economy is not, in her judgment, an unalloyed good. Even so, for her,

> State control remains the most important obstacle to democratization of communication. Indeed, if there is one single important idea that is offered by a Western liberal model it is the relative autonomy of the press. The struggle for this autonomy must be the first step toward democratizing the news media in China.[6]

Zhao's judgment that, in the sphere of information, commercialization must be judged relatively – not wholly – benign, is echoed in an important study of US politics and media in the first half of the nineteenth century by historian John Brooke. Brooke sees the 1830s in the United States as marking a fundamental "transformation of the public sphere" from "classical forum to liberal marketplace, from the freeholders' commonwealth toward universal participation." And he adds pointedly:

> The motor of this transition was the commercializing of the public sphere, to which Jurgen Habermas objected so influentially in The Structure Transformation. But commercialization had its virtues. In effect, the reading public became a free market in which editors – still gate keeping, but with lots of competition – had to sell their wares. The entire reading public became drawn into the process of assessing public affairs.[7]

This seems to me a well grounded interpretation. If we can shed the triumphalist, smug tone of Whig history, the view that the commercial-professional media that developed in the nineteenth century enhanced and enlarged the public sphere deserves reconsideration and more careful assessment. What in the information marketplace adds to and what retards the autonomy of the press, the liveliness of political discourse, the variety of viewpoints made accessible to large numbers of citizens? What protects public expression from the worst ravages of the marketplace? What is the importance of preferred stock arrangements that keep voting power in publicly traded corporations in the hands of private families (as in the case of the *New York Times* and the *Washington Post*)? What is the importance of a concentrated group of elite readers large enough to sustain a profitable elite-oriented news organization? (*The Times*, *Post*, *Wall Street Journal*, and *New Yorker* all come quickly to mind.) What importance is there in an empirically minded, fact-obsessed culture and the devotion of professional journalists to it? Or, in contrast, of a more belletristic culture of philosophical and political essays and a journalistic culture that is a part of a somewhat exclusive intellectual life? I am obviously contrasting here the stereotyped distinctions between American and French journalistic cultures, noted clearly by Tocqueville in the 1830s and still present today.[8] What should be said about the relative difficulty or ease of market entry and how this changes over time? What can be said about the role of press-friendly state intervention and its history? Historian Richard John has been emphatic in pointing to early US subsidy of the press through the post office and the preferential postal rates granted to newspapers.[9] How useful or effective have been the direct state subsidies to news organizations in northern Europe in the twentieth century in protecting or reviving a diversity of opinion available to a general public? What do we know – if anything – about the relationship between a lively marketplace of ideas in print and political participation? Brooke's research on the early nineteenth century suggests that in states and regions with the largest number of newspapers per capita, voter turnout was lower, not higher, than in regions with fewer newspapers per person.[10] Why should that have been the case? What are the various factors that contribute to a participatory, democratic public life? What, in the twentieth century and since, is the importance of a strong public broadcasting service with relative independence from the state? What does the weakness of public broadcasting in the United States mean for American public life? Or does the continued growth of National Public Radio suggest that to some degree Americans' own concept of the weakness of our public broadcasting requires some revision?

Besides Whig history and Habermasian history, there are other influential approaches to an appreciation of the place of journalism in human affairs, but the most celebrated of them offers more scenes than story, that is, a view in which a historical dimension seems to be incidental. For Benedict Anderson, the media are transmitters of and creators of "imagined community."[11] As Anderson himself observes, nearly all communities are and always have been imagined. Even Emile Durkheim's dispersed aboriginal groups are only briefly unimagined – that is, only during their brief, periodic reunions do they exist as a committee of the whole in face-to-face interaction; the rest of the time these groups' collective consciousness is a matter of memory, itself a form of imagination, and of anticipation of the next reunion, anticipation being still another form that imagination takes. To acknowledge this sharply reduces the likelihood that the concept of "imagined community" is tailor-made for societies dominated by mass media. Anderson's concept is instructive, and it has obviously been a valuable reference point for many studies, but it offers little in the way of historical orientation.

Likewise, Robert Darnton's view that historians should study "how societies made sense of events and transmitted information about them" is also surprisingly ahistorical.[12] He simply sees the social life of information as part of the dynamics of any society at any time and urges that historians attend to it as one of the features or aspects of life to be described and understood and woven into any causal explanations of events. This is fresh and appealing in its encompassing anthropological reach. Still, it offers no historical trajectory and it is perhaps of some significance that in the paper of Darnton's I have focused on here, he is at pains to deny that he has implicitly proposed a causal sequence even when, plainly, he has. The lesson Darnton wants to draw is really something of a cautionary note, reminding scholars that old forms of communication do not necessarily die when new ones appear, that new wine gets deposited in old bottles, that profound themes of how human beings understand themselves cut across both media and moments. It is not that there is nothing new under the sun, but that we are never so modern and enlightened as we imagine ourselves to be, a conclusion that these days seems all too poignantly and tragically true.

Paul Starr's account is cautionary in its own right, but without relinquishing a sense of historical motion.[13] Starr insists on a comparative framework for understanding political development and change. The unfolding of the media in America, for Starr, is a story that demonstrates how important contextual factors are to understanding media development. Starr rejects both the liberal rapture with the market and equally the gloom of the Habermasian rise-and-fall story. For him, nothing is inevitable. It all depends. It depends, according to Starr, on circumstances and particularly on political circumstances. Politics is not just what happens when you count the existing economic and social forces at a moment and award political power to whichever set of forces is largest. Politics is about what political movers are able to do with social forces and economic assets, not to mention rhetorical assets and personal capacities to connect to popular moods. For Starr, more than for the others, history actually matters – that is, the constellation of political forces at a particular moment can push social change in one direction rather than another, that when two roads diverge in a political wood, it really matters (as it does not, in the Robert Frost poem, incidentally, but that's another story) which road one chooses. Human action makes a difference. History matters. It is not just an endless recycling of folk themes or an all but inevitable crushing of the human spirit by market forces or an equally inevitable triumph of liberty over the forces of reaction and repression. Instead, history actually makes a difference.

The comparative element in Starr's work is very important. Historians have long known that Americans in the nineteenth century were newspaper readers to an extent that repeatedly astonished European visitors. One British visitor called Americans "the newspaper-reading animals." This is old news. And today it must be qualified. As Daniel Hallin and Paolo Mancini observe, three very different patterns of newspaper penetration in European and North America consolidated by the late nineteenth century and persisted until very recently – Southern Europe at the bottom, the US and UK in the middle, and Scandinavia with a veritable mania for newspapers at the top.[14] Norwegians, not Americans, are the newspaper-reading animals today. For the mid-nineteenth century United States, Starr aggregates familiar information in a way that places it dramatically before us. He notes, following Richard John, how important the post office was in the development of both American democracy and American journalism. By 1828 there were 74 post offices per 100,000 population in the United States – 17 in Great Britain and 4 in France. In 1820, when Massachusetts had 443 post offices, Quebec and other parts of what became Canada to the east had 100,000 people but only 7 post offices. One begins to get the picture: there was not simply a better postal system in the United States; it was better by an order of magnitude. A rough estimate from a late nineteenth century British writer making his best guess about the year 1840, is that total weekly newspaper circulation in the United States, with a population of 17 million, was larger than that of all of Europe, with 233 million people.[15]

That astonishing figure should stop us cold. How could this be? And how is it that there has never been a gathering of historians to discuss "The Quantity of Journalism in America: Causes and Consequences"? We know something about the causes. We can infer something about the consequences. But never, to my knowledge, have historians beyond journalism history confronted the mind-boggling significance of such numbers and their implications for understanding American character and American social structure and, if you will pardon my evoking another set of debates, American exceptionalism. Nor has this discussion taken place inside journalism history because US journalism history has been so provincial and not comparative.

There is a striking essay by Jean Chalaby published a decade ago in the *European Journal of Communication* entitled, "Journalism as an Anglo-American Invention."[16] In fact, the evidence in the paper is rather stronger that journalism is an American invention rather than an Anglo-American invention. In Chalaby's terms, journalism is a "fact-centered discursive practice." In the nineteenth century, at a time when most European journalism consisted largely of long-winded political essays aspiring to be literature or philosophy, American journalism was increasingly centered on reporting. If, before the Civil War, European visitors to these shores were stunned by the quantity of newspapers, in the decades after the Civil War, visitors were impressed by – and generally disgusted by – the odd habit in American newspapers of reporting. They were even more stunned, and distressed, to see Americans engaged in a novel practice called "interviewing." In fact, they managed to resist adopting this practice, widespread in US journalism by 1890, until Americans in Europe during World War I encouraged them to try it out themselves, the Americans frequently leading the way and being the first to interview European monarchs, prime ministers, and Cabinet officers.[17]

Journalism is not something that floated platonically above the world and that each country copied down, shaping it to its own national grammar. It is something that – as we know it today – Americans had a major hand in inventing (broadcast journalism, I would say, as it is known around the world today, was in fact an Anglo-American invention and one that the British in fact had the larger role in establishing). It's not a very appropriate time in the world today to be touting the special achievements of American civilization, but it is a time to be attentive to what is distinctive, for better and for worse, about the character of this country and the institutions which it has developed. Historians are in a better position to do this – particularly those with a comparative field of vision – than anybody else, but in the study of journalism, we have scarcely begun.

It is not enough to identify American journalism with a commercial profit-driven business model. The quantity of American journalism was enormous in 1840 even when its producers were small businessmen in print shops scattered across a country where, as Tocqueville remarked, "scarcely a hamlet lacks its newspaper".[18] These were not swashbuckling capitalists. When Tocqueville visited America in 1831, the sharply commercial-minded penny papers had not yet appeared in the seaboard cities and country weeklies still dominated the nation's journalism (although the hour of the urban dailies was just moments away). Nor does the distinctiveness of the US press lie only with a professionalism centered on objectivity. Before it ever aspired to "objectivity," US journalists developed a habit of factuality, routines of reporting, and an intensely competitive spirit to learn "the news" before their rivals did. Before American journalism professionalized, it became socially aggressive, democratic, and populist in the voices it included. There are many questions unanswered, even unasked. If only history departments showed the slightest interest in recognizing journalism as an institution of some importance, worth more than casual and superficial asides, we would have more to work with. But I see no forces among historians likely to change this; serious history of journalism is going to have to come from schools of communication and schools of journalism where news as a human activity linked to democracy and the quality of public life is taken seriously.

Notes

1 Robert Darnton, "An Early Information Society: News and the Media in Eighteenth-Century Paris," *American Historical Review* 105 (2000): 1–35.
2 Darnton, "An Early Information Society," 34.
3 Darnton, "An Early Information Society," 35.

4 Jurgen Habermas, *The Structural Transformation of the Public Sphere* (Cambridge, MA: MIT Press, 1992).
5 Yuezhi Zhao, *Media, Market, and Democracy in China* (Urbana, IL: University of Illinois Press, 1998), 8.
6 Zhao, *Media, Market, and Democracy in China*, 9.
7 John L. Brooke, "To be 'Read by the Whole People': Press, Party, and Public Sphere in the United States, 1789–1840," *Proceedings of the American Antiquarian Society* 110 (2002): 41–110.
8 Alexis de Tocqueville, *Democracy in America* (New York: Penguin Books, 2003), 214.
9 Richard John, *Spreading the News* (Cambridge, MA: Harvard University Press, 1995).
10 Brooke, "To be 'Read by the Whole People', " 96–105.
11 Benedict Anderson, *Imagined Communities* (London: Verso, 1983).
12 Darnton, "An Early Information Society".
13 Paul Starr, *The Creation of the Media* (New York: Basic Books, 2004).
14 Daniel C. Hallin and Paolo Mancini, *Comparing Media Systems* (New York: Cambridge University Press, 2004).
15 Starr, *The Creation of the Media*, 87, 88–89.
16 Jean Chalaby, "Journalism as an Anglo-American Invention," *European Journal of Communication* 11 (1996): 303–26.
17 Michael Schudson, *The Power of News* (Cambridge, MA: Harvard University Press, 1995).
18 Tocqueville, *Democracy in America*, 215.

Chapter 12

How to think about journalism

Looking backward, going forward

Robert W. McChesney

"The condition of American journalism in the first decade of the twenty-first century can be expressed in a single unhappy word: crisis."[1] So began a 2007 report made by a scholar ensconced in the heart of mainstream academia. Such a comment would have been far less plausible in the political mainstream only a decade earlier, and its rapid evolution to becoming the new conventional wisdom among both academics and much of the news media is little short of breathtaking. For the past quarter-century this argument was made primarily by critical analysts of the US news media, especially those from the political economy of media tradition. In the 1980s and well into the 1990s it was subject to categorical dismissal by many journalists and journalism professors, if not outright ridicule. No longer need critical scholars present piles of evidence to make even mild criticism of the status quo. Today it is those who wish to defend the commercial system as doing a superior job at generating quality journalism that must provide the hard evidence. Only a handful of true believers, often those wed materially to the system, make much of an effort to do so.

In this essay I wish to address the contours of the now-roundly accepted crisis in journalism, and suggest how we may most fruitfully consider it. There is an opportunity before us to reinvigorate journalism and, with that, democratic governance in the United States. But we need to correctly understand the source of the problem to prescribe the solutions. There are many prospective solutions before us, but some may turn out to be of limited value for journalism and, of singular importance, for democracy. Or, to put it in more stark terms, and to make clear what is at stake: without journalism we not only make viable democracy unthinkable, we open the door to a tyranny beyond most of our imaginations.[2] I argue herein that the political economy of media is uniquely positioned to provide the insights necessary for constructive action.

The place to start is by understanding what we mean by viable journalism for a democracy, what the crisis of journalism entails and what caused it. What exactly does a democratic journalism entail? I believe it must provide a rigorous accounting of people who are in power and people who wish to be in power, in both the government and corporate sector. It must have a plausible method to separate truth from lies, or at least prevent liars from getting away scot-free. And it must provide a wide range of informed opinions on the most important issues of our times – not only the issues of the day, but the major issues that loom on the horizon. These issues cannot be determined primarily by what people in power are talking about. Journalism must provide our early warning system. It is not necessary that all news media provide all these services; that would be impractical. It is necessary that the media system as a whole make such journalism a realistic expectation for the citizenry. Indeed the measure of a free press is how well a system meets these criteria. Understood in this manner, journalism requires resources, institutions, legal protection and people who work at it full-time to be successful. It may benefit from more than that, but these conditions are indispensable.

And understood this way, our current news media earn a low grade, even using a curve.

What does the crisis of journalism entail? The corruption of journalism, the decline of investigative reporting, the degeneration of political reporting and international journalism, the absurd horserace coverage of campaigns, the collapse of local journalism, the increasing prevalence of celebrity and scandal are now roundly acknowledged by all but the owners of large media firms and their hired guns. *Washington Post* editors Len Downie and Robert Kaiser wrote a critique of journalism in 2002 that was nothing short of devastating in its evaluation of how commercial pressures are destroying the profession.[3] The 2006 Report from the Project for Excellence in Journalism observes, "At many old-media companies, though not all, the decades-long battle at the top between idealists and accountants is now over. The idealists have lost." The same report gave an accounting of the state of journalism that is worth citing at length:

> Most local radio stations, our content study this year finds, offer virtually nothing in the way of reporters in the field. On local TV news, fewer and fewer stories feature correspondents, and the range of topics that get full treatment is narrowing even more to crime and accidents, plus weather, traffic and sports. On the Web, the Internet-only sites that have tried to produce original content (among them Slate and Salon) have struggled financially, while those thriving financially rely almost entirely on the work of others. Among blogs, there is little of what journalists would call reporting (our study this year finds reporting in just 5% of postings). Even in bigger newsrooms, journalists report that specialization is eroding as more reporters are recast into generalists.[4]

In February 2007, the *Washington Post* published an article on the state of international coverage in the American news media by veteran foreign correspondent Pamela Constable. She wrote:

> Instead of stepping up coverage of international affairs, American newspapers and television networks are steadily cutting back. The [Boston]

Globe, which stunned the journalism world last month by announcing that it would shut down its last three foreign bureaus, is the most recent example.

Although more than 80 percent of the public obtains most of its foreign and national news from TV, the major networks are also closing down foreign bureaus, concentrating their resources on a few big stories such as Iraq.[5]

Working journalists routinely state that few outside the newsroom truly grasp how completely commercialism has gutted journalism over the past two decades. Linda Foley, the head of the Newspaper Guild, the union for print journalists, states that the number one concern of her members, by far, is how commercial pressure is destroying their craft. In December 2006 working journalists across the nation held a national day of protest to draw attention to the corporate demolition of journalism.[6] In the 1980s journalists tended to be the strongest defenders of the status quo. That is ancient history.

So thorough is the recognition that the existing corporate system is destroying journalism, that the acclaimed scholar Michael Schudson – who has been a singular critic of political economists who made structural criticism of US news media, and who for years has argued that things are not so bad with the press – is concerned about Wall Street's negative impact on journalism. He wrote in 2007:

> While all media matter, some matter more than others, and for the sake of democracy, print still counts most, especially print that devotes resources to gathering news. Network TV matters, cable TV matters, but when it comes to original investigation and reporting, newspapers are overwhelmingly the most important media. Wall Street, whose collective devotion to an informed citizenry is nil, seems determined to eviscerate newspapers.[7]

In 2002 and 2003 the news media largely abrogated their duty by uncritically publishing administration lies and exaggerations that were instrumental in taking this nation to an unnecessary, illegal and disastrous war.[8] So indefensible was the press coverage that both the *New York Times* and *Washington Post* issued apologies. In 2007, the former *Des Moines Register* editorial page editor Gilbert Cranberg took an arguably unprecedented step of demanding a formal public inquiry into the failure of the news media in reporting the buildup to the Iraq invasion.[9] I could go on and on and discuss Britney Spears and the other salacious idiocies that have become more prevalent in the news, particularly broadcast news, but we are long past the point where one needs to pile on to make this point.

The real concern is what accounts for the present crisis. In much of conventional parlance, the crisis is due primarily to the Internet providing competition to the dominant commercial news media and draining resources from the traditional journalism. This has led to an economic downturn for broadcast news and, especially, for daily newspapers, the guts of news procurement in the United States. As the Internet takes away advertisers and readers, daily newspapers lay off journalists, board up newsrooms, and prepare to join the horse-and-buggy in the annals of American history. And the marketplace has provided no economic alternative to generate the resources for journalism as we know it on line so society loses. The market has spoken, for now at least. Technology killed the goose that laid the golden egg. To add insult to injury, in the minds of some professional journalists, for all the blather about "new media" and their empowering effect, on balance the Internet has hastened the degradation and commercialization of news values across the board.[10]

The solution, to listen to the media corporations, is to permit existing media companies to merge and combine and become effective monopolies at the local level. Governments should, in effect, ratchet up their inducements, privileges and direct and indirect subsidies to the media giants so they will have the resources to provide us with the journalism we need.[11] And we need not worry about monopoly because the Internet is providing a forum for everyone else.

The strength of this argument is that it has an element of evidence to support it. Newspaper revenues and profits are falling as its readership has flattened and is skewing older, much older. Moreover, at present, it is nowhere near profitable to transition from ink and paper to digital production and online distribution for newspapers. One study concluded "that a newspaper needs to attract two or three dozen online readers to make up for – in terms of advertising revenue – the loss of a single hard-copy reader."[12] But to stop the analysis here is misleading. Newspapers remain profitable on their operating expenses. They may not be raking in the monopolistic profits that made the balance of the business community envious for much of the twentieth century, but very few are shuttering their doors. And newspapers may well find a way to remain viable in the digital era.[13] The matter is less clear with regard to broadcast news media, which have gone even further in abandoning journalism. But the merger of broadcast news with Internet operations is advancing as well.

The weakness of the "Internet has killed the economic basis for journalism" is that the crisis in journalism emerged long before the Internet. In the 1980s and certainly by the 1990s news media were cutting back on reporters and resources. They were doing so when they were flush with money, because it was the profitable thing to do in the short term, and in the long run we will all be dead. News media were discouraging hard-hitting and expensive investigative reporting and softening their standards on trivial but commercially friendly news stories about celebrities and the like. By the early 1990s, in fact, a small but vocal group of prominent journalists were already declaring the "death of journalism." In their view, from their experiences, the corporations that dominated the US news media – and that had become fewer in number due to considerable consolidation – were running it into the ground as they sought ever greater profits.[14] The corporate mindset had little respect for the autonomy of professional journalism and was inclined to seeing the news converted into an immediately profitable undertaking first and foremost.

By then, too, before the World Wide Web, the marked decline in youth newspaper readership was evident. Some, like Ben Bagdikian, argued that if the news media stopped doing actual news ands started doing "infotainment" and "lifestyle" reporting to allegedly draw these young readers/viewers into the fold, it would ultimately fail. Hollywood would easily trump the news media in proving young people with entertainment; once the new media stopped doing original and important journalism they would have a difficult time attracting new and younger readers and viewers. And if young people were not in the practice of being regular readers or viewers of conventional news, it would be much harder to draw them in as they grew older with their media patterns well established.[15]

Put this way, the policy solution offered by the industry and its advocates – to permit increased media concentration so the handful of media giants remains flush with profits – is a nonstarter. The media giants were scrapping resources to journalism when they were swimming in profits, because there was even more money to be made by gutting the newsroom. Good journalism costs money so it is always tempting to water down the fare. Why on earth should anyone believe they are not going to continue to gut newsrooms when their profits are even harder to come by? Indeed the one clear outcome of permitting firms to establish ownership of newspapers, cable channels and broadcast stations in the same community – media company towns, if you will – is that they will eliminate competing newsrooms and have one news-room serve all outlets. With far less competition, that invariably leads to a nonchalant approach to the news and no great punishment for a continued reduction in resources for journalism over time. The sad truth is that the media firms determined long ago that doing journalism was bad for the bottom line, and that conviction is more strongly held than ever, if one looks at these firms' actions rather than listen to their rhetoric. To the extent the Bagdikians of the world made a plausible argument about the long-term wisdom of spending more on journalism in the short term, the response of the media corporations seems to have been to let some other chump test out that theory. If it works, they will join in the party. In the meantime, they will cash in their chips.

There is even a larger problem with the conventional wisdom that the crisis in journalism is due to the Internet: it rests on the assumption that all was fine with the world of American news media in the not-to-distant past. Such an assumption is bogus. Part of the problem is the misunderstanding about the origins and nature of professional journalism. The conventional explanation for the emergence of professional journalism had relied upon technology – for example, the telegraph and Associated Press making it necessary to have neutral content acceptable to a broad range of papers – or how it was in the economic interest of monopolistic publishers eager to serve the public-at-large to publish nonpartisan journalism so as not to alienate part of the market. Although these were important factors, what tended to be missing was a crucial component: the immense public dissatisfaction with the sensationalistic and decidedly conservative journalism of the times. New research, including extensive work by Ben Scott, highlighted just how significant a factor this public controversy was in pushing the emergence of professional journalism. In addition, there was a concurrent intense struggle between newspaper publishers and journalists to define professional journalism and gain control over the newsroom.[16] This struggle boiled over in the 1930s and 1940s with the organization of the newspaper Guild. I will not keep you in suspense: the journalists lost.

Understood this way, professional journalism, which emerged over the course of the first half of the twentieth century, was far from perfect. The type of professional journalism that emerged was one more conducive to the needs of media owners than to journalists or citizens. Professional journalism's capacity to keep implicit commercial values out of the news was always nebulous, as the power to hire and fire and set budgets always resided with the owners. It allowed a certain measure of autonomy and independence for journalists from commercial and political pressures – and it certainly looked to be an improvement over what it replaced – and it has a commitment to factual accuracy that is admirable and perhaps its greatest legacy. Professional journalism's core problem, and by no means its only problem, is that it devolved to rely heavily upon "official sources" as the basis of legitimate news. Official sources get to determine what professional journalists could be factually accurate about in the first place. It gets worse. When elites were in general agreement, as was often the case concerning fundamental economic and foreign policies, professional journalism spoon-fed the conventional wisdom, which was often dead wrong, and offered little protection for the citizenry. But from the Gulf of Tonkin to Operation Iraqi Freedom our finest professional journalists did spoon-feed the misleading propaganda accurately.

There are some who suggest – argue may be too strong a word for this position – that concerns about the decline of conventional journalism are greatly exaggerated because people learn about politics and the world around them through many other means than the news media. In particular, entertainment media such as The Onion and the Jon Stewart, Stephen Colbert and Bill Maher comedy shows are increasingly where young people learn about the world.[17] Ben Barber has noted that one antidote to the commercialization of society (and toothless journalism) may come from Hollywood films, which in his view have demonstrated surprising and impressive social awareness in recent years.[18] Popular music, too, often addresses social and political issues. Maybe we don't need the news after all, or its importance has been exaggerated?

The problem with this reasoning is that the social commentary of comedians, filmmakers and musicians is predicated upon a certain baseline understanding of the world which is provided by journalism. Jay Leno once
commented that he has had to "dumb down" his political humor considerably and he now sets up his jokes with elementary background information: e.g. "You know Democrat Harry Reid is the Senate majority
leader ... " Much of Stewart's and Colbert's humor is that by avoiding the
increasingly counterproductive practices of mainstream journalism they can get
directly to the truth of the matter, a truth largely obscured in the news, hence
highlighting the asininity of much of what passes for contemporary political
journalism.

No better example of this comes with the build-up to the US invasion of
Iraq in 2003. In January 2008 a comprehensive study by the nonpartisan
Center for Public Integrity determined that there were fully 935 lies – with
several hundred coming from President Bush and Vice-President Cheney – told
to the American people to generate popular support for a war in Iraq. These
were not "gray area" statements, as the CPI's detailed data base makes clear.[19]
Nor were they oversights or merely clumsy missteps. As the report concludes,
the lies "were part of an orchestrated campaign that effectively galvanized
public opinion and, in the process, led the nation to war under decidedly false
pretenses."[20] In mainstream professional journalism this has all been filed
away in the dark memory hole, to the extent it is even acknowledged. When
the same people who lied us into Iraq present fantastic and unsubstantiated
claims about how swimmingly the Iraq war is going and about why the United
States may well need to invade or destabilize a number of other nations, the
respected professional journalists takes these claims quite seriously and at face
value. Those who call the administration and its publicists liars are accused of
making "solidarity-seeking buzz phrases," and certainly not of sufficient rectitude to report the news in a professional manner.[21]

Comedians need not suspend judgment and regurgitate what those in power
say. They can simply tell the truth and let the chips fall where they may.
Sometimes merely repeating what the president or a pro-administration pundit
says verbatim can produce waves of laughter because of its absurdity. But,
again, this is not necessarily reason for celebration, and it certainly does not
solve the media problem in the United States. Ralph Nader once commented
that the finest political satire and humor he ever saw was in the old Soviet
Union. The humor was so biting and embraced because the official news media
were so deplorable. Few, if any, would argue the people of the Soviet Union
had a plausible political information system for a free society. Although it is
well and good that, unlike in the old USSR, social critics are not imprisoned or
working underground and are treated respectfully as long as they are enter-
tainers and comedians; it would be far better if the same viewpoints were not
dismissed as outside the range of legitimate debate, even lunacy, as soon as we
entered the world of journalism.

So if having viable journalism is mandatory for a self-governing society, the current crisis is at the very center of what type of world we will be living in for the coming generations. And here, as with the disastrous invasion and occupation of Iraq, the place to look for answers is not with the people who created the problem or ignored the smoke signals and pooh-poohed the critics until the status quo was up in flames. Instead, the prudent course would be to look at the critics whose analysis best explains the current crisis of journalism and whose analysis has been on the mark the longest. In short, this is where we need look to the political economy of media.

It is arguable that nowhere has the power of political economy of media been more evident than in its critique of journalism. Many of the main insights are now roundly accepted, though often without acknowledging the political implications. It has provided the foundation for understanding the present crisis in journalism and therefore it may provide keen insights into the solutions. The starting point for a political economic analysis is that structure matters. Institutions matter. They matter a great deal. The importance of structures, of institutions for shaping journalism and media content directly and indirectly is well understood when looking at other nations; it is only recently that American exceptionalism in this regard has begun to erode. It is not that owners and advertisers and managers need to directly interfere with or censor editors and journalists; it is more the case that organizational structures transmit values that are internalized by those who successfully rise to the top.

From political economy of media research there are a handful of propositions to guide understanding, scholarship and action. I discuss these in great detail in Chapter Three of *Communication Revolution*, so for our purposes I will summarize them in brief forthwith.

First, media systems are not *natural* or *inevitable;* they are the result of explicit policies and subsidies. The types of media systems societies end up with are strongly influenced by the political economy of the nation, but it is not a mechanistic or vulgar relationship. That commercial media is not a "default" system is clear from liberal democratic political theory: Free people opt for the institution of private property because they regard it as the best way to advance their values. Likewise, a free people opt for commercial media because they determine it is the best way to promote the type of press system they deem desirable. And of course, in democratic theory, a free people may decide to have a noncapitalist economy, and likewise they may decide to have a noncommercial media system.

But, to be clear, the two matters are distinct in theory and in practice. Even in capitalist societies, it is not a given that the entirety of the media or communication system will be run for profit. Capitalist societies, including the United States, have had elements, sometimes significant, of their communication systems operating outside the marketplace during their history. When telegraphy came along, or radio broadcasting nearly a century later, the United States was certainly a capitalist nation, but there were debates about whether these emerging industries should be conducted by private profit-maximizing concerns, even by people who favored capitalism otherwise. Even today, professional journalism, perhaps the defining characteristic of our free press in our media textbooks, is explicitly a public service that does not, at its best, follow the commercial logic of the companies that house it. A core principle of professional journalism is to provide a safe house for public service in the swamp of commercialism.

In short, media systems are created, even if the playing field is sloped at an ever greater angle toward dominant commercial interests.

Second, the First Amendment is not a piece of protectionist legislation meant to grant special privileges to investors in the communication sector to be exempt from government regulation.[22] It does not lock us into the status quo and render all structural media reforms unconstitutional. The oft-stated "libertarian" or neoliberal position – the idea that the Constitution requires that capitalists be the natural rulers of all media to do as they please without government interference, regardless of the nature of the content they provide – is dubious, if not bogus. The "libertarian" position holds that almost any regulation of media is unconstitutional. Media companies have consistently argued that it violates the First Amendment to, among other things, limit how many broadcast stations or cable companies a corporation can buy. Their argument rests on the assumption that media companies are just like individuals and that a good democracy must treat them like individuals.

C. Edwin Baker has done trailblazing research on the relationship of freedom of the press and freedom of speech. Baker concludes that court interpretations of the Constitution clearly see the press as a necessary institution distinct from people exercising free speech rights, and also as distinct from other commercial enterprises.[23] But in academic discourse the question is usually framed as: "Does the press get special privileges individuals do not have?"[24] It is not usually framed as: "Can the media be saddled with extra obligations that individuals do not have?" or "Can the people enact policies to create a press that meets its constitutionally understood functions better than the existing press is doing?" Baker's theory, although supported by the evidence, is outside the mainstream of constitutional law at present, and the implications have not been addressed by the Supreme Court, but it could become important in the years to come. Baker has argued persuasively that the First Amendment permits the government to play an active role in creating media and structuring the media system.[25]

During the founding period, when freedom of the press was being discussed, often by Jefferson and Madison, there was no sense they regarded the press as an inherently market-driven institution, where the right to make profit was sacrosanct.[26] Accordingly, Jefferson and Madison were obsessed with subsidizing the distribution of newspapers through the post office and supporting newspapers through printing subsidies as well.[27] An institution this important is not something you roll the dice of the commercial marketplace on and hope you get lucky. They understood the press in a precapitalist, if not non-capitalist, sense – and primarily as a political institution.[28] Nor did Madison or Jefferson have a romanticized notion of journalism. Jefferson's correspondence from his years as president is filled with screeds against the press of his day as an agent of destruction.[29] That pushed him not to censorship, but to policies to promote a better press.[30]

Moreover, when the Supreme Court has actually pondered what freedom of the press means under the First Amendment, it has not endorsed the neoliberal model of maximum profits equal maximum public service.[31] In some of the most important cases, the opinions suggest that freedom of the press is not an individual right to do as one pleases to make money. To the contrary, freedom of the press is in the Constitution to make self-government possible. The extraordinary majority opinions in the 1945 *Associated Press v. United States*,[32] and the 1971 Pentagon Papers (*New York Times v. United States*) case[33] make that clear.[34] The spirit in several of these opinions is that the state has not only the right but the *duty* to see that a viable press system exists, for if such a media system does not exist the entire constitutional project will fail. If the existing press system is failing, it is imperative that the state create a system that will meet the constitutionally mandated requirements. At any rate, these opinions hardly suggest that the First Amendment is meant to provide a constitutional blank check to corporate media to do as they please, regardless of the implications for self-government.

At the same time, this is nothing if not a complex matter. The problem of establishing a press system, providing direct and indirect subsidies, yet preventing censorship and state domination defies a simple solution. And there may be no ideal solution, only a range of solutions where some are better than others.

Third, the American media system is largely profit-driven, but it is not a free market system. The media and communication systems in the United States have been the recipients of enormous direct and indirect subsidies, arguably as great as or greater than any other industry in our economy. When communication firms claim they work in free markets, it should provoke more howls than a Jerry Lewis film festival in France. All commercial enterprises benefit by government spending, and, hence, get indirect subsidies (roads, public health, public schools, etc.). But the subsidies provided to media and communication firms go far beyond that. One need only start with the value of the monopoly licenses that are given for free to commercial radio and TV stations or to spectrum for satellite television, or monopoly cable TV and telephone franchises. The best estimate of FCC staffers of the market value of the publicly owned spectrum today – which is given to commercial broadcasters at no charge – is around $500 billion.[35] When one considers all the wealth created on the backs of the free gift of spectrum to broadcasters since the 1920s, all the empires built upon it, the total transfer is certainly well into the hundreds of billions of dollars. Nor are the public gifts to broadcasters, cable companies and telephone companies the only subsidies, as I chronicle in *Communication Revolution.*

The term "government subsidies" tends to be held in disrepute in the United States, unlike "business investment," which is sacred, so let me be clear about this. I think subsidies can be good, and I think that in principle they are necessary. Subsidies are costs that are supposed to have benefits. It is in our interest that the extent and role of subsidies in our media system be recognized and appreciated. Copyright, for example, is a necessary evil, a "tax on knowledge," as the Founders understood it in the Constitution. It is necessary to give authors an incentive to write books, for creative people to generate content. The benefit of the massive printing and postal subsidies in the first few generations of the Republic, for example, was the establishment of an extraordinary press system and, with that, arguably the most advanced political democracy in the world. Our Founders regarded subsidies, in effect, as the price of civilization, or at least a viable republic. Many of our major communication revolutions, from the telegraph and radio to satellite communication and the Internet, were spawned as a result of massive government subsidies.

Even if one wanted a truly "free market" media system, without direct or indirect subsidies, it would be awfully difficult, if not impossible, to construct. And, ironically, to implement and maintain anything remotely close to a truly competitive market would require extensive government coordination, probably far beyond what currently exists.[36] It would never happen naturally. But the last thing the dominant commercial interests want is their subsidies removed; as far as I can tell, the "free market" think tanks are dedicated to promoting corporate domination in concentrated markets of the heavily subsidized communication system, rather than ending the heavily subsidized communication system. One need only look at how the self-proclaimed pro-free market editorial page of the *Wall Street Journal* carries water for AT&T and the big government-created telephone and cable powerhouses to see how the notion of free markets in the realm of media and telecommunication is mostly a rhetorical ploy to protect entrenched monopolistic power.[37]

This argument over subsidies leads directly to the fourth proposition: the central importance of the policymaking process in structuring a media system. The question is not whether we will have subsidies and policies, but rather, what will the subsidies and policies be, what institutions will they support, and what values will they encourage and promote? When we talk about media, what most of us are concerned with, ultimately, is the content the media system produces and what effect that has upon our lives. But the content is shaped to a significant extent by the institutional structures of media systems, which is why political economists devote so much time to studying that issue. And the institutional structures are determined by policies and subsidies, which are in turn determined by the policymaking process. So that takes us to the nucleus of the media atom.[38]

The policymaking process in the United States has grown increasingly undemocratic as media and communication have become ever more lucrative industries. The policies and subsidies are made in the public's name but without the public's informed consent. That is pretty much how communication policymaking has been conducted in the United States. Monopoly broadcast licenses, copyright extensions and tax subsidies are doled out all the time, but the public has no idea what is going on. Extremely powerful lobbyists battle it out with each other to get cushy deals from the FCC, whose members and top staffers almost inevitably move to private industry to cash in after their stint in "public service."

Above all else, the FCC has been dedicated to making the dominant firms bigger and more profitable. Congress too is under the thumb of big money. The one thing the big firms all agree upon is that it is their system and the public has no role to play in the policymaking process. And because the news media almost never cover this story in the general news, hardly anyone outside of the industry – until recently – has any idea what is going on. If anything, they are fed a plateful of free market hokum, extolling an industry that "gives the people what they want."

The empirical evidence is devastating: in the first six months of 2006 alone, communication and technology firms spent $172 million on lobbying in Washington, more than any other sector or group.[39] How serious is this lobbying army? Rep. Edward Markey of Massachusetts states that the largest communication firms each have a lobbyist assigned to *each* member of Congress on the relevant committees.[40] In January 2007, AT&T convened a meeting of its Capitol Hill lobbying army. A standing-room only audience attended in a conference room described as "the size of a stadium."[41] These firms also spend commanding amounts in candidate contributions and for public relations. When these firms do engage with the public on pressing policy matters, it is often in the form of phony "Astroturf" front groups – that is, the "fake grassroots."[42] Combine this with the extraordinarily high percentage of FCC members and top FCC officials (as well as members of Congress and congressional aides on the relevant committees) who leave the agency through the "golden revolving door" and go on to lucrative careers working for the firms and industries they were once theoretically regulating in the public interest.[43]

The fairy tale of free markets protects the corporate media system from the public review it deserves. The propositions of the political economy of media undercut the positions of communication corporations and their advocates by shining a light on the two great and indefensible blind spots upon which their arguments for the status quo are based. The first blind spot was the "immaculate conception" notion of the American media system, the idea that corporations "naturally" assumed control because it was the American way. It requires the "immaculate conception" for industry and its defenders to shift seamlessly into a righteous lather about transgressions of the state. I recall being invited on to the Milt Rosenberg program on (Tribune-owned) WGN radio in 1999 to discuss my book *Rich Media, Poor Democracy*. To provide the home team perspective, Rosenberg also invited an editor from the *Chicago*

Tribune to join us. Both the editor and Rosenberg conceded that some of my criticism of the media system was accurate, but waxed on about the evils of government censorship and how WGN had a First Amendment right to operate as it pleased. When I was asked to respond, I merely asked why WGN had been granted the monopoly license in the first place. Why not the Chicago Federation of Labor or some other commercial enterprise? Why did we assume that WGN was the rightful steward of that frequency? Initially flummoxed, both the editor and Rosenberg conceded the point and quickly moved to another topic.[44]

The second blind spot is the extent of public subsidies. Communication firms and their advocates love to wave the flag of free market economics; acknowledging the extent of their massive public subsidies blows up the free market argument. What was striking to me during my research was that the four main "free market" think tanks in Washington – the Cato Institute, Heritage Foundation, American Enterprise Institute and Progress and Freedom Foundation – which often weigh in on behalf of communication corporations and against government "interference" with free markets, did no discernible research on the extent of subsidies.[45] When the state funnels tens of billions of dollars in subsidies to the firms that often bankroll these think tanks, it is not worth noting; if pressed, they confess it is troubling and move to another topic. But when the government asks for anything in return for those subsidies, it is like the Sword of Damocles is being held over the very survival of freedom in our land.

Once the importance of the policymaking process is understood and the corruption of the process is grasped, our understanding of communication changes dramatically. Consider the term "deregulation," which is used frequently by journalists and scholars to describe the situation when big media firms look to see media ownership rules relaxed or eliminated. If we had a free market media system, this use of the term would be accurate, in the sense that market forces would play a larger role than the state in setting the terms of competition. But in telephony, broadcasting, cable or satellite communication, the term is pure propaganda. It is meant to imply a competitive market outcome, when as often as not this "deregulation" leads to far less market competition.

So political economy of media not only explains the crisis of journalism, it explains how we get the institutions that produce the crisis in journalism. Accordingly, it points the way forward: structural change, through policy reform. We have to create a system that makes it rational to produce great journalism, and the clear lesson we have is that the really existing marketplace will not do the job. It has failed. As our friends in public relations like to say, we have to go in a different direction.

The prospect of engaging in policy reform and structural change is a difficult pill to swallow for many journalists and citizens, weaned on the notion that we have a press system entirely independent of the government, and that any government involvement puts us dangerously close to a slippery slope to tyranny. Even recognizing the failures of the marketplace and the cornerstone role of government policies and subsidies in building our press system, for many observers the notion of recognizing the state's role remains anathema, and there is an almost palpable desperation to find an alternative that avoids politics. This is understandable, but a frank recognition of the government role should also make possible a careful consideration of enlightened government policies. It is simply untenable and serves only to protect entrenched corporate interests to presuppose that there are two and only two alternatives for the American people: either a corporate status quo that guts journalism or *1984*. There are innumerable other models for a press system, many arguably superior to what exists, if we only open up our minds and expand our horizons, and look to our own history.

There is more than a little irony to hear proponents of the status quo raise concerns about the dangers of state interference and censorship in our media system if measures are taken for constructive structural change. The same media corporations that raise these concerns often acquiesce to government policy – especially on military matters, where dissidence is most important. It was striking that public and community broadcasters in the United States – who receive direct government subsidies in addition to indirect subsidies through their monopoly broadcast licenses – showed more criticism of the US government during the invasion and occupation of Iraq – though at times, not much – than the "independent" commercial news media.[46] Moreover, these same firms that are so obsessed with government intrusion on the press demonstrate little concern about the expanded police state activities of the government, or, of direct pertinence, of increased government secrecy. This is true for their actual news coverage, and with their lobbying arsenals in Washington. For every lobbying dollar these firms spend to battle for open government, I suspect countless hundreds of thousands, or millions, or tens of millions, are spent to promote corporate rights to hold an ever larger number of government monopoly licenses, and to generally promote their profitability above all else. The relationship may be impossible to compute mathematically because in most cases the former number is likely to be zero.

Not that the concern with state censorship is illegitimate. Quite the contrary. Direct state censorship is unacceptable. It is imperative to have policies that protect the integrity of freedom of speech, and promote a climate that is welcoming to dissent. What political economy recognizes is that the policies, and the structures they foster, implicitly encourage certain values and discourage others, encourage certain types of content, and discourage alternatives. Enlightened policy making recognizes that and seeks to create a range of structures that can provide for the information needs of the people, and that allows for as much openness, freedom and diversity as possible. That is freedom of the press.

This does not mean that reforms that do not directly challenge the commercial system are meaningless, merely that they are insufficient on their own to get the job done. Nearly all of the seemingly non-structural solutions to the crisis in journalism are worth pursuing and have some value.

The importance of policy is particularly striking with the Internet and the digital revolution, and it is here that people often regard the Internet as some sort of magical technology unaffected by policy. As noted before, media chieftains argue that ownership restrictions are irrelevant today because the Internet has blasted open the system generating millions of new media. They are not the only ones. Critics of corporate media and capitalism sometimes join the chorus, stating that citizens can do whatever they want online, as long as they get their act together. Technology has slain the corporate media system, and the future is very much up for grabs. The blogosphere is democracy's tidal wave to overwhelm the commercial news media status quo. The King is Dead. Long Live the King.

Wouldn't our lives be easy were this true? The argument is fatally flawed: The openness of the Internet is due to policy as well as technology. Telecommunication companies and cable companies have the power to censor the Internet and work hand-in-hand with the governments that grant them monopoly license to do exactly that. We see that in nations like China where major US firms work with the Chinese authorities to create a tightly controlled web and digital communication world.[47] But it is also true in the United States, where the largest telecommunication companies worked closely with the Bush Administration to illegally spy on American citizens. In 2008, after a contentious debate, the Senate overwhelmingly approved an extension of the Foreign Intelligence Surveillance Act which included, chillingly, "retroactive immunity" for the telecommunication firms that engaged in illegal spying on Americans.[48]

This matter deserves more treatment, because for all the understandable hype about how the Internet and digital communication liberate people and revolutionize our lives, they also come at a price, the elimination of privacy as we have known it and allowing the government and corporate interests to know a great deal more about us, generally surreptitiously. The threat of state harassment is greater today than at any time in our history. For many Americans this may seem like an abstract threat, or a concern only to those engaged in crime or terrorism. Far more apparent is how marketers and commercial interests are extending and deepening their penetration of our lives through cyberspace. Back in the early 1930s, James Rorty called advertising "our master's voice," referring to corporations and the power they held in American society.[49] In his view advertising provided a pervasive propaganda for capitalism and corporate domination of society. To the extent that is true, Rorty lived in a noncommercial socialist republic in the 1930s compared to what Americans experience today.[50] These intrusions can be limited, but technology will not do the job for us. To protect privacy and freedom requires explicit policies, and a government committed to the rule of law. Unless we take proactive steps, we may come to regret the day the computer was invented.

There are additional policy issues that must be resolved successfully for the Internet to even begin to fulfill its promise for society, and for journalism. For starters, if the Internet is to provide the foundation for free speech and a free press, it has to be ubiquitous, high-speed, and inexpensive.

Our goal should be to have broadband access as a civil right for all Americans, at a nominal direct fee, much like access to water. This is not simply for political and cultural reasons, but for economic reasons as well. Already the decline of broadband speeds and penetration in the United States compared to European and Asian rivals is a factor undermining economic innovation and growth. A 2007 article in *Information Week* put the US situation in context:

> The United States currently ranks 12th in broadband adoption rates, sig-nificantly down from its ranking of fourth in 2001, according to the Organization for Economic Co-operation and Development, a 30 member-nation group committed to the development of democratic governments and market economies. The International Telecommunications Union lists the U.S. as 21st worldwide for broadband penetration rate in 2005. Point Topic shows the United States is in 20th place by number of households with broadband access and in 19th by individual broadband access. Those ranks have been falling, not rising, in recent quarters.[51]

What accounts for the US decline? The first place to look is the stranglehold of the telephone and cable giants over broadband, due to their government-granted monopoly franchises granted in the pre-Internet era. These firms have no great desire to offer a service to poor people or difficult-to-reach rural areas, and they certainly have no interest in a ubiquitous service. It is far better to have a dirt lane to scare consumers into paying more to get faster service. And because broad-band is an effective duopoly in the United States there is little market pressure to generate the speeds and lower costs that other nations are achieving. That would require enlightened regulation and planning in the public interest, something the battalions of lobbyists these firms employ are commissioned to prevent.

The relationship of the telecommunication and cable giants to the pro-gressive development of the Internet is not in doubt: it is almost nonexistent. As Representative Edward Markey, Democrat of Massachusetts and chair of the subcommittee that oversees the Internet and telecommunication matters, put it in a 2007 speech,

> AT&T was offered, in 1966, the opportunity to build the Internet. They were offered the contract to build it. But they turned it down. Now let me ask you this: what has AT&T done since then to develop the Internet? The answer is: nothing. What has Verizon done to help invent the World Wide Web? Nothing. What did they do in order to invent the browser?

Nothing. These companies did virtually nothing to develop anything that has to do with what we now know as the Internet today.[52]

What the telephone and cable companies are singularly distinguished in is lobbying; their entire business models have been built on wooing politicians and regulators for monopoly licenses and sweetheart regulations much more than serving consumers. It is the basis of their existence.[53] They hope to parlay their world-class lobbying muscle into carving out a digital gold mine in this critical juncture. The boldest effort, and where the most important fight lies, is over their efforts to effectively privatize the Internet. The telephone and cable companies want the right to control which websites and services you can have access to, and which you cannot. If the AT&Ts, Verizons, and Comcasts of the world are able to pull this off, all bets are off for the revolutionary potential of the digital revolution.

This struggle to keep the Internet open, to prevent the telephone and cable giants from controlling which websites get favored treatment is the battle to preserve Network Neutrality. The huge cable and phone companies are champing at the bit to set up a "fast track" on the Internet for their favored sites or those sites that gave them a cut of the action. Websites that refused to pay a premium would get the slow lane, and probably oblivion. The cable and telephone companies claim they need to have this monopoly power to generate sufficient profits to build out the broadband network, but the evidence for this claim is nonexistent. Jeff Chester states that

> Cable and telephone subscribers have paid for a super-fast broadband network several times over. Network Neutrality will do absolutely nothing in terms of denting returns or slowing down deployment. Look, the reason that the cable and phone companies oppose Network Neutrality is they're desperate to extend their monopoly business model from multichannel video to the broadband world.[54]

As an appalled Markey put it in 2007, "And now they say they have a right to put up the toll roads, showing up as though they should own it all."[55] Or as Columbia University law professor Tim Wu described what the phone and cable companies are trying to do:

> You know, companies can do two things, they can either offer more value, or they can try and extract cash from companies because they're in a position to threaten them. The first helps the economy, the second is just extortion. It's the Tony Soprano system, you know, it's like a protection racket, and it's not an economically productive activity.[56]

The stakes are so high much of the balance of the business community, not to mention everyone else in society, is in favor of Network Neutrality, to the extent they know it is an issue at all.[57]

The next great battleground for Net Neutrality is going to be cell phones and wireless communication. "We are about to open a new front in the Net Neutrality wars: wireless," writes Michael Calabrese of the New America Foundation. "Cellular phone and data today is a nightmare image of what the Internet would be like without Net Neutrality – and, as the world goes wireless, it may be the way of the future, unless we push back."[58] Tim Wu and Milton Mueller have launched research into this area, but much more needs to be done.[59] In many ways this is the signal free speech battle of the digital era.[60]

The future of a free press is dependent upon ubiquitous, inexpensive and super-fast Internet access as well as Network Neutrality. In 2008, for example, the *Capital Times* of Madison, Wisconsin became the first American daily newspaper to convert its operations to primarily digital production and distribution – it went from ink and paper to bits. It could do so because of an agreement with the other daily newspaper in Madison that allowed the *Capital Times* a revenue base to cover what would be obvious losses for the immediate future as it entered the digital world.[61] It did this despite concerns that many of its older and poorer readers would lose access to the paper, and recognizing the uncertainty that Net Neutrality would be maintained so the phone and cable companies won't demand a ransom for the newspaper to have access to the public. For the Internet to develop as the viable basis for a free press, ending the digital divide and stopping the corporate privatization of the Internet (and the broader realm of digital communication) are mandatory.

That being said, although necessary, protecting online privacy, establishing a ubiquitous and high-speed Internet, and maintaining Net Neutrality will not solve the crisis of journalism. Among the most important lessons we have learned in the past decade has been that doing good media, even in the digital era, requires resources and institutional support. The Internet does many things, but it does not wave a magic wand over media bank accounts. I recall a conversation I had with a prominent retired television journalist in 2004. He told me with great enthusiasm that with the Internet all of his journalistic needs were met: He could find all the reporting he needed from around the world on his computer. He went on and on about how he now read the great newspapers of the world online every morning. He compared his blissful situation with the Dark Ages B.I. (Before Internet), when access to such a range of news media would have been pretty much impossible, even for world leaders and corporate CEOs. I asked this retired journalist what the Internet informed him on doings in Schenectady, New York. He looked at me quizzically, thinking I must be from Schenectady and probably feeling some measure of sympathy for me. But, as I explained, my point was that the Internet made existing journalism available, but it was not creating lots of new journalism, and by that I mean research and reporting, not just commenting on someone else's research and reporting. And, I told him, it was not clear how existing journalism would segue to the Internet and maintain its revenue base while commercial pressures were lowering the resources going to journalism overall. In community after community, like Schenectady, there was precious little journalism, and *Le Monde* was assigning no correspondents to cover the Schenectady School Board meeting. He conceded the point.

This is not to deny the potential of the blogoshere, social networks and citizen journalists. No matter what happens, their emergence is radically changing journalism, and often for the better.[62] Even beyond the notion of citizen journalists, the digital revolution is opening up the potential of access to information that still boggles the mind, even as we approach the end of the second decade of the World Wide Web. The ability of people to collaborate and work together to share and expand knowledge – exemplified by wikis – is revolutionary, in the literal meaning of the word.[63] But the need for paid journalists who work fulltime, have resources, generate expertise, and have institutional support to protect them from governmental or corporate harassment remains as strong as ever. And having competing newsrooms of such journalists is just as important. Citizen journalism and, social information networks, will flower in a marriage with enhanced professional journalism, not as a replacement for it.

So we cannot sit by and expect the Internet or the marketplace to solve the crisis. In fact, the crisis is so severe, and the stakes are so high, even if we could win the policy fights for more journalism education, more media literacy, more student media, more local commercial media, more foundation support, digital privacy, and ubiquitous inexpensive super-fast Internet access with Net Neutrality, that would be helpful but insufficient to accomplish the task at hand. There is no magic policy bullet to solve the problem, no single policy to pursue to correct the situation. There are three layers of policy solutions, moving from those just mentioned, to the more radical. And, as we will see, even those are insufficient, or, perhaps better put, cannot be won without a broader movement for social reform.

The second layer of policies are those that more aggressively shape the news media system and that are legitimate within the range of policy debates in the United States. These include antitrust and communication laws to promote diverse media ownership as well as using postal subsidies to encourage a broad range of publications. The single most valuable of these may be the tradition of establishing nonprofit and noncommercial broadcast media, specifically public and community broadcasting, and public access television channels. In other nations public and community broadcasters have been a stalwart of quality independent journalism, and buffers against commercial degeneration.

There are two areas where public and community broadcasters cum media can play a central role: First, in the provision of local journalism. The commercial broadcasting system has degraded, if not abandoned, this aspect of its operations. If our public and community broadcasters had BBC-type funding, which would translate into some $20 billion annually, there could be multiple competing public newsrooms, with different organization structures, in scores of communities. That may provide a competitive spur to the commercial news media to get back in the game, especially as they see there is an interest in the material. Yes, I know, people will say $20 billion is a lot of money, and will require massive tax hikes to be justified and nobody will be willing to go for that. But spending that sort of money is small potatoes and hardly subject to debate when Wall Street howls about a crisis or there is a Third World country to invade on the other side of the globe. No one asks where the money is going to come from then; apparently it is a matter of small concern. It is all a matter of priorities. And even with far less than $20 billion, public and community media could do wonders for the currently decimated local news media landscape.

Second, one concern generally under-discussed is how the Internet allows Americans to construct a personalized media world where they share common experiences with fewer and fewer of their fellow citizens. As Cass Sunstein argues, this "Daily Me" that people construct on the web makes them share far less with each other than in the past, especially with people they might disagree with on matters of politics or culture. This may be a form of "freedom" for the individual, but it exacts what may be a very high social cost. What follows is a "group polarization," as people grow less informed, less respectful and more distrustful with people outside their own group. There is a withering of the experiences that provide the bonds that make us understand that we are all in this together. Sunstein concludes that this produces a "real problem for democracy."[64] In addition, this "group polarization" is strongly egged on by the desire or need of marketers to split Americans up into bite-sized demographic groups so it is easier to sell them things. As Sunstein's analysis implies, journalism is at the center of what Americans need to share if we are going to have a viable republic. The evidence is in: commercial journalism is comfortable serving the demographic groups that are most profitable for the owners and desirable to advertisers, and disregarding less lucrative parts of the population.[65] It is public broadcasting cum media that is in the best position to provide the basis for a common shared journalism to which all Americans can relate. Public and community media cannot do this by themselves, nor should they, but they can provide a necessary and valuable foundation.

Even if we win great victories on this second layer of policy measures, I do not think it would be sufficient. I think we need to go to a third and more radical layer, and begin to rethink the structures and organizations of news media in a fundamental way. We need to acknowledge the limitations of the options available in the first two layers of policies, and expand and enhance our options. We need to consider policies to encourage local ownership, employee ownership, and/or community ownership of daily newspapers, knowing that newspapers will be largely digital within a generation and, hence, indistinguishable from other media forms. What we are talking about is the social production of journalism. We need to seek guidance from the experiences of other nations and from our own history. As noted above, what is striking when one studies the real history of freedom of the press in the United States, what the political economy of media teaches us, is that the Founders did not regard the First Amendment as authorizing media to be a source of profits above all else. Jefferson and Madison, in particular, promoted a series of extraordinary subsidies – in particular, printing and postal – to spawn a far more vibrant print culture than would have existed had the matter been left to the market. The understood self-government would be impossible without a vibrant press, and the government had a duty to assure such a free press existed. We need to go back to their spirit and attack the problem with an open mind.

In short, it is imperative that we conduct research on alternative policies and structures that can generate journalism and quality media content. The process has begun. More than a decade ago, Dean Baker was arguing for a $100 tax credit that a taxpayer could donate to any nonprofit news medium of her choice. This would spawn a potentially multi-billion dollar subsidy of a non-profit media sector with no government role in selecting the recipients of the money. The idea seemed fanciful then; today it is enlightened. Already, people like Orville Schell, former dean of the University of California – Berkeley School of Journalism, and Geneva Overholser, former editor of the *Des Moines Register* and now director of the School of Journalism at the University of Southern California's Annenberg School for Communication, are putting their minds to this project.[66] Charles Lewis, the legendary founder of the Center for Public Integrity, makes a powerful case for a substantial non-profit sector to be responsible for journalism.[67] The *Columbia Journalism Review*, the flagship for professional journalism, devotes sympathetic features to the issue of establishing policies and government subsidies that might better produce journalism than the commercial system.[68] This would have been unthinkable a decade ago. What was once considered "radical" is now fair game for the some of the more established members of the journalistic profession.[69] We know we are in uncharted waters when, in 2006, the heir to the Chandler newspaper fortune acknowledges the failure of the system that made him fabulously wealthy and calls for community ownership of newspapers.[70]

So this is how the political economy of media diagnoses the crisis of journalism, and how it points the way forward. At this point an occasional response is, understandably, "wait a second, what about the audience, the public? Are they not responsible for this mess? If they really had an interest in the type of journalism you propose as necessary for self-government, wouldn't commercial media be certain to give it to them?" The logic is powerful. The traditional rejoinder from journalists is that journalism is not supposed to be determined by market values, but that is has an innate social duty regardless of how much public interest there might be in the material. Political economists like me like to point out that the public's lack of interest in conventional news may be due to the fact that conventional news is so fruitless. It is the supply-side factors – far lower costs and lack of controversy with powerful political and commercial interests – that pushed the news to celebrity and scandals and natural disasters and regurgitating political spin, not public demand. But once exposed to a steady diet of crap the public has not been able to develop a taste for great journalism, and the market provides less of it as a result. It is understandable people would lose interest in journalism; so there is a downward spiral. Sometimes, flustered, I have barked out that this approach of assigning responsibility for the deplorable state of journalism on the public is tantamount to "blaming the victim." Clearly, I argued, we need to look at the system.

But this response, by journalists or by political economists, and, in occasional fits, by me, is insufficient and inadequate. The criticism concerning the audience is correct at a fundamental level, and if political economy of media stops its analysis of journalism at this point its value is understandably questioned. If ours were a politicized society, where people were engaged with politics as a matter of fundamental importance, even life and death, the sort of drivel that passes for journalism today would be impossible, even in a commercial system. The cause of depoliticization runs deeper than the news media. Our lousy journalism may reinforce depoliticization, but it does not cause it. There is something more profound here. By this logic, changing media alone would not *ipso facto* produce a highly politically engaged democracy. In fact, media reform in isolation from other reforms, if such a prospect were even plausible, probably could only be partially successful.

Far from being a repudiation of political economy of media, this criticism in fact completes political economy of media and its analysis of journalism. There are two sides to the political economy of media coin. On one side, the side upon which this chapter has concentrated, we examine the firms, owners, labor practices, market structures, policies, occupational codes, and subsidies that in combination provide the context for the production of journalism and media. The other side of the political economy coin, however, looks at how journalism as a whole, the media system as a whole, interacts with broad social and economic relations in society. Does the media system tend to challenge or reinforce broader trends within society? It is here that we find the source of depoliticization, and this is a staple insight of political economy and critical theory, drawing from Mills, Marcuse, and Macpherson among others.[71] In short, in a society with significant social and economic inequality, depoliticization is encouraged by those who atop the social structure, especially in democratic societies. Looked at from the perspective of those at the bottom, the further down the social pecking order one goes, depoliticization is a more rational response by a person because it is a frank acknowledgment of how much power an individual actually has. Why waste time learning about a political world you have no influence over? It is only a form of self-torture.[72] The political economy of media has always been about the task of enhancing participatory democracy; media and communication systems are a means to an end, with the end being social justice and human happiness. We need satis-factory journalism and media systems to have a just and sustainable society. We study media so closely, because in a democratic society journalism is the primary means through which the mass of people may effectively equip them-selves to effectively participate. It is a central political battlefield. But media are far from the only variable, as important as they are.

Understood in this manner, political economy of media offers two addi-tional observations about how to think about journalism. The first goes to journalists and those who aspire to be journalists. It is often written, and accurately, that democracy requires journalism. It is not an exaggeration that our entire constitutional system is predicated on there being an informed and engaged citizenry, and the press system is charged with the task of making that possible. That is the point of the most eloquent opinions on freedom of the press by Hugo Black and Potter Stewart. But the converse is every bit as true and even more important: journalism needs democracy. Journalism is not agnostic about whether a society is fascist or authoritarian or democratic. Its survival as a cred-ible entity depends upon their being democracy. If a society is formally demo-cratic, with rampant inequality and vast demoralization and depoliticization, journalism as defined at the outset of this chapter will be especially con-tentious and difficult to conduct, and the news will tend to gravitate toward propaganda. Journalism is committed to ending information inequality and therefore has a stake in seeing the lessening of social inequality. Journalism requires a society committed to openness, the rule of law and justice to prosper. Journalism opposes corruption and secrecy and attacks on civil liberties and therefore has a stake in lessening militarism, as Madison and Lincoln both under-stood militarism: a powerful force that unchecked leads inevitably to corruption, inequality, secrecy, attacks on civil liberties, and the end of the republic.[73]

Some of our greatest journalists, from George Seldes and Haywood Broun and I.F. Stone to Bill Moyers and Amy Goodman and Charles Lewis have understood the importance of democracy for journalism. This did not make them less professional, less concerned with fairness or factual accuracy. This did not make them treat one political party with kid gloves and another party with a guillotine. It did not justify a double standard. It only gave them a much stronger sense of mission and of what is at stake. They saw and see journalism as representing the interests of all those outside of power, those without a voice, those who desperately need journalism to effectively govern their lives in a contest with those who own and dominate the country and see journalism often as a nuisance, and who are none too excited about the pro-spect of an informed population.

The second observation applies to journalists and everyone else. The battle to reform media and to establish the basis for the journalism a free society requires cannot be fought in isolation. It is necessarily part of closely related political movements to make our electoral system and voting systems and political campaigns more fair and open. It is part of broader social and political movements for justice, to democratize the institutions of our society and draw people into the heart of public life. It is only in the context of people coming together to struggle for social change that depoliticization is vanquished and victory becomes plausible, even inevitable. Media reform is necessary to make such democratic politics possible and such democratic politics must enjoy a measure of success for media reform to make any genuine advances. Journalism depends upon media reform; media reform and broader movements for social justice rise and fall together.

Notes

1 William Powers, "Hamlet's Blackberry: Why Paper is Eternal," Discussion Paper Series, Joan Shorenstein Center on the Press, Politics and Public Policy, Harvard University, 2007, 1.

2 See Naomi Wolf, *The End of America: Letter of Warning to a Young Patriot* (White River Junction, VT: Chelsea Green, 2007); Joe Conason, *It Can Happen Here: The Authoritarian Peril in the Age of Bush* (New York: St. Martin's Press, 2007).

3 Leonard Downie Jr. and Robert G. Kaiser, *The News About the News: American Journalism in Peril* (New York: Alfred A. Knopf, 2002). See also: Eugene Roberts, Thomas Kinkel and Charles Layton, eds, *Leaving Readers Behind: The Age of Corporate Newspapering* (Fayetteville, AR: The University of Arkansas Press, 2001).

4 The report details the hard decline in the number of reporters actually covering communities over the past two decades as well as the domination of commercial values of the public interest in the determination of news. See Project for Excellence in Journalism, "State of the Media 2006: An Annual Report on American Journalism." At: www.stateofthenewsmedia.org/2006/index.asp.

5 Paula Constable, "Demise of the Foreign Correspondent," *Washington Post*, February 18, 2007, p. B1. www.washingtonpost.com/wp-dyn/content/article/2007/02/16/AR2007021601713_pf.html

6 Go to http://www.savejournalism.org/

7 Michael Schudson, "Owning Up: A New Book Stops Short of Deepening the Discourse on Media Concentration," *Columbia Journalism Review* (January–February 2007): 58. See also Michael Schudson, *The Sociology of News* (New York: W. W. Norton, 2003), 38, 40.

8 Several authors have assessed the news coverage of the Iraq invasion and occupation. My analysis can be found in John Nichols and Robert W. McChesney, *Tragedy and Farce: How American Media Sell Wars, Spin Elections and Destroy Democracy* (New York: The New Press, 2005).

9 Gilbert Cranberg, "Cranberg Wants a Serious Probe of Why the Press Failed in Its Pre-war Reporting," *Nieman Watchdog*, February 7, 2007. www.niemanwatchdog.org/index.cfm?fuseaction = ask_this.view&askthisid = 00261

10 Neil Henry, *American Carnival: Journalism under Siege in an Age of New Media* (Berkeley, CA: University of California Press, 2007).

11 This argument in defense of allowing greater media concentration has a loud proponent in FCC Chair Kevin Martin. See Kevin J. Martin, "The Daily Show," *The New York Times*, November 13, 2007.

12 See Thomas E. Patterson, preparer, *Creative Destruction: An Exploratory Look at News on the Internet* (Cambridge, MA: Joan Shorenstein Center on the Press, Politics and Public Policy, Harvard University, August 2007), 13.

13 See Jennifer Saba, "The New Math: Putting Numbers to Work for You," *Editor & Publisher* (January 2008): 22–24.

14 John H. McManus, *Market-Driven Journalism: Let the Citizen Beware?* (Thousand Oaks, CA: Sage, 1994); Penn Kimball, *Downsizing The News: Network Cutbacks in the Nation's Capital* (Washington, DC: Woodrow Wilson Center, 1994); James D. Squires, *Read All About It! The Corporate Takeover of America's Newspapers* (New York: Random House, 1995); Doug Underwood, *When MBAs Rule the Newsroom: How Marketers and Managers are Reshaping Today's Media* (New York: Columbia University Press, 1993).

15 For a recent discussion of this issue by an ex-journalist, see David Simon, "Does the News Matter to Anyone Anymore?" *The Washington Post*, 22 January 2008.

16 This is research that Ben Scott has been doing at the University of Illinois, and is the basis of his dissertation: Ben Scott, "Labor's New Deal for Journalism: The Newspaper Guild in the 1930s" (Urbana, IL: University of Illinois, 2007).

17 See Theodore Hamm, *Gloves Off: How the New Blue Media Is Reshaping Progressive Politics* (New York: The New Press, 2008).

18 See Benjamin R. Barber, *Consumed* (New York: W.W. Norton, 2007).

19 Go to www.publicintegrity.org. See also: John H. Cushman, Jr., "Web Site Assembles U.S. Prewar Claims," *The New York Times*, 23 January 2008, A12.

20 See also, Danny Schechter, "New Study Claims Mistruths Shaped Rush to War," Common Dreams website, January 24, 2008.

21 See Carlin Romano, "Big Fish and Small Fry," *Columbia Journalism Review* (January-February 2008): 50.

22 This is the text of the First Amendment: "Congress shall make no law respecting an establishment of religion, or prohibiting the free exercise thereof; or abridging the freedom of speech, or of the press; or the right of the people peaceably to assemble, and to petition the government for a redress of grievances."

23 C. Edwin Baker, "The Independent Significance of the Press Clause Under Existing Law," Presentation to the Reclaiming the First Amendment: Constitutional Theories of Media Reform conference, Hofstra University, Hempstead, New York, January 19, 2007.

24 A classic example is Potter Stewart, "Or of the Press," 26 *Hastings Law Journal* 631 (1975).

25 Whenever I write about freedom of the press issues and the Constitution I find myself invoking the name Ed Baker, because his work provides the foundation on which I stand. It is ironic that a law professor is doing so much cutting edge communication research. His latest book is another example of his enormous talent: C. Edwin Baker, *Media Concentration and Democracy: Why Ownership Matters* (New York: Cambridge University Press, 2006).

26 In what follows do not mistake my position on the Founders and Madison and Jefferson. They are not deities. Although I find their writings on freedom of the press enlightened and extraordinary, they were complex figures and far from perfect, even if viewed from the vantage point of their own historical period. I discuss the anti-democratic aspects of Madison's thought in *Rich Media, Poor Democracy*. A recent talk by my colleague Pedro Cabán delved into the racism and white supremacy of the Founders. Pedro Cabán, Comments for the February 9, 2007 Forum, "Disempowering Racial Oppression, Discontinuing Chief Illiniwek and Other Forms of Racial 'Entertainment,'" University of Illinois at Urbana-Champaign, February 9, 2007.

27 I discuss this at some length in Robert W. McChesney, *The Problem of the Media* (New York: Monthly Review Press, 2004), ch. 1.

28 As Mark Lloyd makes clear in *Prologue to a Farce*, the nature of capitalism in the United States in the founding period through much of the nineteenth century was

quite unlike what we think of as capitalism today. For starters, the majority of people were neither employers nor employees. They were self-employed farmers, trades people, mechanics, etc. And corporations barely existed. In this environment, the idea that private media were regarded as large profit-generating corporate entities was non-existent and would be for a good century. American history from this period is filled with ringing denunciations of the emerging corporate sector from leading figures, both on economic and political grounds. As Lloyd demonstrates, Lincoln made a series of criticisms of corporations, and even capitalism, which were not entirely dissimilar to what Karl Marx was writing at the same time in England. See Mark Lloyd, *Prologue to a Farce: Democracy and Communication in America* (Urbana, IL: University of Illinois Press, 2007), 60–61, 294.

29 See, for example: Eric Burns, *Infamous Scribblers: The Founding Fathers and the Rowdy Beginnings of American Journalism* (New York: Public Affairs, 2006).

30 For some sense of the crucial role of the press in the development of participatory democracy in the United States, see Sean Wilentz, *The Rise of American Democracy: Jefferson to Lincoln* (New York: W. W. Norton, 2005).

31 My point in this discussion is not to reify the Constitution. It is not a flawless document. See Sanford Levinson, *Our Undemocratic Constitution: Where the Constitution Goes Wrong (And How We the People Can Correct It)* (New York: Oxford University Press, 2006); Bruce Ackerman, *The Failure of the Founding Fathers: Jefferson, Madison, and the Rise of Presidential Democracy* (Cambridge: Belknap Press of Harvard University Press, 2005).

32 *Associated Press v. United States*, 326 U.S. 1 (1945) http://caselaw.lp.findlaw.com/ scripts/getcase.pl?court = US&vol = 326&invol = 1

33 *New York Times Co. v. United States*, 403 U.S. 713 (1971) www.law.cornell.edu/ supct/html/historics/USSC_CR_0403_0713_ZC.html

34 *New York Times Co. v. United States*, 403 U.S. 713 (1971) www.law.cornell.edu/ supct/html/historics/USSC_CR_0403_0713_ZC3.html

35 This figure is derived by the staff of Commissioner Michael Copps in consultation with various experts and based upon evaluating the amounts raised during recent spectrum auctions. See "Remarks of Commissioner Michael J. Copps," National Conference on Media Reform, Memphis Tennessee, January 12, 2007.

36 For a detailed investigation of this "irony" of deregulation, see Robert Britt Horwitz, *The Irony of Regulatory Reform: The Deregulation of American Telecommunications* (New York: Oxford University Press, 1989).

37 See, for a recent example, "Net Discrimination," *The Wall Street Journal*, 2 January 2007, A22.

38 Sandra Braman has extended this argument, contending that the nature of the modern state has been transformed in the past few decades from a bureaucratic, welfare state to an "information state," with information policymaking at its heart. Her argument will be a subject of debate and study in the field in the coming years. See Sandra Braman, *Change of State: Information, Policy, Power* (Cambridge: MIT Press, 2006).

39 Amy Schatz, "Industry Braces for Net-Neutrality Fallout," *Wall Street Journal*, 2 January 2007, A3.

40 Comments of Edward Markey, National Conference on Media reform, Memphis, Tennessee, January 13, 2007.

41 Kate Ackley, "AT&T Takes Shape as Lobbying Giant," *Roll Call*, February 20, 2007.

42 See Common Cause, *Wolves in Sheep's Clothing: Telecom Industry Front Groups and Astroturf* (Washington, DC: Common Cause, 2006). www.commoncause.org/ site/pp.asp?c = dkLNK1MQIwG&b = 1499059

43 See Jeff Chester, *Digital Destiny: New Media and the Future of Democracy* (New York: The New Press, 2007).

44 Viewed this way the framing of debates around media looking exclusively or primarily at "media concentration" is wide of the mark, at times even a red herring. Even if concentration in a media sector is not increasing, or may even be in decline, that does not mean all is well in the world. Media concentration tends to be a bad thing, but it is far from the only thing that matters in media. To the "immaculate conception" crowd, once it is shown that concentration is not growing at dramatic rates, the conclusion is invariably that the system works just fine, thank you, and critics should shut up and shop. The real issue is why do we create and subsidize media systems built around profit-maximization and advertising in the manner that we do. I am reminded of the Chinese student dissidents in the late 1980s when they protested the meetings of Chinese government leaders with elected heads-of-state. "Who elected you?" they would chant. That is the question to be asked about the WGNs and AT&Ts in our world: "Who elected you?"

45 I approached the top telecommunication or media researchers at each of the four "free market" think tanks in 2007 asking if they could help me determine the size of the subsidy in a number of specific areas. I thought this might be an area of interest because these think tanks tended to be so adamantly opposed to government subsidies and welfare that they might be interested in determining the extent of such practices. I received gracious and thoughtful replies in three cases; in each response, I was informed that this was an area they knew nothing about and they knew no one who was working on the subject. The other think tank did not respond, and on none of the websites did I find any research remotely close to this topic. It is worth noting that some economists raised concerns about the "rents" AT&T received as a result of its monopoly status back in the 1960s and 1970s. The point then was more to open up the telecommunications market to other firms than to consider what the public might rightfully demand in exchange for those rents.

46 See chapter 4, and Robert W. McChesney, *The Problem of the Media* (New York: Monthly Review Press, 2004).

47 Due to government polices, the Internet in China is very different from the Internet elsewhere. See "Alternative Reality," *The Economist*, 2 February 2008, 69–70.

48 "Spies, Lies and FISA," *The New York Times*, 14 October 2007.

49 James Rorty, *Our Master's Voice: Advertising* (New York: John Day, 1934).

50 And not just Americans. Digital technology has converted China into a nation filled with video screens pummeling people with advertising. See Frederik Balfour, "Catching the Eye of China's Elite," *Business Week*, 11 February 2008, 55–56.

51 Richard Hoffman, "When It Comes to Broadband, U.S. Plays Follow the Leader," *Information Week*, 15 February 2007. www.informationweek.com/story/showArticl e.jhtml?articleID = 197006038. This piece draws from: S. Derek Turner, *Broadband Reality Check II: The Truth Behind Americas Digital Decline* (Free Press, September 2006). Available at www.freepress.net/docs/bbrc2-final.pdf

52 Comments of Edward Markey, National Conference on Media Reform, Memphis, Tennessee, January 13, 2007.

53 For a discussion of how AT&T came to dominate the South through dubious political influence, not providing good service in the market, see: Kenneth Lipartito, *The Bell System and Regional Business: The Telephone in the South, 1877–1920* (Baltimore, MD: Johns Hopkins University Press, 1989).

54 Kent Gibbons, "Five Questions for Jeff Chester," *MultiChannel News*, 5 February 2007. www.multichannel.com/article/CA6413144.html?display = Opinion

55 Comments of Edward Markey, National Conference on Media Reform, Memphis, Tennessee, January 13, 2007.

56 Quoted in PBS Bill Moyers special, "The Net at Risk," broadcast in October 2006. www.pbs.org/moyers/moyersonamerica/print/netatrisk_transcript_print.html

57 Even a former top executive in the telecommunication and cable industries has spoken up on the crucial need to preserve Net Neutrality. See Leo Hindery, "Let Cable Companies Compete in Battle for Broadband," *Financial Times*, 18 January 2008, 9.

58 Michael Calabrese email to the author, February 9, 2007.

59 Tim Wu, "Wireless Network Neutrality," Social Science Research Network working paper, January 2007. http://papers.ssrn.com/sol3/papers.cfm?abstract_id = 962027; for Milton Mueller's work, go to: http://blog.internetgovernance.org/blog

60 Because this chapter addresses journalism specifically, I will stop the discussion here, recognizing that digital communication is radically overturning most media industries.

61 Phil Rosenthal, "Cap Times Puts Cap on Print Editions," *Chicago Tribune*, 10 February 2008.

62 See Scott Gant, *We're All Journalists Now: The Transformation of the Press and Reshaping of the Law in the Internet Age* (New York: Free Press, 2007).

63 See, for example, Cass R. Sunstein, *Infotopia: How Many Minds Produce Knowledge* (New York: Oxford University Press, 2006).

64 Cass Sunstein, "How the Rise of the Daily Me Threatens Democracy," *Financial Times*, 11 January 2008, 9.

64 See the September–October 2007 edition of *Extra!*, the publication of Fairness and Accuracy In Reporting, for a special issue on how the news media ignore the issues of concern to the poor and working class.

66 Overholser is working on developing a variety of structural policy measures. See Geneva Overholser, "On Behalf of Journalism: A Manifesto for Change," paper published by the Annenberg Public Policy Center, University of Pennsylvania, 2006. www.annenbergpublicpolicycenter.org/Overholser/20061011_JournStudy.pdf. For background, see Geneva Overholser and Kathleen Hall Jamieson, eds, *The Press* (New York: Oxford University Press, 2005).

67 Charles Lewis, "The Nonprofit Road," *Columbia Journalism Review* (September–October 2007): 32–36.

68 Bree Nordenson, "The Uncle Sam Solution," *Columbia Journalism Review* (September–October 2007): 37–41.

69 As Geneva Overholser wrote to me: "I used to feel that there was hope in addressing corporate governance. I was part of a group of former editors pressing for such measures as more retired journalists on boards, committees to audit journalism and the like. I think it's too late for that now, the crisis is too advanced. We need more sweeping reform proposals that might provide dramatic change to address the magnitude of this crisis." Geneva Overholser email to the author, February 26, 2007.

70 James Rainey, "Scion offers ideas for Times: In an opinion piece to run Sunday, Harry Chandler proposes community ownership," *Los Angeles Times*, 11 November 2006; Harry B. Chandler, "A Chandler's advice for the L.A. Times: The newspaper can only thrive if its owners and editors make drastic changes," *Los Angeles Times*, 12 November 2006.

71 See, for example, C. Wright Mills, *The Power Elite* (New York: Oxford University Press, 1956); C. B. Macpherson, *The Life and Times of Liberal Democracy* (New York: Oxford University Press, 1977).

72 This is why collective action – e.g. independent labor unions – is the foundation of mass democratic political action, and why it is despised by those who benefit by the existing division of power.

87 In November 1864, for example, as the postwar era was on the horizon, Lincoln wrote: "I see in the near future a crisis approaching that unnerves me and causes me to tremble for the safety of my country. As a result of the war, corporations have been enthroned and an era of corruption in high places will follow, and the money

power of the country will endeavor to prolong its reign by working upon the prejudices of the people until all wealth is aggregated into a few hands and the Republic is destroyed." See Mark Lloyd, *Prologue to a Farce: Democracy and Communication in America* (Urbana, IL: University of Illinois Press, 2007), 60–61, 294.

Index

Abbott, William ('Bud') 72
Abercrombie, N. and Longhurst, B. 104n6
Ackerman, Bruce 215n31
Ackley, Kate 215n41
adaptation, refinement and 3, 46
Adorno, Theodor 67
advertising and design 145
Advertising Council 128–9
Advertising the American Dream (Marchand, R.) 71
ahistorical scientism 168
Alasuutari, Perti 104n4, 104n6
Alldredge, Charles 88n28
Allen, Gracie 72, 73
Allen, Robert C. 88n15
almanacs 114
Althusser, Louis 131
Altick, R.D. 99–100, 106n43
Altschuler, G. and Blumin, S. 86–7n3
Amadae, S.M. 134n19
American Journal of Sociology 79–80
American Journalism 163, 170, 171, 173, 174, 175, 177
American Sociological Association 79–80
American Town Meeting of the Air (NBC Radio) 81–3
American Women (Kennedy Commission on Status of Women) 72
analytical bibliography 167–8
Anderson, Benedict 139, 164, 182, 185–6
Anderson, James A. 64
Angrosino, M. 105n14
anthropic principle 29
anti-suburbanism 84
Appadurai, Arjun 104n7
archeological record 22
archival accumulation 32

archival research 121, 122, 125–6, 127, 129, 131
Associated Press 138
Associated Press v. United States (1945) 199
AT&T 200, 201, 205, 206, 215n41, 216n44, 216n45, 216n53
audiences: audience-researcher interaction 131; diffusion in notions of 103–4; media history and practices of 103–4
audiences past, textual analysis as window on 66–76; 'common sense' 65, 69, 74, 76; content analysis, public opinion data and 70; context and legitimacy of textual analysis 70; contradictoriness in media texts 69, 70, 76; cultivation analysis 69; Douglas' work on 1960s female powers 71–2; empathy, value of 71; fragmented subjectivity 68; Hall's encoding/decoding model 67; incoherence in media texts 69; inference from textual sources 66; internalism, fallacy of 68, 69; intertextuality 69, 70, 74; Marchand's *Advertising the American Dream* 71; masculine authority, anxieties for exemplified in radio texts 73; mass media studies, elitist bias against 67; meaning-making of media texts 66, 68, 69, 70, 74, 75; media history, development of 67–8; media texts, consumers of 67–8; motherhood, images of 74; multiple media texts, analysis of 69; radio, studies on nostalgia for 72–3; repetition of representations 70, 76; skepticism, value of 71; sophistication of textual

history; history as communication
problem
Denning, Michael 74
Denny Jr., George 82–3, 88n22
deregulation 123, 202, 215n36
Derrida, Jacques 115
Des Moines Register 192, 210
Dewey, John 19, 35, 38, 41
Diall, Gideon 87n10
Dicken Garcia, Hazel 156n49
Dickens, Charles 98–100, 102
Dickinson, John 116–17
digitization of newspaper production
153–4
dispersed audiences 93, 94, 95–6
Disraeli, Benjamin 102
documents: authenticity of 26;
documentation and communication
21–4
Doisneau, Robert 74
Dombey and Son (Dickens, C.) 100
dotcom bubble 52
Douglas, Mary 3
Douglas, Susan J. 8, 63–5, 66–76, 91,
92, 139; work on 1960s female powers
71–2
Downie Jr., Leonard 191, 213n3
Durkheim, Emile 3, 185
Dworkin, Ronald 37

Eagleton, Terry 174
early warning, journalism as system
for 191
Ebel, E.W. 134n21
Edward Reed, E. 134n18
e-government 51, 52
Eisenstein, Elizabeth 17, 50, 111, 138,
139, 167
Eliot, George 30
Ellis, John 34n33
emotion: contagion of audiences by 79;
possession of audiences by 80
empathy, value of 71
employee ownership of media 209–10
enterprise networks 52–3
entertainment media as information
sources 195–6
Erickson, John E. 178n10
Ernst, Wolfgang 33n16
ethics: 'ethical incompletion' 122; history
as communication problem 28
ethnography 63, 64, 90–91, 95, 103, 175;
auto-ethnography 72; historical 93

European Journal of Communication
187
evidence: delivery of 26; emergence of
23–4

"family audience," construction of 92
"fan audience" 101–3
Farrar, Ronald T. 165
FCC (Federal Communications
Commission) 82, 83, 124, 199, 201,
213n11
Febvre, L. and Martin, H.-J. 179n13
Febvre, Lucien 47
The Feminist Mystique (Friedan, B.) 72
Ferry, W.H. ('Ping') 126, 134n18
Finkelstein, D. and McCleery, A. 163, 164
Fish, Stanley 12n5, 169, 173
Fisher, J.W. 102, 106n54
Flood, John L. 117n5
Foley, Linda 192
Fones-Wolf, E. 134n13
Fordism 52–3
The Form of News (Barnhurst, K.G. and
Nerone, J.) 167
Foucault, Michel 3, 125, 135n26, 173, 174
fragmented subjectivity 68
Fraisse, Genevieve 87n14
Frankenheimer, John 84
Franklin, Benjamin 115
Fredriksen, Paula 33n20
free competitive elections 36
free market media system, fairytale of
200, 201–2
free speech: freedom of press and 198–9;
traditional rights of 78
Friedan, Betty 72
Frost, Robert 186
Fund for the Republic 126–8, 129, 130
future: back to the future 11, 54–6;
mega-trends 55–6; *see also* journalism,
looking backward, going forward

Gant, Scott 217n62
Garfinkel, Harold 21, 23, 26
Garvey, Ellen Gruber 173–4
Gauntlett, D. 104n3
Geertz, Clifford 91–2, 93, 97, 104n10
generic boundaries, dissolution of 103–4
Gerbner, George 69
Gibbons, Kent 216n54
Giddens, Anthony 164
Gilbert, G. Nigel 3
Gilens, Martin 69

research 121, 122, 125–6, 127, 129, 131; audience-researcher interaction 131; *Cavalcade of America* (DuPont) 123–4, 130–31; civil rights 126, 129; commercial sponsorship of public service 123–4; community service 123, 124; context and decontextualization 121; definitions of democracy, emergence of 120–21; democratic participation 121; democratization, measuring levels of 119–20; 'ethical incompletion' 122; Fund for the Republic 126–8, 129, 130; governance and public service broadcasting 119–20; governmentality 131–2; industrial films 121–2; *Industry on Parade* (National Association of Manufacturers) 123; interest group realpolitik 125; language of liberal pluralism 122; market pressures, protection from 123; media and citizenship orientation 119–20; media effects, assumptions about 121; mediated democracy 119–20; mediation of diverse interests 125–6; noncommercial broadcasting 122–3; ownership and accountability 122–3; pedagogical political opportunism 124; political culture, influence of public service voice on 132–3; process of production 125–6; production of public service films 122; propaganda films 121–2; public relations advertisements 121–2; public relations and public service 124–5; public service as discursive relationship 124; public service media 119, 121–2; public service obligation 124; race relations 128–30; reception and efficacy of strategies 130–31; religious programs 121–2; sociopolitical possibilities of television 122; sponsorship and citizenship, links between 125, 132–3; technocratic fantasy of 120; viewing and civic action effects, relationship between 126–8; welfarist liberalism 123; *see also* newswork, technology, and cultural form; printing
television audiences (1950s) 77, 83–5
Temple, Shirley 73
terseness in newswork 142–3, 145
Tetzel, John 112–13

Tharoor, Shashi 59n40
Theorizing Communication (Schiller, D.) 139–40
Thompson, Dennis 37, 38
Thompson, Edward P. 47, 78, 87n4
Thompson, John 68
Thompson, Michael 33n13
Thussu, Daya 46
Tocqueville, Alexis de 19, 185, 188
Tom Sawyer (Twain, M.) 171
Tomlinson, John 56n3
Tompkins, Jane P. 179n22
training for textual analysis 66, 74–5
transcription protocols 22
transmission 7, 16, 20, 24–8, 29, 95, 138, 142, 143–4
transportation and communication 140
triangulation 75–6
truth in journalism, deficiencies in 196
Tucher, Andie 173, 174, 175
Tuchman, Gaye 174
Turner, Victor 91, 104n8
Twain, Mark 170, 171
typewriter, impact on newswork 151
typographical unions 149–50

Ulrich, Laurel Thatcher 23
uncertainty of the past 30–31
underdevelopment of studies in journalism 181
Underwood, Doug 214n14
UNDP (UN Development Program) 59n38
United Kingdom *see* Britain

vagueness 30–31
van Braght, Thieleman J. 172
Varela, Juan 112
Veeser, Harold A. 179n20
Verne, Jules 98
Vincent, D. 98, 105n39
Vlock, D.M. 99–100, 106n44
Voltaire 136

Wall Street Journal 171, 185, 200
Warner, Michael 120
Washington, George 115
Washington Post 67, 171, 185, 191, 192
Weaver, Sylvester ('Pat') 126–7
Weber, Max 136
Weber, Steven 59n47
Weed, Thurlow 141–2
welfarist liberalism 123
Welles, Orson 74